MESSENGERS
of
GOD

MESSENGERS
of
GOD

THE SENSUOUS SIDE OF SPIRITUALITY

BY
ARTHUR O. ROBERTS

ASSISTED BY ROBIN ROBERTS

BARCLAY PRESS

MESSENGERS OF GOD
The Sensuous Side of Spirituality

© 1996 by Arthur O. Roberts

International Standard Book Number 0-913342-80-7

Library of Congress Catalog Card Number: 96-085288

Cover by Donna Allison
Cover photo by Åke Lundberg
Design, composition, and lithography by
Barclay Press
Newberg, Oregon 97132, U.S.A.

DEDICATION

To my siblings, Lucille, Marjorie, and Warren.
We share memories of loving parents,
a stable home, and strong communities
of work and worship.

CONTENTS

Controlling access to nature
Touch and the artificial world
Egoistic Touching
Touching ourselves
Touching things
Touching others
Bearing pain
Experiencing joy
Tactile behaviors
Empathetic Touching
Family touch
Erotic touch
Friendly touch
Healing touch
Touch as investiture
Godly Disciplines of Touch

Acknowledgments

Many persons have contributed in some way to the writing of this book. My granddaughter, Robin Roberts, did the background research for the psycho-physiological aspects of sensing and wrote the descriptive text found within each of the chapters and in the Appendix. She also served as a helpful critic of my ideas. My wife, Fern, read each draft carefully both for content and for clarity of expression. I am grateful to my sister, Lucille Adams, for editorial assistance, especially in regard to grammar and syntax. Gene Dykema and Dwight Kimberly, colleagues at George Fox College, read the manuscript and offered helpful suggestions. So did Gary Fawver, with whom I engaged in profitable discussion about sensuous aspects of spirituality, during the whole process of research and writing. Many of my ideas were forged in the crucible of the classroom by several generations of students at George Fox College, and were crafted into shape through various philosophy and Bible classes. One of these helpful students of former years is Richard Foster, who kindly agreed to write the Foreword.

I am grateful also for many authors and professors whose own lectures and books have helped shape my understanding of the world without and the world within us. Those most relevant to this book are acknowledged with appropriate attribution in the footnotes, and in the bibliography. All learning occurs in community. Who can claim exclusive title to one's own thoughts and expressions? But within such limits I accept accountability for the ideas expressed, however richly or poorly expressed, hoping that this book will contribute creatively to a common quest for wisdom in daily life.

Biblical citations are from the New Revised Standard Version (Collins Publishers, copyright, The Division of Christian Education of the National Council of Churches of Christ of the United States, 1989) unless otherwise noted.

The Christopher Pearse Cranch quotation heading the Prologue is from poetry selections from "Correspondences," *American Poetry: The Nineteenth Century,* ed. John Hollander, Vol. 1 (New York: The Library of America, 1993).

The Nicodemus quotation heading Chapter Two is from *Handbook of Spiritual Counsel* in *Classics of Western Spirituality* (Paulist Press, 1989), p. 70.

The quotation used to head the Conclusion is from Thomas Mann, *Joseph in Egypt* (Knopf 1938), p. 152.

FOREWORD

Two distinct movements mark Christian spirituality: world affirming and world fleeing, incarnational and ascetical, the *via positiva* and the *via negativa.* Without denying the importance of the second movement, Arthur O. Roberts provides us with a cogent analysis of the first—world affirming, incarnational, the *via positiva.* In *Messengers of God* he shows us a clear path between ascetic denial and hedonistic indulgence.

Building upon St. Augustine, Dr. Roberts sees the senses as "the messengers of God," especially when "reason interrogates the senses." This is, in the best understanding of the term, a sensuous spirituality; that is, a spirituality of the senses. By "senses" Roberts is referring literally to our hearing and seeing and smelling and tasting and touching. Perhaps few of us have thought of these everyday experiences as having much to do with spiritual life. But Arthur Roberts sees them as crucial. "This book," he writes, "is about being spiritual in sensory ways. About how our eyes and our ears function as receptor/transmitters of divine revelation, about how taste and smell signify truth, about the triangularity of touch—oneself, the other, and God....A practical spirituality acknowledges that God is in the communications loop made possible by our senses."

With the skill of one at home in the contrasting worlds of science and poetry, Arthur Roberts has taken masses of technical data about the senses and made them understandable to us, even significant. Like me, you too will marvel at the labyrinthian wonders of the senses. We are indeed "fearfully and wonderfully made."

This book is packed with analytical insight and practical counsel. Some of the phrases will startle you—"Conversation is auditory intercourse." At other times the insights will sting—"People too sophisticated for high-powered religious banter, blithely accept secular hucksterism on talk shows and television commercials." Still other words will soothe and counsel—"If your ears are...too burdened to find the soul's still center, let your feet find familiar paths among silent trees, or let your hands engage in ruminative routines, such as knitting or woodcarving, and let your memory recover for inward hearing some melodies of past joy."

In the midst of reading *Messengers of God*, I took a hike in a lovely canyon area near our home. I was accompanied only by my carved redwood walking stick and a water bottle. In the springtime this canyon is filled with the sights and smells of columbine and larkspur, golden banner and Indian paintbrush. But not now. We are in the fall of the year and earth tones dominate. Leaves crackle under my feet, drab and dry. Even the ponderosa pine are darker now, blending in with the browns of gambel oak and mountain mahogany. Walking through the forest, I can see that the sap is retreating deeper and deeper into the interior of the trees in preparation for winter's cold.

The vanishing of leaf and flower makes the boulders of the canyon stand out in rugged relief. They are always there, of course, but in the fall they fill the landscape, like giant sentinels. It's mostly conglomerate rock, reminders of the vast prehistoric sea that once covered this area. I like the rock—hard and durable. I brush my hand over boulders studded with stones, all cemented together by ancient pressures.

This is my favorite time of year in the canyon. In the spring and summer numerous hikers enjoy the beauties of flora and fauna; but few venture out in late fall and winter. I can hike miles of trail without sight of another *homo sapiens*. So it is today. As a result I do not speak...but I do listen. Always I hear the rush of the creek winding through this little canyon. I am never fully out of ear shot of its perpetual babble. It is a pleasing sound, which in a strange way both calms and energizes. There are other sounds, of course. Chipmunk and squirrel scratching for food. In the trees or high above are hawk and jay, American goldfinch and dark-eyed junco. The great variety of tracks on the trail remind me that I have many more neighbors than I ever see or hear.

The sun flees the canyon early, and I feel a chill beginning to set in. I pull my jacket tight around my ears, regretting my decision not to bring hat or gloves. Clutching the water bottle, my fingers feel icy.

As the early evening comes on, I meet a herd of deer grazing in a brown meadow. Several bound away, but others only watch in a disinterested sort of way, making sure this stranger does not come too close. They remind me that I am only a guest and visitor here; they are the permanent residents. Noting the pink on the eastern horizon—the afterglow of the sunset over the Rockies—I realize that darkness—and genuine cold—

will come quickly. I pick up my pace and finish the trail loop just as Orion begins to appear.

On my way back home I stop at Colima's. Family owned and family managed, it is unpretentious in every way. That is what I like about it. The patrons eating here, the family running it, the building itself (being nothing more than an old frame house of a bygone era) are all unpretentious. On the wall, amidst giant sombreros of green and orange and purple, is a handwritten poster of the specials of the day—Carne Asada, Mole de Pollo, Carne Adobada, Tacos al Carbon.

Two young teenagers do the serving. Older brothers (or perhaps cousins) work in the kitchen, their voices mixing with Latino music from a local radio station. The mother, quite dignified and in charge, is the hostess, and the father sits at the cash register. At the table next to me are two Anglo kids practicing their Spanish. I dislike the sound of their words—flat, emotionless, classroom. But they are just kids. From others I hear a mixture of English, Spanish, and some Tex-Mex. The owners' voices are different, but I can't quite identify the accent. It sounds almost Castellano, but not quite. Looking at the postcards displayed at the front counter—all scenes of the city and state of Colima, Mexico—I surmise that this family has moved from there to here not too long ago. I'm too shy to ask. Besides, they do not need another *gringo* nosing into their business.

I like the sights and sounds and smells here. I like the people. Each one is different, each one with a story to tell. I think back to my canyon hike and I try to integrate it into the utterly different experience here at Colima's. I am struck by the infinite variety in God's creative act.

With my Carne Asada and two Soppapillas for dessert, I suddenly realize that the insights of Arthur Roberts have become lived experience for me. My senses have become the media of revelation. In complete silence I place my money on the table and push open the screen door.

Arthur Roberts invites us into a way of living that is world affirming and life giving. It is a way that involves "the intelligent interrogation of the senses acknowledged as the messengers of God, with appropriate disciplines to follow. A spiritual life can be a sensory life, but it need not be a vain and extravagant one." This is a way of living worth our best efforts. *Messengers of God* will help chart our course.

—Richard J. Foster, Thanksgiving, 1995

Every object that speaks to the senses was meant for the spirit.
—Christopher Pearse Cranch

Memory retains certain melodies a long time. I can still hear the words of
this little jingle that someone (perhaps my mother) taught me:

> Oh, be careful little eyes what you see,
> for the Father up above is looking down in love,
> oh, be careful little eyes what you see.
> Oh, be careful little ears what you hear,
> for the Father up above is looking down in love,
> oh, be careful little ears what you hear.
> Oh, be careful little hands what you do,
> for the Father up above is looking down in love,
> oh, be careful little hands, what you do.

The exhortation omitted reference to smell and taste, apparently because these gates to the soul were not considered as vulnerable to the influences of good and evil as were sight, sound, and touch. Nonetheless,
the exhortation called this child to a life of reverent morality. Why have
I remembered that song all these years? I don't know, some powerful influences grooved these words in my mind. Perhaps they were the influences of love and truth.

One could easily be amused by this little song. It seems so out of date,
so simplistic. Many persons would consider such a chorus sung by a mother to a child unimaginable, let alone effective, in a culture in which children hear (with visual animation) a hundred variously voiced ditties on
television before mother gets out of bed on Saturday morning. And yet,
the song's simplicity, like Shaker furniture, haunts us. Our memories
strain to recall more idyllic times when spiritual maturity was conveyed
from one generation to another along understated but forthright lines of
disciplined moral life. A quickly surfacing cynicism, our first response to

that simple call for discipline, upon reflection is firmly countered by a more thoughtful response: an underlying hope that certain values may be reaffirmed.

This little song implies three basic values. One, that God's love includes both judgment and grace. Two, that persons, even small ones, can make choices about good and evil influences. Three, that discipline of the senses is spiritually important.

This book is about being spiritual in sensory ways. It's about how our eyes and our ears function as receptor/transmitters of divine revelation, about how taste and smell signify truth, about the triangularity of touch—oneself, the other, and God. Given the subtlety of sin, practical discipline is ever a concern of sensitive people. People use the senses to communicate with each other. Linguistic and non-linguistic sign systems interrelate in complex ways, forming a common culture and a civil society. Through the languages of our senses we convey who we are—body, mind, and spirit. We evidence our relationship with God and others. A practical spirituality acknowledges forthrightly that God is within the sensory communications loop.

Health clubs abound and fitness programs flourish everywhere, for people are rightly concerned to discipline the body. Education is a major social enterprise, offering many ways to discipline the mind. But for what purpose? Is weight lifting an end in itself? Is good diet merely a survival mechanism? Are spelling bees and graduate exams ends in themselves? I knew a man once who greatly admired his new car, cleaning it so often he wore off the paint! He idolized this long-awaited automobile instead of letting it serve him (elegantly) for transportation. Physical exercise can be like that with the body. Mental exercise can be like that with the mind. Such exercises can become idolatrous, even narcissistic, unless linked to proper spiritual discipline (even "spiritual" exercise can become idolatrous and narcissistic). To be whole the body must function in the image of God. Those aspects of the self we call body, mind, and spirit are so interdependent that for right functioning they require godly and harmonious exercise.

Despite the superficial secularity that characterizes modern society, a deep spiritual hunger persists. There is a hunger for God and for goodness. This hunger for wholeness has not been nourished by hedonistic idols. Mental gymnastics have not filled the spiritual void. This hunger has not been satisfied by a spirituality that ignores the body, nor by a spirituality that idolizes the body. The notion that science and religion signify worlds of discourse that never intersect or merge is not convincing.

People yearn for a coherent view of things and events. They seek coherence through spirituality.

The quest for spirituality occurs within and apart from institutional religion. Many books reflect upon or nurture this search for the holy, but few correlate the enhancement of the senses with the development of spirituality.[1] This book deals specifically with such a correlation. The first chapter supports the theme from several perspectives and subsequent chapters consider each of the senses in turn.

Notes

1. Virginia Stem Owens, in *A Taste of Creation* (Valley Forge: Judson Press, 1980), and *And the Hands Clap Their Hands, Faith, Perception, and the New Physics* (Grand Rapids: Eerdmans, 1983), deals in a Christian manner with a creation physicality, that is, that the body is the locus of spirituality. She is at pains to distance spirituality from mind-body polarities.

In his books on spirituality, beginning with *Celebration of Discipline* (Harper & Row, 1978), my friend and former student, Richard Foster, assumes aspects of what we make explicit: a vital correlation between the senses and spirituality.

A book by Virginia Ramey Mollenkott, *Sensuous Spirituality: Out from Fundamentalism* (New York: Crossroad, 1992), despite its title, has a quite different focus from our book. Her book is based upon a panentheist interpretation of biblical theology that includes an apologetic for a lesbian/gay lifestyle.

CHAPTER ONE

THINKING ABOUT THE SENSES

...all these messengers of the senses
report the answers of heaven and earth
and all the things therein, who said,
"We are not God, but he made us."
—Augustine

In this chapter we show the importance of thinking about the senses, drawing upon historical, cultural, philosophical, psycho-physiological, and religious perspectives. It seemed important for us thus to establish a rationale for sensuous spirituality. Readers who consider one or more of these topics burdensome may wish to move on to the next chapters.

Historical Perspectives

To correlate sense and spirit is a timely exercise. Fortunately, we can gain insight from an earlier period of cultural upheaval. During the closing years of the imperial Roman era, a North African scholar, Augustine, thought deeply and wrote insightfully about body and spirit. Augustine offers a relevant historical perspective for our thinking about the senses and spirituality. During the time he lived (A.D. 354-430) Christian spirituality had increasingly become defined in habits of discipline that treated the senses as barriers to holiness. During this era Christians reacted (overreacted, perhaps) against the decadent sensuality characteristic of a dying civilization. It has been generally asserted that Western Christian mysticism reflected the social triumph of a Platonic view of self, one that denigrates the body, and that Augustine contributed significantly to this unfortunate conquest. To some extent that assessment is correct. Augustine's dramatic adult conversion to Christianity did mark a personal, agonized, dramatically articulated turn from sexual promiscuity to chastity. The vow of chastity became his test of obedience to God. Putting away his mistress instead of marrying her seems to most people in our culture to have been a misguided choice. It seems so to me. Perhaps we underestimate how shackled Augustine had become to an indulgent lifestyle, and how for him divine grace could heal only by a radical break with sexual addiction.

Augustine was too complex a thinker, despite his personal mode of achieving spiritual discipline, to be blamed for the restrictive asceticism that came to mark the Christian quest for holiness. For our purposes it is sufficient to recognize that Augustine expressed in very human terms a universally experienced struggle between what St. Paul termed flesh and spirit. That struggle, subsequently expressed in systems of rationalism and empiricism, espousing respectively the ascendancy of mind and body in cognition, became a major philosophical issue in Western civilization.

This issue need not concern us now, although it does signal a profound mystery to understanding.[1] Of greater concern here is how the senses may be instruments of righteousness, apart from whether sensory impressions develop into mental concepts experientially or whether they arise from innate mental equipment.

To ascribe value to human actions, and meaning to communication about such actions, presumes a condition of freedom. To be spiritual assumes such freedom. People are not wholly preprogrammed, whether by God, genetic coding, or mind-sets; but they are not wholly autonomous, either. Freedom requires some necessities. Metaphorically speaking, we may be clay molded by the Lord, but we are not inert. Divine molding requires human consent. Furthermore, morality (if it is other than personal or social preference) presupposes either divine creation or incarnated revelation. Christian theology accepts both.

Augustine's reflections about how reason interrogates the senses, comparing "the voice received from without" with "the truth within" are therefore instructive for a spirituality that acknowledges the body to be a temple of the Holy Spirit, that seeks an earthy rather than an ethereal holiness. A quotation from Augustine's *Confessions,* Book Ten[2] illustrates as well as anything in literature the struggle to love God with the whole body, mind, and spirit.

It is not with a doubtful consciousness, but one fully certain that I love thee, O, Lord. Thou hast smitten my heart with thy Word, and I have loved thee....

But what is it that I love in loving thee? Not physical beauty, nor the splendor of time, nor the radiance of the light—so pleasant to our eyes—nor the sweet melodies of the various kinds of songs, nor the fragrant smell of flowers and ointments and spices; not manna and honey, not the limbs embraced in physical love—it is not these I love when I love my God. Yet it is true that I love a certain kind of light and sound and fragrance and food and embrace in loving my God, who is the light and sound and fragrance and food and embracement of my inner man—where that light shines into my soul which no place can contain, where time does not snatch away the lovely sound, where no breeze disperses the sweet fragrance, where no eating diminishes the food there provided, and where there is an embrace that no satiety comes to sunder. This is what I love when I love my God.

. . . . I replied to all these things which stand around the door of my flesh: "You have told me about my God, that you are not he. Tell me something about him." And with loud voice they all cried out, "He made us." My question had come from my observation of them, and their reply came from their beauty of order. And I turned my thoughts into myself and said, "Who are you?" And I answered, "A man." For see, there is in me both a body and a soul; the one without, the other within. In which of these should I have sought my God, whom I had already sought with my body from earth to heaven, as far as I was able to send those messengers—the beams of my eyes? But the inner part is the better part; for to it, as both ruler and judge, all these messengers of the senses report the answers of heaven and earth and all the things therein, who said, "We are not God, but he made us." My inner man knew these things through the ministry of the outer man, and I, the inner man, knew all this—I, the soul, through the senses of my body.

Human beings share with animals a diversity of senses, mused Augustine, but are distinguished from them by a "huge hall of memory" into which each experience (not the thing in itself, but the image of it) enters by its own door, and richly furnishes the soul with treasures. In this spacious hall of memory songs resonate though the throat be silent, and in the darkness colors reappear. Here the self cogitates about these experiences retained in images, impressions, imaginations, and judgments. Here the self meets itself, not only to recall actions but also judgments and attitudes about these occurrences. What a wonder it is, ponders Augustine, that travelers rightly marvel at high mountains, ocean waves, the heavenly orbits, and "yet they neglect to marvel at themselves!"

Augustine's words from the twilight years of the Roman Empire retain a certain cogency for our times. He understood how important sensory input is for the self and society. We know that too, and are busy enhancing the sensorium with electronic languages and machinery. He knew how sensuality can become depraved. He understood how a distorted sensuality can destroy persons, homes, communities and civilization, itself. We know that, too, and shudder at the devastating effects of a rogue sensuality.

Augustine understood that the senses must be interrogated rationally by the inner self, with awe before the Creator, if life is to be rightly lived. To "interrogate" implies a certain reciprocity, "to ask between, or among." To ask is to engage in a dialogue between the world coming to us and the world reaching out from us. Between God and the self, between the macro and the micro, between the created and the creating, between the self and the other. We understand that, too, but find such dialogue difficult in our society.

We are awakened to this need for interrogation, however, by the furor over whether, or how, sophisticated artificial sensory stimuli contribute to violence and social blight. Or how they can be consecrated to uplifting purposes. Underlying the erosion of value is a mind-set difficult to overcome: that perception is basically a "calculus of probability" offering opportunity to manipulate whatever stands external to one. This mind-set is fostered by a reductive use of scientific method and reinforced by an equally reductive use of religion. Ecological concern has challenged this secular cult of objectivity, and a recovered biblical theology of creation has rebuked the idolatry implicit in such a view. Now, as in the days of the Roman Empire, violence correlates with political hubris. Augustine's own agonizing struggle to overcome youthful egoistic, culturally-driven, secular sensuality adds weight to his soliloquy about the senses and the soul, and pertinence to our own quest. His reflections hold up for us a useful mirror.

Augustine accepted the fivefold designation of the sensorium that had been so categorized by the Greeks centuries earlier: hearing, seeing, tasting, smelling, and touching. Over the centuries attempts to add to or reclassify the senses have come and gone. Recently some persons wonder whether smell is adequate to account for certain sexual chemical interactions (pheromones). Should another sense be identified? Should touch be divided into internal and external perceptions? Perhaps the kinesthetic should be distinct from the external, added to the other senses? I have chosen to consider it an aspect of touch, however, and have stayed with the traditional categories of five senses. Early Celtic Christians spoke of the need "to tune the five-stringed harp" to the presence of God in the natural world with all its creatures. It's a good exhortation.[3]

Contemporary Reasons

Why is it important currently to study how we hear, see, taste, smell, and touch? For several reasons, and not just because of historical parallels, the philosophic mind-body problem, or semantic confusion about biblical words like "flesh" and "spirit" and "worldliness."

First, it is important to think about the senses because our culture has heightened sensory stimulation to such a degree that freely chosen, consistent responses to the world about us are increasingly difficult to make. Consider sexual touching. How confusing are the mixed signals sent and received! Seductive inducements for early and recreational sexual activity bombard people on every side, and these signals conflict with confusing social standards for casual touch. What is appropriate for casual touch during the exhilaration of athletic competition, for example, isn't permissible at work. In the office if a man pats a co-worker on the rear he risks charges of sexual harassment. At a ball game it's different. If a woman enhances her natural aroma with seductive perfume, and thus assails a man's olfactory receptors, she is just being "sexy." This is considered admirable. Should a man respond with a caress it may be construed as harassment. Just smell, just look, but don't touch, seems to be the socially correct signal. Occasionally, now, if a woman dresses too provocatively, or flirts too openly she may get fired, but the burden generally rests upon the man. These examples illustrate how difficult it is to establish social boundaries for sensory interaction.

Second, our technological culture has enhanced the range of our sensorium, offering a bewildering array of manufactured sights, sounds, smells, tastes, and tactile experiences. There's a down side to such enhancement. Our senses are also increasingly subject to the will of persons or agencies who program them for their own purposes, beneficent or malign. We grope to maintain the integrity of our persons within roles programmed for us. It's as if we are asked to perform in a human drama beyond the original script, with cues thrown at us from all sides. Consider the enormous industry (billions of dollars annually) that provides sensory intercourse through video games, television shows, movies, cassettes, advertisements, interactive software, and workplace simulations. Add to this artificial environment the emerging virtual reality hardware and software, by which immediate bodily presence is replaced by simulated presence. Add, further, a complex industry that transfers sensory stimuli into "smart" weapons that can destroy others at a physically and aesthetically safe distance. Or a technology that can spy on us in many secret ways. Talk about being "led by the nose" or "grabbed by the ear," this technological culture has enormous power to program our lives, not all of it for good.

The French sociologist Jacques Ellul has hammered home the significance of the technological era in which modern humanity finds its current home—its milieu.[4] Ellul believes humankind has lived in three milieus: nature, society, and technology. In each environment people find meaning and encounter, and they wield power. Each milieu provides sustenance for body and soul, and elicits symbols of regeneration. The symbols of renewal are for nature, the feast; for society, the sacrifice; and for technology, consumption. Each milieu poses dangers and the human response is ambiguous. We are both attracted and repelled, fearful and hopeful. The natural milieu has plagues as well as pristine forests; the social milieu has tyrants as well as courthouses and colleges. What about technology? It definitely has its good side: better housing, less arduous toil, rapid transportation, medical care, global awareness, variety in food and clothing, effective communication tools (such as the word processor I am using). It also has its down side. In consuming ever increasing amounts of goods and services technological culture abuses nature, marginalizes a percentage of the human population, tramples traditional morality, and weakens social civility.[5] Technique is employed to manipulate not just nature but also people. Freedom is threatened. Celebrities replace sages. In technological culture celebrities are those who model play, not work or social leadership, and celebrity images become icons for consumer devotees. Such consumer-driven worship correlates with a consumer-driven economy offering fewer and fewer creative, well-paid, labor intensive jobs. As a result the gap between rich and poor widens and revolution hovers like a dark cloud everywhere on the planet.

The specter of irresponsible genetic alterations, for example, may be no more awesome a prospect than the alteration of the self by technological manipulation of the senses. When an electric system gets overloaded it blows. Power shuts down. When social systems get overloaded, they fail; order shuts down, anarchy prevails. There are many reasons for social collapse. One reason for disorder in our times is sensory overload. Sensory overload endangers human community and threatens civilization as greatly as at any time since the Roman era in which Augustine lived.

Despite its foibles and hypocrisies, religion over the centuries has sustained human community to a remarkable degree. It has provided philosophic foundations for scientific inquiry, a context for ethical and aesthetic values, and motivations for political justice and acts of mercy. The spiritual life has often been described as a journey. Appropriately so, for the human spirit moves toward God through manifold experiences in time and space. Spirituality leavens society. In the community of faith one generation conveys to the next the acts of God in history and within human experiences—and their continuing significance. Spirituality is a journey both for the individual and for the group, reinforced by shared history, shared worship, and shared stewardship of ideas and actions. For biblical people time unfolds inwardly and outwardly with purpose infusing the soul and the cosmos.

But there has been a breakdown in the conveyance of these truths and values. There has been a breach in vital tradition. Ethos has become blurred or reduced to a modern tribalism. The sensory antennae once attuned directly toward God's revelation, or even, in the modern era, toward philosophical concepts embodying universal principles, are now subject to exponentially expanding artificial stimuli, unchecked by a transcendent order or by covenanted standards of value. Our era may aptly be designated technological humanism.

As sensory overload occurs in this culture, the journey of the spirit stalls. People become confused about the road ahead. Classical literature and art no longer awaken the mind to wonder and creativity. A glut of merchandised pop art overwhelms the more expressive folk arts and creative handicrafts. A glut of pop therapy offers quick fixes to troubled people. The voice of the evangelist does not quicken the conscience of the sinner, nor do hymns offer hope to the despairing. Education loses social direction and propaganda gains from that default, as manipulators exploit media to distort both human goals and political purpose.

It is not that people now are more evil and insensitive than people used to be, but rather that the imagination has been hemmed in by a thicket of sensory barriers. It's hard to work our way through, even to see which way to go. There isn't time to sort the impressions that entangle us, no time to classify them, no context in which to ponder their significance and to make comparative judgments and applications. Physically, our sensory receptors become exhausted by the effort. A shortened work week once gave people needed time for personal growth. Now this makes little difference for people whose senses are bombarded constantly with manufactured stimuli, whether at work or at home or on vacation. Lacking memory's perspective of the past and hope's perspective on the future, the self easily becomes trapped in an all-encompassing (and sometimes overwhelming) present. Without disciplined effort, the self more readily becomes a jaded consumer of commercial goods and entertainment, morally confused and spiritually immobilized.

In the mid-nineties the public became outraged over seductive violence patterned by video images. One program, "Night Trap," was withdrawn by its producers because the bloody scenes were considered too evocative for impressionable children. Public leaders groped for means to preserve freedom of expression while preventing exploitation of vulnerable people through increasingly sophisticated sensory stimuli. Do certain interactive video games constitute child abuse? With the advent of virtual reality into media, has fantasy lost its historic power to evoke creative responses within the real world? Has fantasy become, instead, a terrible force for trapping people in illusion? Will the information highway instruct or seduce? Having witnessed a cause and effect relationship between diet and physical health people are now drawing similar inferences about a relationship between sensory ingestion and psychological wholeness.

Our technological culture enables us privately and corporately to invade the privacy of others with technological extensions of eyes and ears and hands. When are such invasions honorable? When they have political status (the good of the state or tribe), corporate status (the good of the company), survival status (the good of the individual)? When they are freely consented to by the receivers? Or when they offer praise and glory to God, the creator, and dignity to humanity sculpted in God's image?

We have noted that our culture has greatly heightened sensory stimulation and (through technology) enhanced the range of our sensory antennae, but at a risk to personal freedom. There is a third reason why thinking about our senses is important. Urbanization of living space has increased artificial stimuli while proportionately diminishing natural ones. We hear traffic noise instead of surf. We see buildings instead of forests. We smell automobile exhaust rather than fecund soil. Convenience foods condition tastes from early childhood on. Manufactured smells overwhelm natural ones. Programmed touch merchandises tactile delight with selective focus on sex, sports, skin lotions, and wearing apparel.

For these reasons it is important to do a "zero based" analysis of what we take too readily for granted, our senses: hearing, seeing, tasting, smelling, touching. To recover title to them may enable us to yield our bodies as instruments of righteousness, to become personally a praiseworthy temple of God, and socially a people with a divine covenant.

Philosophical Reflections

Before dealing with the specific senses, certain words should be noted and certain concepts examined. If in an earlier sentence we had written *"sensuous"* instead of "sensory" ("being spiritual in *sensuous* ways"), would our expectations have been different? Probably. If we had chosen "sensual," "sensational," "sensate," or "sensible" as adjectives to describe spirituality, the meanings conveyed would vary from notions of sexually compromised or hyped religion, to the decline of Western civilization, to prudent conduct. These words that cluster about the activity of sensing differ in how they function as communicative signs, but they share common language roots. They depict how we experience the world and acknowledge it through an intricate network of physical sensation and mental interpretation.

Sensory is a neutral, descriptive term. It simply refers to sensing. But other words are value loaded, and acquire social connotations that must be acknowledged. So definitions are called for. Let's stipulate contrastive meanings to the words *sensual* and *sensuous*. When the mind drives the body to fulfill selfindulgent desires, *sensuality* is the appropriate descriptive word. In sensuality the body is enslaved by the mind. When the mind accepts and delights in the rhythmic functions of the body, *sensuousness* is the appropriate descriptive word. In sensuousness the body is liberated by the mind and in synch with the spirit. To illustrate: sexy commercials are sensual, ice dancing is sensuous. A materialistic culture accents the sensational, and hence can be characterized as sensate. A humane culture accents the sensible and hence can be characterized as sensuous. Under secular influence humane culture stresses the aesthetic form of the sensuous. Under religious influence humane culture stresses the ethical aspects of sensible conduct as well as the aesthetical aspects of divine-human encounter. When a culture is truly spiritual, it lifts the aesthetical and the ethical into a sensuality that includes God, the created world, and humanity within a network of living, passionate beings. The sensuous person accepts embodiment sacramentally. The body is a living sacrifice in praise to God, who honors it as the temple of the Spirit.[6]

Concepts are those cluster words by which we organize the impressions that arise from our senses and are shaped into perceptions. Philosophers acknowledge the primacy of perception for knowledge and experience. This is the case, obviously, for empiricists who assume that mind is a *tabula rasa* (blank sheet) upon which impressions write (blindly or by divine election) the script to personal identity and action. It is also the case for rationalists who assume innate ideas *a priori*, or a coherent network of universal ideas (software for the mind), or boundary categories for receiving and processing impressions.

An Irish bishop in the early eighteenth century concluded there was no abstruse entity called "matter." George Berkeley's motto, "esse est percipi," "to be is to be perceived" is well known: nothing exists independently of knowing minds, God's and ours. He didn't ignore "stuff" out there, but denied to it any sort of general unperceivable substance. Nature exists not in itself but as God's language. Terms such as figure and extension don't exist in things to be viewed by the eye, but in the mind. There are no generalized images, only particular ones, e.g., no eternal triangles, only perceived ones. This view, called radical empiricism, followed Locke in rejecting innate ideas. But Berkeley anticipated, and tried to answer, the implications that might arise from this view, ones that David Hume drew, namely, that all impressions are random and without transcendent purpose, no telic cause informs the world. Hume's view left little room for memory, morality, or freedom, let alone for God. The good bishop, Berkeley, who lived for a time in the American colonies, and wanted to start a college in Bermuda, has had his critics, but at least he offered a philosophical rationale for sensuous spirituality. It's a better option, in my judgment, than the fatalistic behaviorism that developed early in the twentieth century as a corollary to Humean empiricism. It was said of that materialistic trend: first philosophy lost its soul, then it lost its mind. In consequence, body became a thing. This was unacceptable to personal self identity.

Whatever terms we give to personal identity, "self" or "mind" or "soul," this personal center is accessed through the senses. Through the senses we communicate. The other modes of knowing—reasoning and intuiting—affirm the primacy of sensory perception and seek to bring it under rational control and into spiritual coherence. The body is not just a collection of sensors that receive impressions from external objects, but rather a center for consciousness, which interacts with other centers of reality (and with itself) through the neurological functions of hearing, seeing, tasting, touching, and smelling. These other centers of reality we sometimes lump together under the heading "nature." Sometimes we act as if nature is wholly other than ourselves, forgetting that we too are part of nature, part of the creation. The human temple of the Holy Spirit has walls of flesh and blood, and reacts to the Given with its sensory receptors. In some ways human beings stand within and outside nature, part of it, yet not part of it. Theologians commonly distinguish humanity's uniqueness on the basis that they are made in the image of God, that is they reflect the likeness of the creator. But as Langdon Gilkey has pointed out, nature also represents an image of the creator, particularly in its manifestation of power, order, and value. The trace of the sacred is everywhere discernible, thinks Gilkey, and religious intuition universally affirms this to be so.[7]

Knowing occurs in three ways: through sense, reason, and intuition. These modes of knowing shape our experience of reality. How we know determines in large measure what we know. Cultures weigh experience differently, depending upon characteristic modes of knowing. Often specialized societal needs foster weighted combinations among subcultures, typically characterized by two dominant and one recessive mode of knowing. Thus some people are basically sensory-rational in their understanding. They don't trust intuition. Others are sensory-intuitive. They don't trust reason. Others (like traditional mystics) are rational-intuitive. They don't trust the senses. Good and evil are viewed from these epistemic perspectives.

These complementary ways of knowing can be illustrated as a "Kingdom of Light." Picture three lands approximately equidistant from a central headquarters island, all set within an ocean that faces into darkness at the perimeter. The island is the energy source, the administrative center, the organizing mind for this universe of discourse. One continent is sense, another is reason, and the third is intuition. We are describing the geography of thought, with the Word (logos) as the divine center, and the darkness constituting a demonic periphery. Salvation is first the restoration, then the sustenance, of life connected to the Center. The relationship may be diagrammed thus:

The Kingdom of Light

A study of the realms of the holy and the sinful

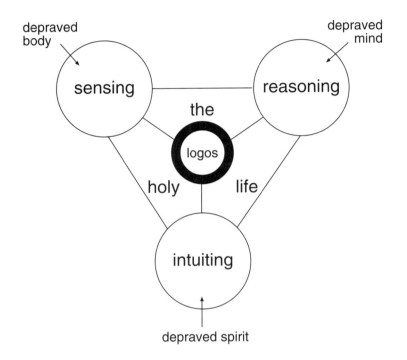

In this "Kingdom of Light," rational-intuitives tend to see clearly the sins of the flesh—pornography, for example—but they may be blind to greed. Sensory-intuitives tend to see clearly the sins of social rationalization—the military-industrial complex, for example, but they may be blind to the demonic grip of drugs. Sensory-rational people see clearly the dangers of the occult but they may be blind to spiritual pride. Conversely, in respect to righteousness, rational-intuitives may undervalue the ministry of artists; sensory-intuitive persons may undervalue the spiritual value of accountants and administrators; and sensory-rational persons may undervalue intuitive gifts of discernment. With the Logos (Christ) drawing us toward the center, demonic temptations at the periphery can be overcome. All the devils aren't in multinational corporations or governing bodies, or in sexually explicit art shows, or in New Age cults. The periphery is demonic at all points outside the circle. Conversely, holiness occurs all along the rim, as long as the Center holds within the orbit of truth. The physical senses can become messengers of God when they connect in useful tension with both the divine center of truth and with reason and intuition.

When sensory perception gets overloaded, especially by enhanced technological stimuli, reason and intuition also suffer. Then there isn't enough space and time for reflective judgment or for intuited feelings. Then choices that seem nearly endless in a sophisticated technological society become sapped of significance by real life restrictions upon the freedom of the will. "Which brand shall I buy?" hasn't the same weight as "how shall I honor God by my actions?" but under constant bombardment it seems to. The self, already limited by genetic boundaries, becomes further restricted by technological determinants. The self ceases to be free, but becomes instead a programmed organism, a product as it were. Many children are shaped by MTV, many adults by commercial hype, without realizing they have been controlled. They are free but only narrowly so.

It is not taking in each other's wash (sharing specialized labor) that drives the economic engine now, but mutual programming. We are in the information era, as many social commentators have noted, in which knowledge, not manufacture or agriculture or government offers the driving force. Even in war, assert Alvin and Heidi Toffler, the media is the star of the spectacle.[8] People are understandably fidgety about this heightened role of media. In such a manipulative culture not only do ordinary people protest being exploited, but the manipulators are beginning to as well. Note the rising publicity given whistle-blowers. Who programs the programmers is a question for our time. The rise of a psychically programmed class may be even more ominous than the threat of a new economic underclass. Bread and circuses, so Rome managed its underclass. But that palliative policy only accelerated the fall of empire, that and lead plumbing! It doesn't take much imagination to draw parallels: convenience food and sensational entertainment—oh, yes, and ecological disaster. With these components, now as ever, the stage is set for a modern Babylonian fall. The "four horses of the Apocalypse," it seems, are stabled nearby.

When primary perceptions are strong, and subjected to reasoning freely applied, however, then logic shapes these perceptions into scientific theories, social paradigms, political covenants, narrative myth, geometric models, metaphoric imagery, analogs, and artistry. So the social order achieves design and function. One generation passes the torch of knowledge and values to the next. In multiform ways we use sign, signal, and symbol to remember and convey the meanings we perceive and construe in categories of the understanding. Through a diversity of signification culture transmits the meaning it attaches to things, persons, and events. Historians study and interpret the records of such transmittal; anthropologists, its artifacts. Semiotics is the science that studies the signs and symbols of communicative behavior.

The human senses are not equally good receptors and transmitters. So cultures develop linguistic ways to borrow from the strong to enhance the weak. Sight and sound are formally alphabetized (and touch for the blind). They carry their own signification but also through metaphor and simile stand in for smell and taste and touch. But each sense is capable of some form of language, which cultures in various ways incorporate into mores and memes that influence human behavior. "Body language" is more than twisting one's back to encourage a golf ball to drop into the cup.[9]

Governed by the will, perceptions yield knowledge of the good, the true, and the beautiful, and of their contraries—the evil, the false, and the ugly. Directly through the senses, and indirectly through derived concepts, we acknowledge reality. We apprehend the wonder of the world, we frame that mystery with systems of understanding. When intuition judges perception, this perceptive knowledge becomes subjective; we feel the mystery of God beyond the boundaries of our systems of understanding. World views become internalized into personal belief. Truth, as Kierkegaard says, becomes "truth for me." Logical conclusions cease to yield merely propositional conclusions or indefinite abstractions; they impel to faithful action. The world, accessioned by the senses, interrogated by the mind, and transmitted by language, under intuition becomes "my lived-in world." I am present in the world with integrity, free within God-given boundaries, and hence accountable.

But physical sensing occurs first, before constructions of mind and spirit yield their interrogation of the senses in experiences of aesthetic ecstasy and moral obligation. It is a biblical teaching that our bodies are designed to be instruments of the Holy Spirit. Apostle Paul exhorted us to "glorify God in our bodies."

Psycho-physiological Perspectives

It may help us glorify God if we understand better how the senses function. So in psycho-physiological terms we will describe the sensorineural mechanisms and the way the cerebral cortex provides clues for understanding the interactive and often conflicting aspects of patterned and volitional behavior.

Before beginning a discussion of the physical nature of sensation perception, it is important to address the dynamic interplay between physical stimuli and human cognition. Science is remarkably acute in describing the process by which we come to have knowledge and feel emotion about something in our environment, but it may never be possible to break down the entire human condition into the sum of its physical processes. Gaps exist as to how we make the quantum leap from experiencing a sensation to developing a memory trace for that sensation to forming an opinion or attitude about it that will persist over time.

We are not passive receptors of information, like a computer. Nor are we able to record the events and experiences of our lives like a video camera or cassette recorder. We "color" our world and our perception of it through four interrelated conceptual modes: attention, memory, prior knowledge, and emotion.

Attention can be construed as the point of clarity when conscious thought and willful application of mind and body exists with regard to a particular object or situation. We have all been caught daydreaming, or gawking at the scenery when we should have been watching the road. However, a more fundamental notion of attention stems from the fact that it is one of our few ways to combat the constant onslaught of stimuli in a modern, multi-media-driven, society.

Often we feel at the mercy of our eyes and ears and long for an amorphous "peace and quiet." Boredom has now become a condition of overstimulation, not understimulation. Research shows that, contrary to popular opinion, selective attention is crucial if information is to be retained in memory. Unattended information, at most, may act as a clue to understanding attended information, if presented simultaneously. Generally speaking, unattended information itself is not encoded into memory and is almost virtually irretrievable.

In some significant way, the consent of the will is needed for information to be processed. The attendant has to open the gate. How vital, then, it is to protect the freedom of the will!

Memory is another way the mind controls the internal environment, especially in respect to prior knowledge and attitude formation. Memory is the storage and recall of previous experiences. Scientists throughout history have been unable to reduce the phenomenon of the memory process to a set of physical occurrences. What is clear is that memory is a function of the brain that seems to be diffused about the entire brain structure. The research of the psychologist Karl Lashely in the early 1950s involved searching for the "engram" or individual memory trace in the activity of the brain. This led him to believe, after a lifetime of work and study in the area of learning and memory, that neither existed at all in a concrete, physical presence. Of course, subsequent researchers have taken a more optimistic view! Recent research supposes that memories are a product of a permanent change in the synapses (communication points) of neurons that results in a retrievable change in the pathway of that neural circuitry. However, the hypothesis has not, as yet, proven a causal relationship between sensation and memory.

Although memory defies physical description, its function and interaction with sensation perception are significant and can be noted. It has been proven that the way stimuli are perceived is dependent, in part, on the attitudes and prior knowledge base of the individual. So an event witnessed by different people could yield entirely different and conflicting accounts, based on the previous experiences of those individuals and the emotional content associated with them. K. Buehler, in 1908, eloquently described situational context as "zeinfeld," and its companion, "symbolfeld," or symbolic field of knowledge, through which zeinfeld might be interpreted.

Situational context could include the present emotional state of the observer (distress, embarrassment, joy), any external constraints on the observer, as well as features of the external environment. A particularly applicable example of the role of emotion with relation to sensation and memory formation is the powerful relationship between odor and memory recall. The presence of a particular odor in conjunction with an emotional event creates a memory of the event that can be triggered by the mere presence of the odor, even many years later. Researchers suspect that the odor itself is not a particularly strong cue, but rather the emotional context that made for a strong memory and ease of retrieval.

The symbolic field, or prior knowledge base, could include formal education on a topic, previous experience in a similar situation, and the attitudes and opinions held by the observer. It is important to note that the prior knowledge base of an individual is perhaps as dynamic and changing as situational context, because new information is being added to it all the time along with the biases of previous experiences, attitudes, and opinions. Thus the nature of situation and content appears to be circular. We use our prior knowledge base to make inferences about our experiences. These experiences will, in turn, become part of the prior knowledge base (memories) used to judge new experiences.

We seek patterns in our perception, meanings that are comprehensible to us, if not to others. By attending to particular information, we gain experience. As we gain experience, we are inclined to feel a particular way (and vice versa). Experience and emotion are the building blocks by which we make sense of the world. Thus, perceptions enter a personal field of judgment and are marked by it.

To understand more fully the patterns of cognition it may be helpful to have an overview of neuron structure and function. The Appendix provides this overview.

Physiologically speaking, the body is a communication system, receiving, processing, storing, utilizing, and imparting impressions from without and within, throughout the myriad cells making up the organism. This communication loop is linked to a cosmic network with all other entities, sensing and being sensed. In our view it is reasonable to consider that network open instead of closed, dynamic rather than static, meaningful rather than meaningless. It is reasonable to acknowledge that "in [God] we live and move and have our being," as the apostle Paul told a Greek audience, citing their own sages (Acts 17:28). The intricacies of our sensory system can be described in helpful detail, but cognition is not enclosed by explanation. Mystery looms always at the horizon of the understanding. Only those jaded with life or overwhelmed by its burdens would choose ignorance. That our bodies participate in a mystery must be intuited. This condition is no barrier to rational inquiry, but rather a stimulus. Likewise the horizon of mystery is no threat to faith in God, but rather an invitation to greater faith and to a spiritual discipline that yearns for the body to be more fully the temple of the Holy Spirit. Mystery is a summons to receive God's revelation as wholly as possible, including what comes through the senses.[10]

Religious Perspectives

Religious experience, like other truth claims, must "make sense," in respect to those bodily activities that we label sound, sight, smell, taste, and touch. The senses serve as our antennae to the world. The senses function as messengers of God, receiving signals from all sorts of senders, natural, supernatural, artificial. These signals are received and interpreted by the mind and through such perception the world is experienced. The senses are so much a part of us we sometimes neglect to ponder their essential function, but only try to keep them physically operable. So we go to the optometrist for glasses, to the audiologist for a hearing aid, to a gourmet restaurant to whet our taste buds for nutritious food, to the perfumery for olfactory enhancement, and to the health club for muscle toning. But the inner monitor must function rightly. Discipline is required. Jesus lamented folk who had eyes but did not see and who had ears but did not hear. Our sensory antennae are designed to receive the divine Word.

In theological terms the senses are media of revelation, the means whereby God accesses the self in the mystery of reality. Mystery implies reality, not fantasy. As noted previously, Augustine used more poetic language, declaring that "the senses are the messengers of God." Groping for words to explain mystery he drew upon metaphor. Although educated a Greek, Augustine reflected a Hebrew understanding of the evocative power of verbal language and its resulting metaphors. When the psalmist wrote, "As the deer pants for streams of water, so my soul pants for you, O God" (Ps. 42:1 NIV), he used an observed occurrence to describe an inward yearning. The psalmist's word picture signified an abstraction, "the knowledge" of God.

As we scan these words centuries later with our eyes or trace them with our fingers, or listen to them with our ears, these alphabetized symbols for seeing and touching and hearing connect us to the Lord for whose presence David longed. Such a bridging of thought we label metaphor. Poetic metaphors signify reality more intimately than do abstracted concepts, because they are closer to the sensory flow of perception.

This book, to repeat, is about being spiritual in a sensory way. It's about using the body as a temple of the Spirit. As a response to struggles between flesh and spirit, so vividly depicted by Augustine, medieval Christian mystics feared that yielding to the senses would lure them away from God. Indulgence would destroy the soul. As noted earlier, a Platonic world view (that ideas are more real than things) and a horror at Roman licentiousness fed this fear. Medieval spirituality therefore required a rigorous denial of bodily urges. Persons hungering for holiness took seriously, if not literally, the admonition of Jesus, "If your right eye causes you to sin, tear it out and throw it away; it is better for you to lose one of your members than for your whole body to be thrown into hell." (Matt. 5:29) To serious medieval Christians the self was more fully realized through spiritual union with God than by physical self-fulfillment. Sensory deprivation became a major spiritual discipline.

Jacapone da Todi illustrates this monastic retreat from the sensual. This thirteenth-century Franciscan wrote clever verse about the senses, each one claiming merit for being the shortest-lived, with "lustful Touch" the loser. One poem is entitled "On Guard Against the Senses." It conveys admonitions to shield eyes from what can wound the heart, to close the ears to vanity, to be wary of the poisonous excesses that accompany the joys of taste, to guard against what a new scent can convey and the doom touch can bring. In general the theme is to keep fire (passion) away from the gates of the city (the self).[11] Perhaps this is the historic source of the little chorus I learned as a child, "Be careful little eyes what you see...."

Such monastic spirituality seemed elitist at best and perverse at worst to many European Christians of the Reformation era. They welcomed as a significant event Martin Luther's marriage to the nun, Catherine von Bora. They enjoyed it when he rhapsodized about married love ("pigtails on the pillow"). To jokes about the famous doctor of theology hanging diapers on the line, Luther said, "let them laugh; the angels rejoice." Luther's answer symbolized a return of holiness from cloister to hearth. It called for a spiritual discipline based on the body as the temple of the Holy Spirit.

Medieval monks rightly wanted to restore self-control, so that the spirit would be free from bondage to the flesh. But a trail of moral failure by celibate priests suggests this historic approach is a frustrating path for spiritual discipline. Luther rightly wanted to reaffirm a good creation, including the human body. But a trail of moral failure by married Protestant clergy, and promiscuity by the laity, suggests that Luther's exuberant espousal of passion required good discipline.

In contrast to monastic spirituality, some modern "health and wealth" Christian speakers affirm bodily indulgence, and, then, to public amusement, get caught up in sex or greed scandals. These Christian advocates want to gain acceptance by aping materialistic culture, while drawing the line at selected moral excesses of that culture. So supermarket churches stress being "with it" culturally. No longer do people cast their jewelry into the offering plate to purge the soul of vanity or to support missions. Glamour sells religion, as it sells beverages, condiments, medicine, household cleaners, and automobiles. In earlier times sex and religion were culturally intertwined, temple prostitution, for example. Some current cultural patterns accent that ideological blend. Perhaps some people will become so sickened by the gross sensuality of contemporary culture that monastic spirituality will appeal again to earnest Christians. The pervasive force of technology, however, makes asceticism an unlikely option for most people.

There is a better way for most of us than ascetic denial or hedonistic indulgence. It involves the intelligent interrogation of the senses acknowledged as the messengers of God, with appropriate disciplines to follow. A spiritual life can be sensory, but it need not be vain and extravagant. The good life can be sensuous without being sensual. We turn next to what this disciplined way can mean for each of the senses.

Notes

1. The tension between knowledge understood as the implication of innate ideas and knowledge understood as inference from sense data has led to a general intellectual acknowledgment (at least as ground rules for public inquiry) of certain paired boundaries to cognitive paths, boundaries such as subject and object, public and private knowledge, and the specific and general nature of truth.

2. Translation by Albert Outler, Vol. VII of *The Library of Christian Classics* (Philadelphia: Westminster, 1955).

3. I am indebted to my colleague, Gary Fawver, for this phrase found in David Adam, *The Cry of the Deer* (Wilton, CN: Borehouse-Barlow, 1987).

4. The earliest of his several books was *The Technological Society, 1964*. I draw here from *What I Believe* (Grand Rapids: Eerdmans, 1989), pp. 99ff., which is cited in a provocative article by Richard Stivers, "The Festival in the Light of the Theory of the Three Milieus," in *The Journal of the Academy of Religion* (Fall 1993).

5. Paul Hawken, in *The Ecology of Commerce* (New York: HarperBusiness, 1993), considers that social disaster threatens the world through the continuance of wasteful commercial practices. He is not just a prophet of doom, however; he makes a strong and realistic case for business not just to clean up waste, which he considers insufficient, but to redesign industrial processes with cyclical rather than linear pattern, in such a way as to prevent waste. He follows the theories of Nicolas Pigou, commerce must be required to bear the full costs of production, including external environmental costs.

6. For clarifying distinctions between sensual and sensuous I am indebted to Charles Davis, *Body as Spirit: The Nature of Religious Feeling* (New York: Seabury Press, 1976); see pp. 41-45.

7. See his article "Nature as the Image of God" in *Theology Today* (April 1994), and his book *Nature, Reality and the Sacred* (Minneapolis: Augsburg/Fortress, 1993). The contingent aspect of nature, its non-self explanatory character, Gilkey thinks, points to the logic of God as creator.

8. *War and Anti-War* (New York: Little, Brown and Company, 1993), p. 170. Note also an interview with the Tofflers, *Psychology Today* (Vol. 27, Jan-Feb. 1994), pp. 26-31, in which the writers brood over the proliferation of nuclear weapons and the danger this poses in an information-based civilization.

9. We have gained insights from Diane Ackerman, *A Natural History of the Senses* (New York: Random House, 1990). Although not written from an overtly religious perspective, her description of sensory function is depicted and elaborated helpfully.

10. The following books have been helpful in preparing the descriptions contained in the preceding paragraphs and in the following chapters.

John D. Bransford, *Human Cognition: Learning, Understanding and Remembering* (Belmont, CA: Wadsworth, Inc., 1979).

Morton A. Heller and William Schiff, *The Psychology of Touch* (Hillsdale, NJ: Lawrence Erlbaum Associates, 1991).

C. Romero-Sierra, *Neuroanatomy: A Conceptual Approach* (New York: Churchill Livingstone, 1986).

H.R. Schiffman, *Sensation and Perception: An Integrated Approach* (New York: John Wiley and Sons, 1990).

Gordon M. Shepherd, *Neurobiology* (New York: Oxford University Press, 1988).

We have followed with interest the workings of Harvard University's Mind, Brain, and Behavior Inter-faculty Initiative (MBB). See a progress report by John DeCuevas, *Harvard Magazine* (November-December 1994). The report acknowledges the enormous complexity of the brain, and that mapping the brain's neurons, although helpful for human welfare, falls far short of unraveling the mystery of the mind.

11. See Lauds 5 and 6, in Jacopone da Todi, *Classics of Western Spirituality* (New York: Paulist, 1982), pp. 76ff.

CHAPTER TWO

HEARING

Because this mind of ours is enclosed within the "palace" of the body...
God has chosen to create the five senses of the body
to serve as so many openings to the world around us.
—Nicodemus of the Holy Mountain

In this chapter we consider how our ears connect the world outside to the world within us, and how through hearing we discern the voice of God. Two stories set the stage.

Introductory Scenarios

STORY ONE: Lyn and Gladys are widowed persons who have rediscovered romance. Their happiness in a recent marriage is obvious. They live in Gladys's beachfront house, built years ago by her first husband. The surf crashes a few yards from their window. Occasionally a sneaker wave flings foamy water upon their lawn. A seagull, Gertrude, shows up every morning to beg food. Turnstones flash their feathers in formation just above the crests of the waves. Whales cavort offshore. It's a pleasant, peaceful place. These octogenarians are truly helpmates; he is nearly blind, she is quite deaf. The sounds of surf and seagulls and the church choir are good, but Lyn misses the bustling excitement of the city. He is a retired professor of music, who has conducted bands and composed music. Life is slipping toward the edge, he realizes. So one day he and Gladys decide to live it up a bit. They will go to New York and see the opera *Carmen*. A travel agent sets up an itinerary. On the appointed day they sally forth from their village on the central Oregon coast to the "Big Apple," a continent away. First they flag a bus along Highway 101. It takes them to Portland. Then they ride a city bus to a hotel. The next morning an airport limousine enables them to catch a flight to New York, changing planes at Chicago's O'Hare Airport. Arriving at Kennedy Airport they discover their baggage has been lost. Gladys is distraught but Lyn is undaunted. Pounding his white cane on the floor he informs the agent they require proper apparel for attending the opera tonight. He is persuasive. Airline voucher in hand they take a taxi to their hotel, then to a clothing store to secure with airline funds a tuxedo for Lyn and a formal dress for Gladys, plus appropriate accessories.

Thus equipped they rest a bit, eat a hearty meal at the hotel, dress up in their new finery, and take a taxi to the theater for the performance of *Carmen*. Gladys can't hear much of the operatic score but she enjoys seeing the action, the costumes, the staging. Lyn can barely see the stage, but Bizet's lovely music blesses his soul. For him *Carmen* indeed means a song, triggering recollections of ecstasy accompanying his own past musical performances.

They return home the next morning via airport limo, airplane, and bus. Gertrude, the pesky seagull, awaits them on the lawn, loudly complaining of neglect. The ocean waves rise, crest, and crash, reassuring the eyes of Gladys, the ears of Lyn. They are home.

But soon they must move to assisted living housing. Then Gladys begins to fail, but not before the carillon, which they purchased for the church, peals joyous hymns of praise to the Lord. Soon it's nursing home time, then death. Lyn is alone again. For solace he draws upon a rich store of musical memories, not the least of which is the recent hearing of the opera *Carmen*. Then, he dies, full of faith in God, and in God-gifted human artistry.

STORY TWO: *Immortal Beloved* is playing locally. It is the story of Beethoven's later years, when deafness frustrated his musical artistry and complicated his search for love. Few patrons attend this weekday matinee. Most are senior citizens. They select rear seats in the small movie house. One couple, however, is young. They choose seats near the front, kissing each other happily as the lights dim. The "coming attractions" display gratuitous violence: combatants snarling, swords slashing, guns blazing, buildings burning. The word *kill* is the major verb used. There are titillating flashes of flesh suggesting violent copulation. It's grossly sensate, ugly, disgusting to the seniors, boring to the kids. How could the actors sell themselves so cheaply? How could producers face their neighbors? At least that's what the seniors think.

The feature film is quite the contrast. What magnificent cinematography! The story line, the acting, and the photography provide a compelling dramatic frame for the pathos of Beethoven's tortuous but creative life. The sound track of the film uses the best orchestration in the world, the best recording technology. Sometimes it whispers, sometimes it cries, sometimes it shouts, but as Beethoven's music reverberates in the theater it surges through the ear and into the heart of the hearer with power and poignancy. After hearing the "Ode to Joy" whose heart is not touched to forgive?

Or so it seems to the senior couples who remain in the theater after the kids slip out. They stay in place, hands laced together until the credit lines run out and the last note fades away. Until silence falls. A silence in which to dry the eyes. To regain composure. To face their worlds also (if not as dramatically) mixed with terrible sadness and inexpressible joy.

Except for hearing-impaired persons, the ears are antennae for much of the reality we perceive. In contemporary culture the marketing of vocal and instrumental sounds constitutes a major industry worldwide, and through audiovisual pairing in television and motion picture, media has become an enormous social force. Electronically reproduced sounds are widely marketed through television and radio programs, records, cassettes, and CD's. They have become adjunct to or a substitute for immediate experience and memory as a way of savoring sound. Audio technology has revolutionized our culture so profoundly, has become so enmeshed in our daily life, that it is difficult to find either an exterior quiet time or an interior silence with which to judge the meaning of auditory events. Impressions are conveyed so powerfully that they often short-circuit the more laborious process by which the mind interprets data.

Newer sounds threaten to displace many older sounds that traditionally served to carry meaning from one generation to the next. Hymns, classical music, authentic folk music, neighborhood sounds, and story telling are among the threatened sounds.

For purposes of reflective judgment it may be useful to make an inventory of sounds that strike the ear. For convenience we group them in these categories: passive hearing, conditioned hearing, egocentric hearing, empathetic hearing, and godly hearing. In each of these categories we will suggest how sounds can constitute a godly use of this sense, that is, how the mind can interrogate these messengers to discern and act upon the will of God.

But first we describe what happens physically when we hear, how sounds move from physical sensation to mental understanding, and note how sounds function individually and socially.

Basically, the stimulus required to initiate the sensation of hearing is a wave of "sound." Sound waves travel from their source through the air, much as ripples travel through still water from a point of disturbance. They vary in frequency, or rate of successive waves; and in amplitude, or force of air displacement. An increase in frequency, for example, would correspond to a perceptual change in the pitch of the sound, while an increase or decrease in the amplitude of a sound wave would be perceived as a change in volume. A sonic boom, created when a plane travels faster than the speed of sound, makes us aware of these aspects of sound waves.

Human ears detect sound waves between frequencies of 20 hertz and 20,000 hertz. Hertz are the standard unit of measure of sound waves, as one hertz corresponds to one cycle (wave) per second. Our ears are best attuned to frequencies between about 1,000 hertz and 5,000 hertz. It is no coincidence that this is also the level at which we communicate through voice modulation, or language. The precise means by which people communicate with one another through spoken word is far from understood. However, a loose hierarchical framework offers a pathway to better understanding. As sound comes into the ear it is coded as to range and frequency. Then it is stored in short term memory in the form of phonemes (a unit of sound). Phonemes are grouped as to syntax, from which meaningful sounds (words and sentences) are formed. The next phase is semantic, analyzing and interpreting speech within an appropriate environment and context of experience.[1] This summarizes the auditory loop from sensory stimuli to understanding.

Some understanding of the physical properties of sound may be helpful. If a measure of amplitude (volume) is added in decibels along with the range of frequencies in hertz, a chart can be plotted that creates "isophonic curves," or equal loudness contours, along which each point is perceived at the same intensity. For example, on an equal loudness contour, 100 hertz at 70 decibels would be perceived as the same intensity level, loudness, as 1,000 hertz at 60 decibels.[2]

It is important to consider sound intensity because it is the factor involved in damage to the auditory system at high levels. For example, a rock concert may be in the 130 decibel range and at that level a person will actually start feeling the vibrations of the tympanum in the ear. The next step would involve pain (140+ decibels) and consequent hearing loss or damage at a given frequency.[3]

Although receptor cells in lower animals regenerate throughout their lifetime, in humans, the hair cells that receive and transmit sound information are produced only in the embryonic stage of fetal development. Consequently, damage to the receptor cells through overstimulation or other means is irreversible.[4]

We receive and interpret sound physically through a chain reaction of events. When a wave of sound comes in contact with the ear, it is captured by the pinna, or outer ear structure, and enters the external auditory canal. It is amplified in the small space and funneled down to the tympanum, or ear drum. The tympanum is a thin membrane that forms a seal between the middle and outer ear, creating an environment in the middle ear that is under a higher air pressure. As the sound wave strikes the tympanum, it vibrates and this vibration is transmitted through a structure of three bones in the middle ear.

The first bone, the malleus, is connected to the top portion of the tympanic membrane and translates the vibrations into hammering motion on the second bone, the incus. The incus is connected to the third bone, the stapes, and translates the hammering movements of the malleus to it. The stapes is anchored by the incus on one end and the entrance to the inner ear, called the oval window, on the other. There are two small muscles (tensor tympani attached to malleus and stapedius to the stapes) connecting to ear ossicles. When these muscles contract, they mute the sound so that the ossicles cannot conduct the same level of vibration to the inner ear, thus protecting it from some overexposure of noise. An interesting phenomenon is that of "attenuation." This is easily understood when one reenters a car and the radio volume is so high it hurts your ears but yet no one turned it up since you drove it. You are listening to the same music volume but with "fresh ears" that have not been attenuated to the "noise." The movements of the stapes at the oval window create waves in the fluid-filled environment of the inner ear, or cochlea. The force of the vibration of the tympanum is duplicated on the much smaller oval window by the mechanism of the bone structure and the higher pressure of the middle ear environment.

The cochlea is a fluid-filled tube coiled upon itself about three times in a spiral pattern similar to a snail shell. The inner structure of the cochlea is divided into three canals. The middle canal, the cochlear duct, is divided from the upper and lower canals by Reissner's membrane and the basilar membrane, respectively. It is along the basilar membrane that lie the hair-like structures that are the receptor cells for sound perception.

As a wave travels along the cochlea, it has a point at which it displaces a maximum amount of fluid, depending on the frequency. At maximum displacement, the cilia receptors begin to oscillate. In this way, the basilar membrane acts, in the words of pioneering psychologist George von Bekesy, as a "tonotopic map of the frequency content of sound." Sounds of a high frequency displace the hair cells closest to the oval window; lower frequency sounds stimulate the hair cells toward the end to the cochlea.[5]

Each hair cell is actually made up of bundles of filaments, called stereocilia, that are arranged in an increasing stairstep structure. The stereocilia contain a substance called actin that aids in transduction of neural impulse when the stereo cilia bend. There are also two types of receptors, inner hair cells and outer hair cells. There are many more outer hair cells than inner, but the inner hair cells form connections with over 90 percent of the 50,000 nerve fibers that transmit their information to the brain.

In other words, many neurons converge onto a single inner hair cell and carry its information. Con-

versely, the prolific outer hair cells must converge onto the remaining nerve fibers in a 10:1 ratio. Subsequently, it is theorized that the inner hair cells provide the kind of sensitivity and sound discrimination information necessary, say, to enjoy a night at the symphony. Additionally, tuning properties like resonance and bass are thought to be achieved through electrical properties in the hair cell membrane, in the stairstep arrangement of the stereocilia, and the location along the basilar membrane. From the cochlea of each ear, the hair receptors create impulses in the surrounding nerve fibers. This information reaches the auditory nerve of the ear and is relayed through a series of structures and neural pathways that act as transfer stations to different areas of the brain. The cochlea also provides information about equilibrium and sense of balance through a web of vestibular filaments that run along the base of the hair cells.[6]

Some impulses provide information in the way they travel. For example, more information coming from one ear provides clues to the location of the sound in the external environment. Along the way, valuable signals go back and forth to initiate physical responses, communicate memory information, and assimilate the other sense messages coming in at the same time.

How Sounds Function

Hearing is so basic to understanding the world that we take it for granted. Sharp noises startle the fetus within the dimness of the womb; singing a lullaby calms a troubled child. Before sight gives focus to touch, surrounding sounds define our place in the world. When darkness falls, sounds enhance the mystery of the night; they offer eerie tokens of unknown presence, of mystery beyond the reach of light and the warmth of fire. Our names are sounds that link us to other persons and identify us among them. Before language is written for the eye the word is spoken and heard. These sounds occur in random or rhythmic sequences and at varying levels of intensity and cadence, but all within a context of silence. Silence provides the frame for sound, defining its character and accenting its meaning. By using framing intervals the mind provides first order and then significance to auditory impressions that come through the door of the ear.

There are natural sounds, artificial sounds, and spoken sounds. We receive natural sounds as locating markers on life's journey. These sounds warn of danger, they communicate events, and they afford aesthetic pain or pleasure. We seldom question them. The auditory environment is diverse. Wind blowing in the trees, waves crashing on the rocks, the cascading of a creek, rain beating on the roof, footsteps crunching on the pathway, thunder rolling through the night, geese honking in flight overhead, crows cawing from the tops of trees, calves bawling in the barn, horses neighing in the pasture, crickets chirping, frogs croaking, dogs barking, cats purring.

The psalmist (Ps. 104:4) said God makes the winds his messengers. Can we engage in poetic license and let the wind speak for all natural sounds that throng about our ears as messengers of God? What do these sounds mean? Do we hear them? Do we cherish them? Above all, do we interrogate their meaning? Do we let God speak through them? Do we heed them?

Artificial sounds constitute markers on life's journey, too, and for urban people these sounds dominate auditory perceptions. (Most of the time nature is rather quiet.) Automobile traffic, the whir and clatter of kitchen and shop equipment, jets taking off from the airport, the hum of computers, copiers, and fax machines, these are some of the major artificial sounds in a technological culture. Indeed, our fascination for technology is in part a wonder at the sound a machine makes. That is why young people modify mufflers on their automobiles, wanting to unite more fully the energy of their animate bodies with that of the inanimate machines under their control. That is why youth turn up the volume on radios and tape recorders, yearning to stretch hearing into the territory of touch and thus experience at its fullest the throbbing beat of music. Artificial sounds evoke territoriality. The noise of my neighbor's lawn mower bothers me more than that of my own. His sound is intrusive noise—it hurts my ears; my sound is extrusive—a mechanical extension of mind and muscle—and I am in charge.

Manufactured sounds can be interpreted as extensions of natural or linguistic sound-making activities. A jackhammer extends the sound of hands breaking things, a saw the sound of hands ripping things apart. A saxophone extends vocal sounds mechanically. Electronic equipment amplifies the range of sounds projected. Recording devices preserve sounds for future secondhand experience; they serve as a repository for remembered experiences.

Linguistic sounds are those personal, culturally learned, vocal noises we call speech. These sounds receive social context through cultural conditioning, agreed-upon alphabets, memory storage, and electronic amplification. Speech is a major system of social intercourse, especially when correlated with seeing. We term language that system of communicative signals that traverse the major sensory corridors of persons and other creatures. Spoken language seems "natural" to us and our kind when we are accustomed to it, and "foreign" when we hear "strange" linguistic sounds spoken by others and their kind. It may be debated whether porpoises and other sentient creatures use language, but they do communicate along the sensory corridors by which they are connected to the external world.

For human beings, in any case, body language includes activities other than linguistic speech. Non-alphabetized sounds include sighing, laughing, weeping, foot tapping, drumming fingers, whistling, humming, booing, coughing. These are aspects of the auditory system by which we communicate with each other or express emotions, wishes, and sometimes coded information. In addition to alphabetized and non-alphabetized sounds there are other forms of "speech" that convey meanings powerfully through physical movements such as eye contacts, posture, and gestures. Some of these will be noted in the other chapters.

As a function of the body, the voice is an instrument for righteousness or unrighteousness. On both cognitive and affective levels the voice can convey to listening ears either truth or falsehood. The sounds of speech inform or deceive, they hurt or they heal. Consider the ear, then, as a gate to truth or to deception, to persuasion or to propaganda. Thus speech ought to be honored by truth saying. "Simply let your 'Yes' be 'Yes,' and your 'No,' 'No,'" said Jesus; "anything beyond this comes from the evil one." (Matt. 5:37 NIV) A return to this first principle enables persons to offer a powerful witness against a demonic sophistry whereby propaganda subverts truth as the aim of speech. Consider how much human time and energy is wasted in calculating how to circumvent truth and to evade its moral implications. Think of the sophistry involved in applying politically correct "spin" on the speech of public officials, and in media speculation about whether the nuances were well or poorly done. Here, as in other instances, the aesthetic best is used to avoid the ethical good.

Important social activities take place in the conventions of speech: simple instructions, public policy proclamations, affirmed affinity with another person. The vocal locutions that bond us to others vary in significance from "this is how to lay the shingles," to "this is how the health care system should be changed," to "I love you, sweetheart!" The ear plays host to many visitors in the home of the spirit, and seeks to accommodate them harmoniously.

In this temple of the Spirit can be heard, also, litanies of worship, from "God, be merciful to me, a sinner," to "praise to the Lord, the Almighty." Godly hearing does not require a special nonauditory track, but, to use Augustine's terms, it does require a right interrogation of the outer self by the inner self. And for this interrogation the self must be sufficiently free from external programming so that real choices in respect to sound can be made.

We turn now from a general description of how sounds function to a consideration by category of how they serve as agents of the Almighty.

Passive Hearing

In passive hearing we receive auditory stimuli uncritically. Generally these ordinary sounds wash over us. They are the sounds we don't have to respond to actively or analyze for meaning. We are accustomed to them, they don't threaten us. Ordinarily we don't fight these sounds, or try to soften or control them. Within acceptable decibel levels and rightly framed by silence, these sounds define our physical and social location. They help us to be comfortable where we are—to be at home. Our ears stick out (farther for some persons than for others!) as receivers to catch the common sounds of our living space. For impaired persons hearing aids and cochlear implants open the ear gate to the world of auditory perception. Passive hearing is an important part of spirituality.

Many sounds in our daily experience are manufactured; some threaten our inner stability while others do not. The rhythmic putt-putt of a tractor flows over the farmer and serves as a litany of divine blessing upon useful labor. Machineried sounds can also serve as prophetic reminders to work responsibly. The tumbling of a clothes dryer in our home says we live here. Auditory rhythms affirm the dignity of a truck driver or a backhoe operator, a roofer or a typist, a dentist or a drill press operator, a writer or a teacher. All this clatter of marvelous and intricate machinery speaks into a worker's ear a reassuring word: "People are served by my labor; the expenditure of my time and energy is honorable and it is worthy of just recompense."

What are the manufactured sounds common to our daily experience? What sound waves baptize our work as a service to others? What auditory sensations reinforce within us a joyous love for God who has made humanity of one blood, to dwell on the face of the earth?

Other common sounds washing over us are natural within the boundaries of our particular location: the roaring surf, wind in the trees, the patter of rain, the chatter of squirrels, the cawing of crows. Social sounds that provide background noise may include babies crying in the next apartment, children playing in the park, people conversing in a restaurant, youth laughing on the street, a choir singing in a church. What are the sounds common to our daily experience? Do these sounds enmesh us in the beauty and wonder of God's creation? It isn't so much that we need to question these particular sounds as to acknowledge them as part of the environment in which we feel at home and are accepted. We hear them as hovering angels.

Whenever we become overly tired, or ill, or fall into a jangly mood, or become overwhelmed by burdens of the world, by its tragedies, and by our own losses and failures (or even by too much noise), then these common sounds (natural or manufactured) can irritate us. Then we are tempted to retaliate noisily against the conveyers of these sounds. So we yell at the poky driver when the light turns green, or slam the window against the cry of a neighbor child, or kick the whimpering dog out the door. Or mutter at the spouse going about household duties. When this mood comes upon us, sounds that ordinarily reinforce our sense of location become a cacophony that alienates us from ourselves, and, subsequently, from other people. And from God.

Passive hearing is easily exploited. How can we cope when our auditory environment gets dominated by sounds we don't like or when ordinary sounds run amok within our minds? I suggest the following practical ways. The order may vary according to one's needs.

First, *find space for silence.* Find a place as well as a time to rediscover the silence that frames environmental sound and thus accents its significance. The time can be as brief as a few moments of meditation on a rest break or as long as a month's retreat. The space can be as small as your room or as large as a forest. During this quiet time put aside all noise under your control—television, radio, traffic, machinery, family conversations, and clamorous activities. Ask your eyes to cooperate by shutting down images received. If your ears are still too burdened to find the soul's still center, let your feet find familiar forest paths, or let your hands engage in ruminative routines, such as knitting or woodcarving, and let your memory recover for inward hearing some melodies of past joy.

Most of us require a combination of outer and inner silence in order to recover from emotional distress. However reached, such silence clarifies who we are and where we are going. Having experienced such silence we can then resonate with the psalmist: "For God alone my soul waits in silence; from him comes my salvation. He alone is my rock and my salvation, my fortress; I shall never be shaken." (Ps. 62:1)

Silence provides space to work our way through overwhelming daily clutter or through tragic events. "Waiting" is the biblical word for bearing difficult burdens, for coping with losses. The book of Lamentations teaches, "It is good to wait quietly for the salvation of the Lord." (See Lam. 3:26-28.) Personal, even lonely, silence is a spiritual discipline recommended for the young, who often try to avoid the necessity of prayerful reflection by surrounding themselves with noise. It is also a good discipline for adults who sometimes substitute criticism for prayer. "Waiting" is not pious resignation to fate but rather a discipline that enables one to hear God's voice in a tumultuous world. Waiting is a prelude to intercessory prayer for yourself or for others.

Second, *pray.* Catch the Creator's ear, whether in silence or crying out to God from the silence. This is the secret of the psalmist. He sought God's ear in prayer when he became distressed: "Hear my prayer, O God; listen to the words of my mouth." (Ps. 54:2 NIV) Such prayer restores our senses to their function as messengers of God. We yield our bodies to divine will. The sound waves get sorted out and given priority. In prayer we acknowledge that God is the creator and sustainer of the world. Whatever signals we receive through the ear gate of the body, natural and artificial, find significance when heard as the voice of God.

Third, *enhance the hearing of the natural sounds.* People often go to the beach to be soothed by sounds of the surf, or climb the mountains to be sustained by the whisper of wind in the trees and the rippling laughter of a stream tumbling its way from source to sea. In short, they take a sound break. Lacking opportunity or time for such retreats, center down in your own spirit and open your ears to the natural sounds within your own environment. Listen to the birds in the neighborhood whose chirping goes unnoticed unless you remember to tune them in. Or, use recordings of natural sounds. Secondhand is better than nothing.

Fourth, *send forth your own sounds of joy.* Some people restore harmony to their lives by singing or playing a musical instrument. My father used to hum hymns while standing one foot on the fence, watching the hogs eat their slop. He filled ordinary, mundane, even messy chores, with the sounds of inner joy. I honor his memory. Do you find music uncongenial? Try speech. Talk to the squirrels, or to the flowers, if necessary! I know a woman who chats with a blue heron every day while the friendly bird carefully snatches anchovies from her hand. Greet passersby, not for the sake of an audience, or to convey factual information, but for the sake of your soul. Offer an aural sacrifice to God, who has heard your prayer, and whose creation—including humanity—is the object of redemptive love. In offering praise you may hear anew the sonorous world of God's natural and social creation.

Silence, prayer, immersion in natural sound, and praise—these disciplines enfold the common sounds of daily experience in a circle of coherence. Having regained peace, we resist that subtle temptation to sustain control of sound by blaming or hurting someone or by exploiting their auditory space. Why nurture pique or exact a retributive tax from others in an effort to secure your own tranquillity? As God hears our prayer and we heed the Spirit, ordinary environmental sounds begin to roll over us rhythmically. Our ears receive them as God's messengers of grace. We rejoice in a world of interdependent people, appreciating the rattle of labor-easing machinery, the patter of rain, the barking of dogs, and even the whir of a dentist's drill. The noise of children and truck drivers, farmers and teachers, customers and store clerks renew joy in the gift of life. Such is the tranquillity that comes when passive listening is infused by the Holy Spirit.

Conditioned Hearing

Much of our perceived reality is auditory in form. By poetry and music we add human creativity to celebrate that reality. It is as if God has given us an array of sound and said, "Enjoy it!" Even much of what the eye receives through print media, especially poetry and lyric prose, communicates best when heard directly by the ear, or indirectly by the mind replaying harmonious syllables inwardly.

A study of linguistic media is well beyond the purposes of this book. Much has been written recently about the conditioning power of mass media, from Marshal McLuhan on. For our purposes a query may suffice to reflect upon how sounds that aim to influence us can be questioned for conformity to divine purpose. What is the most widely heard exhortation today? Certainly not the religious summons, "Repent!" Modern culture finds that call for a moral turnaround impolite at best and boorish at worst. Maybe it was all right for Jesus to exhort the Pharisees thus in Bible times, but not for us moderns! An indirect question, such as, "Have you ever considered…?" is about as hortatory a religious question as people will tolerate.

What, then, is the most widely heard exhortation today? It is "Call now!" This vocal appeal assails the ears of millions of persons daily through hundreds of television commercials. Television time is so expensive that narrators are chosen who can enunciate rapidly. This effort at speedy speech has reached a point of absurdity! Phone numbers are flung across our ears so fast that few have time to remember them or write them down. Apparently the advertising psychologists assume that noisy repetition will din the message home after multiple hearings. Saturation appears to be the operating mode of such advertising.

This "call now" exhortation to a materialistic discipleship appears in a daily barrage of advertisements. Actors sing, scream, screech, and yell into our ears to get us to buy what their sponsors want to sell. Ironically, we pay to get yelled at; the high costs of such promotional sound contribute substantially to the price of the goods.[7] Promotion often costs considerably more than the material used or the labor expended in manufacture of the product touted.

Do we like being yelled at, especially in our own homes? No. We feel trapped in a materialistic culture, which evangelizes at high entrepreneurial volume, turning every day into a noisy carnival. We put up with such auditory nonsense in order to hear the news or view a program, or a movie. It is tolerated because we hope things will improve. Our hope for improvement is based upon a notion that our culture may be at an early stage of the technological revolution, and that the worst excesses will diminish, that in the future this auditory abuse will seem as deaf to human values as abusive child labor and slavery was in the early stages of the industrial revolution. But anxiety brackets our hope: What if this absurd form of patronage just goes on and on?

Certain ambiguities within our culture give evidence of a burgeoning discontent with media control of our lives. People too sophisticated for high-powered religious banter submit placidly to secular hucksterism on talk shows and television commercials. This will change. People who refuse to tip rude waiters eagerly speak their credit card numbers into a numbered telephonic ear after being urged to "Call now!" (Then they wait six weeks for the goods to arrive!) This numb acceptance of commercial noise will change. People who won't buy another car from an agency where the sales manager closed too aggressively still put up with crude and aggressive television programs and commercials. This will change. People who show the door to an overzealous salesperson timidly accept being yelled at in their own living rooms daily by unctuous hawkers of goods and services. This will change. People who become incensed at a child interrupting an adult conversation blithely put up with advertisements that interrupt important news reporting. People who wouldn't use a chain saw without earplugs pay large sums to hear high decibel musical noise unprotected. This, too, will change.

People are getting angry at auditory assault. People are becoming outraged at loud television commercials, ones that compress sounds to eliminate modulations when first recorded, so as to elevate the effective sound level while keeping within broadcast limits. I say this word to industries, telephone companies, radio and television producers and stations, school systems, art studios, music factories, peddlers of background and mood music, symphony orchestras, churches, and electronic software conglomerates: Listen, all of you! Take notice! A revolt is brewing in the land. People want to regain control of their ears.

And why shouldn't they? Ears are important. Other people shouldn't be allowed to beat on them incessantly. Through these ear gates to the temple of the Spirit enter myriad sounds, some ominous, some mysterious, others replete with the wonders and joys of God's creation and of human artistry. Why should passageways for beautiful music, natural sounds, and pleasant conversation become monopolized by commerce? In the name of Jesus let's throw the rude, noisy, money changers out of the temple! Why should outsiders take charge of selecting sounds for our ears without the consent of our minds? Why should auditory garbage clog our ears? Why should false shepherds guard this door of the soul?

So, let's think about our ears and be concerned about godly hearing, lest Jesus' rebuke apply to us as it did to hard-hearted folk long ago, "having ears you don't hear!"

"The voice of the people is the voice of God," was once a populist slogan. This slogan carries a grain of truth. Speech is a route for the Spirit and a sign of authentic human community. But speech is also a channel for abuse when evil prevails. Such abuse is rampant in our multi-media culture. For example, well-modulated voices intoning a beverage commercial about fun in the sun seems to imply a universal experience of the good life that the listener would be unfulfilled to miss. Those voicing this claim are impostors. Posing as champions of the universal good, they are actually hireling priests serving a modern Baal. The sound track gives vocalists, musicians, and actors remarkable legislative and judicial powers, and the video track offers them convenient staging. Traditionally the theater has upheld the universal good, usually in an oblique fashion that appeals to us aesthetically. Demagoguery in the exercise of political power may arise from the theater or the marketplace. Both kinds of cultural power clamor for our ears, and we have to decide whom to hear and whom to heed. In our technological society, however, the theater has become monopolized by commerce, its major patron. Commerce, not governance or religion, now controls the staging of the human drama. Its hirelings are becoming our storytellers.

The use of human speech is an obvious linguistic adaptation of natural sounds. With our voice boxes we communicate with each other and with other creatures. We have alphabetized sound for great social convenience. In this way we expedite the exchange of useful or pleasant information. Conversation is auditory intercourse. Through speech we give and receive.

Speech is too important a gateway to reality to be monopolized by exploitive media and manipulated by those who would seize control over sound. People are grateful for the invention of remote control devices, so that they can relieve their ears from a constant barrage of sound on the television set. We can "zap" off the sound and gain the relief of silence.

We need other kinds of "zappers," interior ones, that judge between sounds that edify and those that do not. The eye is under more direct control; eyes can be shut or averted from images. It is not so easy for the ear to escape the tyranny of those who would manipulate noise to their advantage.

If we are to take charge of our own ears we should consider how the cultural "powers that be" program sounds for us, then make our own decisions about "tuning in" and "tuning out." Are the programmers agents of life or agents of death? Conveyers of universal or parochial values? Affirmers of the good, the true, and the beautiful, or of the bad, the false, and the ugly? The latter trilogy apparently sells more merchandise than the former, for violent scenes and sounds dominate the television media, especially for children and youth.

Musical gimmicks provide a lumpy audio-visual mix of merchandising and political influences. Music has become enslaved to commerce in mall music, MTV, standby music on the telephone, and newscast preludes. Martial airs, rock tunes, country westerns, gospel quartets, rap, and classical music are chopped up to make advertising teasers. The merchandisers seize us by the eyes and ears and won't let us go until they have drained our pockets of money. The sounds of folk and classical music are often drowned out by highly marketed pop music, and public taste is manipulated as brashly as are clothing styles. Even public television uses the Boston Pops, Christmas music, or performers of a bygone day, such as Peter, Paul, and Mary, to garner subscriptions. But in the case of public television, the annual sound bash for high culture is a commendable alternative to the daily bash of low culture.

We certainly acknowledge the power of sound to persuade. In the church, hymns and choruses have that effect. The song "Just As I Am Without One Plea" was so overused in the revival era that it ceased to bear a verbal message but became a mantra, like cultic "om" sounds. More contemporary church choruses help people express their faith intimately, but they may inure worshipers from the thoughtful query that Christian discipleship requires. On the other hand, hymns such as Luther's "A Mighty Fortress Is Our God, a Bulwark Never Failing" have inspired many generations with a call to spiritual fortitude. Hearing "Ode to Joy" played at the demise of the Berlin Wall brought shivers of ecstasy to millions of hearers and provided a marvelous auditory symbol of the human quest for freedom.

But sound can also be used to exploit or to terrorize. Government agents use loud noise as a siege instrument against those it wants to capture or subdue. Governments use the power of rhetoric and music to convey propaganda rather than truth. Martial music reinforces patriotism, but also jingoistic nationalism. Curiously, the national anthem is heard ritually at athletic contests, but not at drama events or at public policy lectures. The triumphalist refrain from the Battle of 1812 about "bombs bursting in air" uses warring metaphors to reinforce the partisanship of spectators and the competitiveness of players at ball games. Or is it the reverse: does the partisanship and competitiveness of the game evoke civic loyalty? Why don't we use "America the Beautiful"? It extols the glories of the nation mellifluously. But no, people prefer "The Star-Spangled Banner" because our society has become addicted to violence, and this piece reinforces a warrior mythology.

There is a story in the Bible about a boy, Samuel, who heard God speak to him in the silence of the night—an experience his parents, Hannah and Elkanah, had the vision to foresee, his mentor, Eli, the wisdom to encourage, and the boy the faith to heed. How difficult it is for our boys and girls to hear the voice of God, despite the good will of parents and teachers, when their ears are captive to merchandised noises, when their earspace has been leased to others!

Contemporary parents, educators, and religious leaders seek to mute the alien and often hostile voices so that the voice of the Lord may be heard by the children they nurture. Tragically these mentors, like those of old, often themselves have been dull of hearing, with no new word from the Lord, but only wistful celebrations of a past when the Almighty spoke. As in the case of Eli's priestly sons, lust for sex and gain shut the ear to God's voice. Seductive sounds are not limited to the marketplace. They also arise from religion, especially from the electronic church, which can manipulate the mind with aesthetic substitutes for the voice of God as adroitly as do commercial corporations. Even in the church there may be little auditory space for the voice of God. This is so whether that voice carries the moral thunder of Sinai or a quiet reassuring Presence.

To find auditory space for the voice of God is a major task for families, educators, and religious leaders. A concert of prayerful concern, fueled by hope rather than by cynicism or despair, will lead to corrective actions. People who unite in a concern for freedom from auditory oppression will find ways to break the bonds that entrap. The Holy Spirit within is stronger than the spirit of the world. Here are some ways to break out of aural entrapment.

First, *educate the mind* to question all the vibrations that swarm about the ears. Or batter them! We are admonished to love God with all the mind. To reason effectively honors and worships the Creator. Educating the mind to hear these sounds and heed their messages constructively involves learning and using certain logical processes. Here are some suggestions for educating the mind to interrogate the voices of the earth and its creatures, and to honor these voices as messengers of the Almighty.

1) Organize sensory impressions into categories of understanding, so that sounds don't flood the memory all higgly-piggly. When it's too

noisy we can't think straight. Various descriptive categories (taxonomies more sophisticated than "animal, vegetable, mineral") are set up through our educational experience. Impressions, learned or innate, almost routinely find their way to these filing systems of the brain. But during sensory overload conscious thought needs to be given to the value categories, so that godly judgments can more easily be made about the sounds that come our way. Your memory of music, for example, ought to be more than an index of performers or genre classifications (e.g. jazz, classical, western, rock, blues). We should have at the ready categories of value, such as those suggested by Paul, "...whatever is true, whatever is noble, whatever is right, whatever is pure, whatever is lovely, whatever is admirable—if anything is excellent or praiseworthy—think about such things." (Phil. 4:8) An efficient and accessible mental filing system is important if we want to make good rather than bad use of what we hear and to assign priorities to the natural, artificial, and human voices that beckon us.

2) Gain skills in inductive, deductive, and analogical reasoning so that truth can be distinguished from falsehood, theory from fact, probability from possibility, aesthetic judgments from ethical ones. Our passions should be guided by the call of wisdom, not by emotional feelings. Our contemporary culture has accommodated overmuch to the goal of self-gratification. Even before a basis for judgment has been articulated, "How do you feel about it?" dominates a discussion of personal and social values. This is the talk show syndrome. Hosts elicit emotional responses that reflect prevailing and relativistic social moods instead of answers reflecting truths or values. Style setters prevail over the seers, whether these media models are athletes or actors or commentators, whether the question is about clothing or politics or religion. Without moral authority that transcends inward feelings, leaders of a society soon lose their authority to lead. They become captive to opinion-makers who pander the basest motives in order to sustain their public positions and not offend their patrons. It's time to pose an old Quaker query: "How is truth prospering?"

3) Make sure the education of children for whom you are in any way accountable includes training in logic and ethics. For the past several decades a philosophy for children program (founded by an American philosopher, Matthew Lipmann) has demonstrated that if logic is taught early with age-appropriate curricular aids, the ability to process information through the eye and the ear is enhanced tremendously. The child who learns how to think will be better equipped than otherwise to question

sensory stimuli intelligently. The child who does not learn to think is at the mercy of programmers and propagandists.

Some religious leaders, seeking to sustain leadership, would substitute religious for secular conditioning. But such conditioning does injustice to the mind and sullies the image of God. Sooner or later, religiously conditioned children either exaggerate the coerciveness of such conditioning and turn into narrow-minded zealots, or fall into the hands of cult gurus, or react against religious authority and become militant backsliders who transfer their allegiance to secular systems; or they may slide into cynicism.

Religious elementary and secondary schools often focus too much upon values and not enough upon critical thinking. Public schools often focus mainly on scientific method and ignore values. Recently, however, many public schools have discovered there are ways to teach universal values such as fairness, honesty, and respect. These schools will not be able to offer religious foundations for these virtues, but the church can. Church educators should respect scientific method and let it become a friend of faith. Christians shouldn't hassle the public schools about their efforts to provide religiously neutral value instruction. All truth is God's truth, even if unacknowledged. Educators should be grateful that the good is lifted up and should not worry overmuch about attribution. You start with God, you come to truth; you start with truth, you come to God. The church can offer the credit line (actually, the world view required to support values). Furthermore, the church can reach beyond actions to the heart from which good or bad actions arise. The church can show how law rests upon divine revelation and how civility and social cohesion flow from God's teachings and the experience of redemptive grace. If Christians demonstrate what they teach, others will hear the message.

4) Discern your responsibility for these aural messengers. What does the Lord require of *you* in actions obedient to the light of knowledge? To paraphrase the rhetorical question asked by the prophet Micah, "How do *you* love mercy and walk humbly with your God?" Too much abstraction closes the ear to living truth. Convincement and conviction grow out of what we hear from creation and from other persons. It takes heartfelt discernment to act responsibly and consistently upon rational convictions.

The second way to escape aural entrapment is this: *Reduce or eliminate "junk" sounds,* like the constant patter of radio and television programs. To educate the mind requires time and space. There isn't room for everything that comes buzzing along the airwaves. Our ears get heavy with the load of sounds they have to bear. Some people get addicted. They become sound junkies, always feeding a hungry ear with electronic sounds. To get rid of junk sound requires a disciplined will. Studies have shown that children retain in their memory the jingles and slogans of advertisements ostensibly aimed at adults, such as beer commercials at sports events. It isn't easy to reduce the quantity of sounds that batter our ears or to cut out those that debase. Because the television media is so pervasive and powerful, concerted actions are called for, as well as learning when to turn off the tube. Families will have to ask themselves hard questions about their media diet. The coming of a much expanded information network will either flood us with more junk or stimulate us to be proactive about the management of manufactured sounds. So, let's take the initiative. Let's regain control, become active, not passive. Networks and local stations need to hear from us about programs and advertisements. So do screenwriters' guilds. We can boycott advertisers who pander to sensuality and patronize those who act with civility. With the development of the information network the public will have to be careful that people have more, not less, freedom. Infomercial programs offer a retail store for those who choose it, but we must choose wisely. Hopefully this store-in-the-home will reduce the present network patronage wherein half of program time is now used to peddle goods. Citizens may need to band together to prevent the loss of public television, and be willing to pay for it. The airwaves commons should not be monopolized by merchandisers. The public ought to have choice about those to whom they lend their ears.

A third way to avoid aural entrapment is this: *Give more priority to natural and common sounds.* These sounds sing of creation, they tell of a world shared, they ring the orderly hours of human community, they trumpet the gospel word of renewed creation. Godly conditioning springs from the willing interaction of Creator and creation. It does not override choice but elicits consent through the force of truth and love. To give priority to these sounds requires conscious effort to find space for them among the alternatives. All of us, especially children, need to hear more natural sounds in natural settings, such as waterfalls, the ocean surf, crows cawing, horses whinnying, cats purring. Outdoor schools and camping programs frame these sounds with spiritual interpretation, and should be more greatly used by school and church. Family vacations in the quieter places of the earth ought to have higher priority than trips to Disneyland. In these open, uncluttered, places there is opportunity for interaction with the natural sounds of wind and water and wild animals.

Many common sounds are entrusted to the care of the church for transmission from one generation to another. These include instrumental and vocal music and the stories of faith. Let all children *hear* read to them, or told orally, or sung to them, or spoken in dramatic form, those stories of our faith that arose in centuries and millennia past and have become sacred Scripture: the Genesis accounts of creation and human accountability, God's call to Abraham and Sarah, Moses and the burning bush, the Exodus, the heroic episodes involving Joseph and Daniel, David's turbulent faith expressed in narrative and poetry, the stories of Jesus and the disciples and followers who were directly involved in this central event of history. The stories Jesus told are very important. Let the ears of every child hear over and over again about the Good Samaritan, the conversations of Jesus with the woman at the well, the parables of seed sown in the fields, and the redemption of lost coins, sheep, and children. What a tragedy that some children completing their education, even youth at the college level, have never heard these great Scriptures. They are culturally and spiritually deprived. Many of them have heard cartoon stories, sitcoms, and movie stories by the hundreds and thousands. But without the great biblical stories having early reached their ears, their aural store of memory is deficient. These younger people may know the names of pop stars, but they lack the literary skills that foster passion for ideals, for courageous and hopeful living. Distracted by commercial noise, they do not hear those voices from the past that would guide them into the future. Thus they flounder, flooding their ears with pop music that may haunt them with a tragic sense of life but offers few vibrant notes of hope.

It's a simple thing, but many churches need to relearn this discipline: to have Scripture passages read aloud every Sunday, whether these passages relate directly to the sermon or not. Some churches are discovering the value of training persons, young and older, to be effective Bible readers, so that this reading is not just a routine prelude to a sermon, but the word of God spoken within the community of faith every week. It's not enough to stoutly defend the inspiration of Scripture unless the Bible itself is read prayerfully and expressively in the power of the Spirit who breathed life into it centuries and millennia ago.

A fourth way to avoid aural entrapment is this: *Create the kinds of sound that enhance the Kingdom.* Music brings joy to the soul, and our traditions are rich with music that does so. Certain musical fads are best ignored. Just dubbing a few pious lyrics onto "heavy metal" music, for example, is too imitative to redeem the art form. Even set to less extreme kinds of contemporary music, alternate Christian lyrics often lack the evocative power of traditional hymnody and gospel songs. Church musicians should resist the lure of quick popular success. Instead let them work harder to become creative Christian composers and performing artists. The church once again may need to provide patronage. Through such united efforts, contemporary musical sounds can be added to the traditional repertoire of Kingdom music, for the praise of God and for the joy of persons created in God's image.

Egocentric Hearing

Egocentric hearing involves tuning in to sounds that are personally advantageous, and tuning out what is not. First consider the negative side, about being sensual hearers and speakers. Egocentric hearing can be selfish, for example, attending only to talk that feeds pride, or wallowing in the sound of one's own voice, or using loud speech to dominate convivial situations. Egocentric speaking is the flip side of egocentric listening. Selfish sounds are often downright rude and/or hurtful, noises such as yelling, whistling, or stomping down the bleachers when an opposing player attempts to make a "free" throw at the basketball game, or screaming at city councilors or school board members when the vote doesn't go your way, or blaring loud music at neighbors who irritate you.

Cursing is an abuse to the ear. Isn't it time to really question the profane and vulgar sounds prevalent in our culture (abetted by media patterns) that, carelessly or deliberately, batter our ears? Is there no shame, no awe before the Almighty, no respect for humanity created in divine likeness? Surely the right to free speech is an inadequate reason to curse a neighbor in the name of the Holy One! Surely minimal respect precludes bombarding another person with gutter profanity, even if one is provoked or exasperated or unfairly treated. Cursing and profanity signify egoistic bluster. Such speakers announce, in effect, "I am king of the mountain; everything revolves around me, and here is my verbal whip to remind everyone that this is so." If you have fallen into the trap of profanity, repent and let the Lord God mercifully free you from this bondage.

In many ways contemporary culture (especially through mass media) encourages an excessive, even narcissistic addiction to sound. It encourages a constant and high volume of noise that removes from the hearer the frame of intervening silence that enables one to interrogate sound for its significance. To sustain constant aural pressure necessitates increasingly sensational and bizarre sounds. Accordingly, high volume is given to sounds of little significance. Sensationalist reporting used to be restricted to junk newspapers stashed near the grocery store checkout counter. Now sensationalist stories, gory with violence and larded with noisy advertising, appear nightly on television; they are barely masked as news. Bragging, rather than deference to others, marks our culture. Bragging about one's product, one's political party, or point of view is touted as a virtue in modern American society. This is an unfortunate breach of civility. Capitalism requires competition, but does it necessitate defaming others or overstating one's own status? Isn't it all right just to do one's best, rather than have to claim to be the best? An old proverb (Prov. 27:2 NIV) reads "Let another praise you, and not your own mouth; someone else, and not your own lips." Surely a renewal of modesty is in order.

This slide toward degeneracy in basic virtues occurs even in education and religion, supposed bastions for preserving value over time. A neurotic need for novelty and fads in religion is aptly described thus in the Bible, "For the time will come when men will not put up with sound doctrine. Instead, to suit their own desires, they will gather around them a great number of teachers to say what their itching ears want to hear." (2 Tim. 4:3 NIV) Many of the so-called "new age" cults arise from a restlessness to hear sensational things religiously, to be entertained with metaphysical speculation without having to be morally accountable. The weird is newsy, the bizarre attracts attention, the avant garde strokes the ego.

Many secular and religious talk shows pander to itching ears, offering quick fixes for complex personal problems. They readily palliate shame and absolve false guilt, but they seldom assist their clients to acknowledge true guilt, and even less often to acknowledge that guilt penitently before God. Often they excuse bad conduct on the basis of poor environment. They offer therapy but not judgment, assurance without forgiveness. They substitute standards of self-gratification for the moral law of God.

An old adage refers to lack of perceptive hearing as "in one ear and out the other." Biblical judgment on such "tuning out" rebellion appears in the Old Testament and was alluded to by Jesus in the New Testament:

> "Son of man, you are living among a rebellious people. They have eyes to see but do not see and ears to hear but do not hear, for they are a rebellious people." (Ezek. 12:2 NIV)

> "For this people's heart has become calloused; they hardly hear with their ears, and they have closed their eyes. Otherwise they might see with their eyes, hear with their ears, understand with their hearts and turn, and I would heal them." (Matt. 13:15 NIV)

How lamentably frequent it is in American culture to hear a child interrupt adult conversation, churlishly demanding to be heard! Perhaps children learn from adults, who too quickly grab the initiative during the briefest conversational lull, for example, "Lemme respond to that one!" Why rude interruptions should occur among adults on TV discussion forums is a mystery. Presumably programmers of these forums think they must simulate violence in order to sustain interest. Do programmers suppose people will tune out programs that do not have a hubbub of controversy? Is it that they pay so much for advertising—time is so expensive—they don't want a decent interval between speaking and listening? Civilization for its success depends not the least upon civility, and civility requires the courtesy of respectful pauses in conversation, and proper attention to the art of listening.

But all egocentric hearing is not selfish. There is a good and proper side. The self *needs* to hear what is personally advantageous. To personally hear and heed the voice of God in and through natural, manufactured, and social sound is to participate creatively in the wonder and beauty of the world. Each of us is bound within a circle of what is termed the egocentric predicament. All information and perceptions, conceptions, judgments, all choices good or bad—even altruistic thoughts and decisions—pass through the filter of the self. The ego is the center of will and feelings—the center of the soul. Here the will routes multiple streams of causality into chosen responses for which one stands accountable.

The adage "Keep your ear to the ground!" speaks to the primacy of perception. We must be sensible about what is going on. We must be knowledgeable of the world and keep our wits about us. So, how can egoistic hearing receive sounds as messengers of God and interrogate their meaning? Here are a few suggested characteristics.

A first characteristic of good egocentric listening is *to be alert to dangers natural and social.* When the wind screams at a high pitch we take shelter. When machinery doesn't sound right we seek the cause of the problem. Fire alarms depend upon responsible hearing. When footsteps dog us in the night we seek security.

A second characteristic of good egocentric listening is *to hear and heed the prophetic voice of God.* Whether through sermons or conversation, or through interrogating the natural and manufactured sounds about us, the prophetic voice uncovers our sins and leads us in paths of righteousness. When this listening occurs, one who is sensitive to truth repents. Jesus said that if his followers failed to proclaim God's truth the very stones would cry out (Luke 19:40). Many sounds of our civilizations are harsh.

Gunshots in the night warn of danger, but if we listen they also point us to a truth that God loves sinful humanity, seeks its redemption, and calls us to be agents of redemption. When fighter jets roar above the Memorial Day parade, the reverberating sounds bring a certain thrill, an awe at what technology can accomplish. But at the center of the soul conscience asks what do these sounds signify. Do we really need all these sophisticated weapons? Are they useful tools or expensive and destructive toys? If we interrogate dysfunctional social sounds (such as quarreling families) they tell us to be wary, to take heed, but also to listen to the word of God's redeeming grace, to heed the voice of God, to pray more earnestly, "thy kingdom come, on earth, as it is in heaven."

A third characteristic of good egocentric listening is *to recover the simplicity of aesthetic joy.* Young children bask in sound in unsophisticated ways often lost in the process of growing up. Their auditory acuity has not been tampered with, not yet programmed by technological culture to follow a prescribed auditory menu. They simply enjoy the aesthetics of sound, sometimes seeking to imitate. The purring of a cat, the revving of a car engine, rain pattering on the windowpane. They learn to whistle and to talk pig Latin. Once children laid their ears on the railroad tracks to hear/feel the vibrations of a distant train before the eyes could see it. They listened to the Doppler effect, the raising and lowering of pitch, as the train rushes through time from horizon to horizon. For today's children the roar of the jet may be their auditory symbol for human triumph over time. (Perhaps we should now say, "Keep your ear to the sky.") Children possess imagination in respect to sounds. They make stories based on the sounds they hear. Don't let such imagination be destroyed by the noise of manufactured media sounds. Let children grow up free so that their ears can welcome God's angels in all good sounds.

Adults can heed Jesus' admonition to be childlike and apply it to their pattern of listening. With the help of memory and a conscious break with goal-oriented patterns of daily living, adults can recapture the simple joys of listening to ordinary things. Then the patter of rain on the roof or laughter on the street can once again bring messages from heaven. A well-hit baseball or golf ball *sounds right* to a person with childlike imagination. So does a well-tuned motor.

A fourth characteristic of good egocentric listening is *the constructive personal use of music.* Music is so much a part of our culture that this admonition seems unnecessary. But, as noted earlier, the commercializing of music forces us to avoid aural entrapment. We seek the help of creative Christian artists. Music has been cheapened, prostituted, abused, enslaved. Like Hosea's wife, Gomer, music must be bought back from the slave market. To listen or to make good music is an intrinsic value, not just a means to an end. Music may be almost a biological necessity for providing rhythmic order to life that easily gets disorderly. It is a common experience to have remembered melodies dog us for hours at a time, as if we need a metronome for our daily motions and any tune will do. Maybe memory fetches up a tune when boredom threatens. We may not be able to avoid every reappearing tune that annoys us from time to time. But by conscious, attentive, selection of music we can create a reservoir of melodic sounds that can offer rhythmic accompaniment to activities that need a musical cushion to ease their burden.

Music is not just a way to enrich celebrities, to introduce newscasts, to sell products, to entertain people waiting for a telephone connection, or to soothe the ear for financial appeals. Music ministers to the soul by artful combinations of sound. In music the harmonics of the universe are conjoined with human feelings. In music God and humanity praise the creation together.

One value in our technological society is the availability of high fidelity sound systems. This is a boon for nonmusicians. What a wonder that great music can be heard at affordable prices! Symphonies can be enjoyed without traveling to New York or Berlin. What a shame that lack of discipline keeps many people from enjoying great music stored for our use. It is easier to let the junk music assail our ears than to make an effort to secure quality recordings. So, this word to all us nonmusicians, to the consumers of what others produce: Receive great music as a gift from God. Let's attune our ears to classical, spiritual, and folk music. Let's be wary of popular music, asking hard questions about its usefulness. Does it build up or destroy, does it nurture or starve the soul? Does it feed the body or drug it? Does the music and its performance demonstrate integrity of purpose? Does the music open doors to the Divine or slam them shut? Do the sounds that strike the ear enhance or override reason? Let time winnow out the sounds that should stay from those that should be blown to oblivion.

Better that children learn to play a musical instrument to a level of personal aesthetic satisfaction, or to join a combo or a choir, than that they fill their rooms with celebrity hits and their minds with cultic idols. Adults may keep the decibel level lower than teenagers, but they can be enmeshed in music with childlike trust that melody can minister to the soul.

Every week in our town a group of adults, from varying walks of life, get together to play their band instruments, just for the joy of it. It would be a pity if they tried to go commercial, arranging performances at espresso coffee shops. To turn into a commodity what is now a celebration would erode the simple aesthetics of their experience. These people are not overtly religious, that is, as a group. But in their enjoyment of music they enter into the world God has given, and by their participation offer implicit thanks to the Creator. More church combos would do well to operate from this principle and forget trying to become celebrities selling records and doing road shows. There is room for professional musicians. We nonmusicians depend upon them to minister to us. And professional musicians do learn to combine ministry with marketing. The good ones seek to avoid priestcraft. For most ordinary musicians the aesthetics of personal, and shared, auditory pleasure can be destroyed by a subtle consumer mentality that lurks in the wings. What is first marked by spiritual sensuousness only too easily degenerates into idolatrous sensuality. In Nashville, "gospel" is just another musical commodity, a product to be hawked on cable networks by a convenient phone number and urgent exhortations to "call now." We do not need to shortchange ourselves in respect to music. We can take charge of our own ears.

Empathetic Listening

In empathetic listening we "lend an ear" to a fellow creature (usually a person, although maybe an animal). Those whose voices reach our ears may be family members, neighbors, or strangers. Sympathy consoles others in their losses, relating to the other on the basis of similar experiences. Empathy joins more fully into the experiences of others, whether of pain or pleasure. In empathy we respond in a way that affirms their presence, respects their person, and dignifies their spiritual status. We turn aside from passive listening and egocentric interests in order thoughtfully to receive what others need to say and want us to hear. We enter their condition, we make room for their emotions, we share their feelings. The circles of our existence intertwine for the time and to the degree needed. Our ears become a gate opening upon their internal space. Together from that place we listen for the reassuring voice of God.

When a child coughs repeatedly, a thoughtful caregiver questions the cause and takes appropriate action. When cynics scoff, persons of faith listen for undertones of hunger. Empathetic persons listen to other voices in cadence with their own. To the despairing they offer countervailing words of hope framed by shared silence. When ridicule and accusation reverberate, they listen for the Spirit to reveal, directly, or indirectly, whether the challenge is fair or unfair. When the lyrics of music or the discourse of talk shows rumble with rage, people of faith check the social bonds that secure community and ask why they are broken and how they might be repaired. Every fire or ambulance siren is a summons to neighborly concern. Empathy listens with love.

The sounds we receive empathetically are diverse and the languages may be cognitive or affective. The sounds include the following: conversational talk, joyous laughter, songs of faith, formal speech, calls for affection, groans of pain, moans of grief, screams for help, strident judgments upon injustice, and calls to moral reform—sometimes aimed at us.

The idiomatic expressions "Hear me out!" or "I hear you," are more than sound waves vibrating in the atmosphere. They describe using one's ears for the sake of another. Emotional overtones in these vocal summons range from desperation to exuberance. The response of the hearer returns to the first speaker nuances such as understanding, appreciation, petulance, exasperation, fear, reassurance or relief. Mind audits mind through the voice box and the ear. So simple and yet so profound is this sensory bridge between people!

How then can these sounds be received as heavenly messengers? How can we be faithful to those who ask, "Do you hear me?"

First, *listen as those who gratefully receive another's gifts.* Such gratitude prevents us from confusing empathy with therapy. Obviously, counseling is often helpful, and good counseling requires careful listening. But most people who want to borrow our ears aren't looking for therapy, and they become irritated if we try to psych them out. I recall once passionately voicing a prophetic concern to a small group, only to have my message deflected by the condescending remark of one listener: "You feel strongly about this, don't you?" Persons who turn therapist on every occasion of shared confidences risk not only alienation from the speaker but the dulling of their own ears to the divine voice.

Count it a gift from God that others want to share their deep thoughts and feelings along the whole range from despair to ecstasy. Hearing another person thoughtfully is a part of what is meant by the discipline of submission. Mutual submission is foundational to all interpersonal covenants, and especially to marriage. According to the Bible, as husbands and wives mutually submit to each other they evidence devotion to Christ. "Submit to one another out of reverence for Christ." (Eph. 5:21 NIV) Such mutual submission acknowledges the dignity and place of the other, as well as the interdependence that characterizes all social covenants. By really listening we open the doors of the soul to others whom we love as we love ourselves.

Second, *receive the truth revealed through these shared gifts as the voice of God.* Be humble enough to hear truth from unlikely sources. People pour into our ears variant expressions of the good, the true, and the beautiful. We need not limit empathy to intimate conversations, although we will find much truth in both casual and deep conversations. So hear what the neighbor says over coffee. Heed the preacher. Listen to the poets. Ponder the lyrics and the music of artists. Let good hymns, classical music, and folk music convey messages—even prophetic messages—about the world, for example, "Where have all the flowers gone?" "Must Jesus bear the cross alone and all the world go free? No there's a cross for everyone and there's a cross for me." Let such messages convey their truths with artistry and beauty. When form and substance cohere, both the aesthetic and the ethical voices praise the Creator. God may speak occasionally in special visitations, but usually God speaks to attentive ears through people, the creation, and ordinary experiences.

"She has a good ear," we say appreciatively about a friend with tonal acuity. How wonderful to be so aesthetically tuned to the earth! And what a marvel it is that a quartet or choir can hear the pitch pipe, or a note played on the piano and match that sound with the voice. How wonderful that parents can sing to children who are afraid of "sounds that go bump in the night," offering good, loving, lyrics to offset those that lurk in the imagination. They receive their child's emotions as gifts, and act reciprocally.

Third, *train the ear to be a good monitor of the senses, especially of touch.* The ear lets you know that the hand should quit tickling, or that someone needs an arm about the shoulders. A cry signals parents to give hands-on attention to a hungry, sick, or wet baby. A scream protests violence and engraves upon the hearing ear a call for help and justice. The slammed door suggests a need for discipline. A racking nicotine cough calls for non-addictive tactile substitutes. The sound of a coyote or an owl reminds us that we share the earth with other creatures, many of them not under our direct control, but all dependent upon our careful stewardship of the earth. Respect for natural sounds enables us to walk softly on the earth.

"These are the sounds of progress" is a sign posted on construction sites. It is a way of apologizing for intrusive noise and a call to the right handling of scaffolding and tools. Imagine this sign tie-dyed on the T-shirt of a teenager and you may find the right time to hug a hyped up youngster. The ear interrogates the sounds for judgments of moral acuity.

Children yelling at a soccer game is adjudged a more constructive sound than sound track applause on a sitcom. The drone of machinery may be noise pollution but, for a worthy project it can be heard as melodic praise to socially useful shared labor.

Fourth, *practice the discipline of submission.* In empathetic listening we defer to other persons. We are on their turf. They choose the space and control the time. To be good listeners involves a difficult asymmetry. Those to whom we lend an ear pour out their passions, their feelings, their artistry, their troubles, their complaints, their judgments, their insights. We respond best not by providing a kind of cloned replay, but by retaining the capacity for cognitive judgment while affectively sharing their experience. Criticism and challenge may be the appropriate staging for another's dramatic outburst. To listen well can be emotionally draining and morally challenging.

In empathetic hearing transference takes place. The speaker goes home lightened by having been heard; the listener goes home laden with the weight of what was heard. The penitent sinner, freed from the burden of guilt, hums songs of deliverance, while the ejected demons, or their cousins, knock at the conscience of the empathetic listener to claim a home in the soul. One delivered from despair dances with hope while the serpent whispers cynical phrases in the ears of the listener. The poet sleeps like a lamb while the reader tosses through the night with sorrow over the world's pain. The minister relaxes on Sunday afternoon while thoughtful congregants struggle over how to put into practice the searching morning sermon. The producers of a television documentary on the world's hunger go on to other tasks, while hearers brood on how to make a difference in the face of systemic sin. Transference. The listener now bears the pain, the sorrow, the obligations of truth.

It's so much trouble to listen that we often shut out those sounds that tug at the heart. We turn away from persons who would confide in depth. We hear the aesthetics of hymns rather than their lyrics. We praise the poet for how well the lines are read, not for the troubling truth proclaimed. It's easier to give our ears to sounds that don't ask anything of us, like junk music, or idle chatter, or the soothing noise of machinery, than to heed God's message through these sounds.

To listen empathetically brings agony, yes, but also ecstasy. Don't forget it. Spiritually it is worth all it costs. By unselfish listening we acknowledge our interdependence in the world. Pride is leached out. Humility arises. Love flows broadly. The Spirit quickens us in words that cannot be uttered. Christians understand this to be *koinonia*, fellowship, being part of the body of Christ.

The discipline of submission may not make a saint out of you but it will help you to better love God with all the mind, heart, and soul, and your neighbor as yourself. "Carry each other's burdens," is the Scriptural word to us, "and in this way you will fulfill the law of Christ." (Gal. 6:2)

Godly Listening

Godly listening is *letting God speak to us* through the natural, manufactured, and linguistic sounds by which we gain access to the world, and by which we shape the environment in which we live. Infrequently persons may be granted unusual theophanies—God speaking as a voice from heaven. More frequently we hear God's voice mediated through sermons, hymns, poetry, and other anointed proclamations of the Word. But for most of us most of the time, God's voice comes daily through ordinary sounds that vibrate about our ears, natural sounds, manufactured sounds, speech sounds. All of us can interrogate these sounds prayerfully. To keep an open ear signifies obedience to the Holy One. For when we truly listen, we hear God's voice. If we truly listen the good triumphs over the merely pleasing. We can hear God's angels through stammering speech or garbled syntax, in the song of the meadowlark, the lyrics of a hymn, or the blare of the trumpet. God whispers to us in quiet places and shouts to us in the noisy city. To one disciplined in obedient hearing, conversation becomes a sacred trialogue—the self, God, the other. The body functions as the temple of the Spirit. In developing these disciplines of body, soul, and spirit we are guided by the Holy Spirit present within the community of faith, in the Scriptures, and ultimately within the soul.

Thus we learn God's will. We discern truth. We enter into the condition of others. We become effective listeners to the divine voice, capable of receiving from God's many messengers manifold auditory signs and signals. Thus our prayers to be delivered from the Evil One are answered. The creation becomes open to our experience in fruitful ways. We find self-fulfillment, and we learn better how to love our neighbors as ourselves. God is revealed through the word spoken through creation as well as through the word spoken through Scripture.

"Blessed are those who hear the word of God and obey it," said Jesus.

Notes

1. An article by Mary Joe Osberger, "Audition," *Volta Review*, Vol. 92 (4) (May 1990), p. 36, provided data incorporated in the previous paragraphs.

2. See H.R. Schiffman, *Sensation and Perception: An Integrated Approach* (New York: John Wiley and Sons, 1990), pp. 78-79.

3. Schiffman, pp. 78-79.

4. Jeffrey T. Corwin and Mark E. Warchol, "Auditory Hair Cells," *Annual Review of Neuroscience* (1991, 14), pp. 319-320.

5. Ibid. p. 302.

6. Ibid. pp. 307-310.

7. George Gerbner, founder and chair of the Cultural Environment Movement, of Philadelphia, Pennsylvania, considers this added-on cost to be a form of *taxation without representation*. He thinks it unjust that advertisers get a tax deductible business expense for preempting family rights to tell social stories. CEM is one agency actively concerned with media distortion of democracy and the cultural process. See the prospectus offered by the organization, which also lists various publications for members and other interested persons.

CHAPTER THREE

SEEING

The eye is the lamp of the body. If your eyes are good,
your whole body will be full of light. —Jesus

Even though we know "looks can be deceiving," we want to see for ourselves what our ears have heard. Sighted people give high priority to this
sense perception. "Seeing is believing" is an old maxim, and most investigative endeavor is based upon this premise. Visual evidence is important
in judicial disputes and trials, and despite the fact that people see events
partially and within boundaries of bias, it is usually more compelling
than circumstantial evidence.

One of Jesus' followers was called "doubting Thomas" because he refused to take the other disciples' spoken word that Jesus had risen from
the dead. This disciple demanded both visual and tangible proof. When
he saw the nail prints in the hands and touched the wounded side, then
he believed that Jesus was indeed the risen Messiah. Historically, his legacy is the Mar Thoma Church of India, which, according to tradition, was
begun by this convinced believer within two decades of Jesus' resurrection. Thomas may have been gently chided for his weak belief, but many
believers are in his debt. He voiced their need for reliable testimonial evidence for Jesus' claims. Many persons have found belief in the Gospel easier because of his doubt. Doubt is the flip side of faith.

We note the importance of *sensory witness* to religious convictions.
The testimonies that believers read or hear read to them are an integral
part of the Scriptures, an empirical foundation for theological doctrines
and ethical maxims. One biblical writer put it this way: "That which was

from the beginning, which we have heard, which we have seen with our eyes, which we have looked at and our hands have touched—this we proclaim concerning the Word of life." (1 John 1:1 NIV)

Visual witness is central to news reporting. One only has to note the numbers of journalists and photographers who show up at major events, to recognize its importance. And what would political, athletic, and dramatic events be without spectators?

It does not take much reflection to realize that we make and use a wide array of instruments to magnify vision, to help us see farther out and farther in, to gain better evidence, to make more informed judgments. Much of the technology for such viewing is useful to humanity, especially valued in respect to health care, microscopes used in laboratories, or diagnostic scanning devices, for example. Less valued by most of us are secretive spy devices used by government "spooks," which intrude on our living space and verge on being voyeuristic.

To discuss seeing adequately in one short chapter is impossible, so varied and vast are the outward and inward vistas of the world. Accordingly, we will focus on how to use our eyes as instruments of righteousness. To this end it may be useful to organize into categories our visual experiences. For convenience we group them as we did in the chapter on hearing. We will consider passive seeing, conditioned seeing, egocentric seeing, empathetic seeing, and the disciplines of godly seeing. In each category we will suggest how seeing can constitute a godly vision, that is, how to interrogate these messengers that fly about us with the speed of light, and how to discern and act upon the will of God thus perceived.

But first we will consider three foundational topics: the power of visualization, what happens physically from sensation to cognition, and how sight functions socially.

The Power of Visualization

In 1993, a probing novel by Michael Crichton, *Jurassic Park*[1], was made by Stephen Spielberg into a best-selling, largely attended, motion picture. Millions of people read the book, many more saw the movie. In both visual media—print and picture—*Jurassic Park*, with its intriguing story about reconstituted dinosaurs, offered an effective secular prophetic diatribe against dangers latent in technological culture, especially when directed by unprincipled technologists whose greed blinds them to human fallibility and to the limits of human control over nature. The probable can never fully enclose the possible. Actuality eludes even sophisticated prediction. No human system is fail-safe. Crichton's prophetic purpose was unabashedly straightforward: commercialized molecular biology (genetic tampering) will bring unanticipated horrors to humanity. The book/film visualizations constitute a modern parable. Explicitly secular, it uses chaos theory instead of divine judgment to reveal the limits of human knowledge and to expose the disastrous consequences that occur when human pride of achievement lacks ethical boundaries. But this prophetic parable has religious implications.

This particular visualization of what our world was, is, and could become, testifies to the awesome power of the visual image reconstructed through human artistry. People read the book and viewed the movie with their eyes. They were entertained, but also influenced. Was the movie a caricature of research scientists, a technological blockbuster pandering to fears of institutionalized specialists? Yes. But like effective cartoons, the medium carried a message, and attentive people found moral signification beyond the spectacular scenes, the clever simulations, the loud sound track, and a fanciful story line.

Prophetic visualization has a long history. Visions and theophanies abound in sacred text, but visualization also occurred in what today are labeled socio-dramas. The Old Testament prophet Ezekiel, for example, made a spectacle of himself, lying on his side for days on end before a brick model of Jerusalem under siege, and on another occasion dividing his shaved beard into parts and burning the whiskers in the city square. He dramatized a message for persons with eyes to see. Jesus exaggerated in his parables, too, such as saying some people can spot specks in their neighbor's eyes but not logs in their own. Such is the power of the picture, whether alphabetized in a book, framed in a film, or acted out in sociodrama. Something excerpted from reality gets merged imaginatively with communal memories to become through symbols a widely shared experience. In print now for centuries, the word pictures of biblical actions and stories still reach us with evocative force. Whether angels dance on the head of a pin may have been debated by medieval theologians, but that they do dance before our eyes in the natural sights, in vistas of human experience, in words we read, and in film we view, is a testimony of spiritual experience.

In earliest times primary experiences of seeing were stored in memory and reenacted in drama and storytelling, or depicted in art. Later writing, then print, became extraordinarily powerful means for recapitulating experiences, for recovering and perpetuating visions of what has been, is, and might become. Writing has an ancient history. Inscriptions on oracle bones in China may represent the earliest extant forms of writing, but cave walls, stones, papyrus, and many other materials have provided media on which speech has been stored and shared symbolically. The pen has been more powerful than the sword. A few words can convey incredibly compelling images, like "the four horsemen of the Apocalypse." Or the lion Aslan, a Christ figure in C.S. Lewis's fantasies. We rightly honor word pictures and acknowledge them as central to language. Even jargon requires shared residual perceptions, usually visual, to be understood.

In the recent past, certain inventions have enabled images to be stored and communicated as photographs and motion pictures as well as in art, architecture, statuary and books. Computer science has enlarged the capacity of technology to store and exchange cultural visualizations. This revolution in stored images is relatively new, but it is as significant as the earlier development of moveable type. With so many electronic instruments there is a danger that machines, not minds, will become the chief repositories of human memories. We have not yet learned how to make re-visualization techniques our servant instead of our master. A picture may or may not be worth a thousand words, but often it elicits more than that many words in commentary. The invention of instant pictures has certainly changed how events are reported, and how events make impressions on their viewers. Consider the impact made upon you by certain television pictures: the napalmed child in Vietnam, the dogs lurching at the little black children walking toward a newly integrated school, suffering children in Somalia, the tired old mothers of bombarded Sarajevo, the refugee camps of Rwanda, the bloodied victims of the bombing of an Oklahoma City federal building. Or consider the social impact of a widely imitated coffee television advertisement of the 1990s, featuring a lonely man and a woman looking for love.[2]

What power images have to instruct us, haunt us, frighten us, trouble us, corrupt us, inspire us! Sensory images travel the vital freeway that runs between the eye and the soul. These images are grouped into rational categories and subsumed under conceptual labels for comprehension, recall, control, and use. They are the stuff of cognition. But these images overflow all neatly labeled rational containers. They awaken to mystery. They evoke emotion and engender attitudes. They prompt responses and trigger actions. Can they be God's messengers? Assuredly.

Early visualizations imprint the psyche, perhaps not as significantly as touch, but importantly nonetheless. Glance into the recesses of your memory for important picturing. With only a little effort the afterglow of a great painting, seen at an art gallery years ago will move across the stage of your consciousness. And skulking beside this enlightening image may be one left by pornography peeked at briefly years ago—a visual stain on the soul, a sensory scar. Certain tragedies are easily recalled as scenes never to be forgotten although sometimes newly choreographed—a terrible car accident, a crib-dead child, a witnessed murder, a jungle battlefield. Sometimes our dreams constitute a collage of visual memories played out in frustrating or exhilarating scenarios.

The character-shaping force of our early visualizations depends upon how much, and what kind of, attention was given then and later. For example, the modest farmhouse of my childhood contained few aesthetic objects. Mostly the house functioned for shelter—beauty enveloped us outdoors. But my parents had hung a few prints on various walls. One iconically portrayed my mother's heritage: a Dutch woman bowed in prayer over bread and cheese. Another pictured Jesus with the children of the world gathered round. In that latter one I identified with the blond child but accepted the others as God's children, too. This inexpensive print reinforced the message of a song we sang and heard in church school, "Red and yellow, black and white/ all are precious in his sight/ Jesus loves the little children of the world."

Did these inexpensive prints shape my values? I believe so, especially inasmuch as the worth of prayer, generational continuity, and acceptance of plural cultures were reinforced by teachings at home, church, and school. Today, these biblical pictures seem stylized. Why is this? Perhaps because our visual highway bears so much technically sophisticated traffic now that older visualizations seem quaint and out of date, and the transcultural values of the biblical story need new cultural expressions. I didn't anthropomorphize deity by using these pictures. The pictures, rather, signified a transcendent reality wrapped in mystery—not easily explained by descriptive prose.

A danger now is that TV-imprinted children will lack creative imagination adequate for receiving the divine word signified through traditional religious visualizations. What residual image will the cartoon "Roadrunner" leave on children's minds? Will it be stronger than a Sunday school picture? How do God's messengers move along the busy visual highway of our children? Maybe the plethora of moving images will leave as memory only a blur on a dulled imagination, less effective than a single painting on a child's wall, which requires more interaction. Maybe the cartoons will constitute their "child's garden of verses." As children mature, will pop psychology or sports offer substitute visualizations of the God for whom they yearn but can't locate either in pictures or in propositions? If the gate of the eye is closed to God's messengers, then value-laden words, such as *justice*, lose meanings other than those displayed within a secular social order, most likely through corporately profitable dramatic television and motion picture violence. Control of image, rather than fair and truthful service to humanity and a reverence for God, characterizes our current social order. Style swallows substance. Humanity is impoverished by such diminishment. The children especially are affected. An ancient prayer of the psalmist is timely: "Keep me from the trap that they have laid for me, and from the snares of evildoers." (Ps. 141:9)

Our world is united technologically but rent spiritually. Anarchy, predation, exploitation, and ethnic strife characterize this fragmentation. Where do we find a spiritual power both to affirm and to practice virtue for the common good? Historic ethical standards lack persuasive force in a technological culture. The social contract theory, which supplanted an admittedly abused divine right doctrine of morality, has been beached on the shores of parochial, and often petty, national interest. The theory of natural rights has been stripped of its testimony to coherent purpose by the objectification and subjugation of nature. The theory of self-fulfillment has been diluted by a market-driven exploitation of personal desire. The slave ships that now sail the seas (skies) of our culture are owned by management groups and run by advertising agencies. Slavers skulk within the social systems—family, school, entertainment, politics, culture, education—to gather within their power those whose desires can be manipulated to commercial ends. Our children are the easiest to capture. The eye is a major port of entry.[3]

Is there really an effective moral substitute for "God loves the children of the world, all are precious in his sight"? I think not. Apart from divine transcendence neither nature nor society nor the individual self can provide convincing universal standards of morality and the motivation to live by them.

In a seminal document of America's colonial period, William Penn stressed the moral accountability of people to see that governance is good. In the 1682 "Preface to the First Frame of Government for Pennsylvania" the Quaker colonist wrote,

> "Let men be good and the government cannot be bad: if it be ill, they will cure it. But if men be bad, let the government be never so good, they will endeavor to warp and spoil it to their turn."
> Penn thought monarchy, aristocracy and democracy (rule by one, few, or many) each can work, so long as law rules and persons consent to them.
> But without consent, they result, respectively, in tyranny, oligarchy (special privilege) and confusion (anarchy).[4]

Today the capacity to govern effectively (in any "frame") is placed in jeopardy by the privileged power of cultural image makers. Tyranny presently is less a political threat than a cultural one. And social confusion arises from a fear of cultural entrapment—like a dark cloud anarchy hovers over the world. That's why media, especially visual media, is so important to a humane society, to civilization. Who controls the eye gate rules the world.

It is a human conceit that divine sovereignty can be preempted, whether by kings, commentators, actors, or CEO's who think the world is theirs to shape and control. A famous example of image-driven conceit is narrated in the book of Daniel. Here is the scene. A Babylonian emperor, Nebuchadnezzar, enamored of his own importance but insecure nonetheless (as an embarrassing bout with insanity indicated), builds a golden statue ninety feet tall on the plain of Dura and commands citizens and "all people" everywhere to worship the statue whenever the band strikes up the imperial anthem. Nebuchadnezzar's regal countenance darkens, however, when he learns that three of his court favorites consider the decree idolatrous and will die rather than comply. It seems the king has been trapped in his own conceit by clever anti-Jewish advisors. But of course a great and wise ruler can't show weakness by making fumbling exceptions to widely proclaimed policy, however absurdly crafted. But he faces a dilemma. The appeal of conscience to a higher power clouds the image of his sovereignty whether the dissidents live or die. What can his highness do about it? Nothing. Ironically, the Almighty bails him out more mercifully than any current national congress would do an arrogant or errant leader.

You remember how the story unfolds. The three Hebrews pray in the midst of a furnace designed to incinerate dissidents. An angel of God, however, joins them in the fire and shields them from its deathly flames. The distraught king, prisoner to his own pride, runs to the fire pit in the morning and finds the dissidents, incredibly, alive. He shouts, "Shadrach, Meshach, and Abednego, servants of the most high God, come out!" Remember how the king, no longer idolatrous but pagan still, affirms the God of the intended victims and threatens to tear limb from limb whoever denigrates these covenant people? This mighty world leader, who built a famous hanging garden to please his petulant Persian wife and assorted temples to please devotees of Marduk and Ishtar, had stayed in power for decades as much by political savvy as by military might. He can turn a political stumble into personal advantage! So on this particular occasion he loses no time asserting his authority, if not his sovereignty, dispatching a communiqué to all the nations, avowing that the sovereignty of the Most High God is eternal.

Nebuchadnezzar the politician gets front page headlines that day, but the God of the covenant people gets the credit lines in the editorials.

Often obscured in the usual retelling of this story is a stylized version of what the three youth sang during that hot and scary night, huddled together an angel's breath away from death. Pondering it may help us understand their courage and the idolatry of golden images. Read it in Daniel 3. The song thunders with adoration of the sovereign Lord. Praise from the temple, praise from the heavens, praise from the sun and stars, praise from the rain and the dew, from cold and heat, from ice and snow, mountain and hills, sea beasts and land animals, praise from people. Praise because the Lord is good and his love everlasting.

True keepers of the social covenant have eyes to see the creation and thus joyously to acclaim the Creator. Remember what Augustine put in the mouths of all created things which he sought at the reach of his senses? "God made us"! To make crafted images the objects of our deepest allegiance, whether erected on the plains of Dura or displayed on television, even if culturally commanded, is an affront to the Almighty. To recover in our times a biblical awe before God is something fervently to pray for. True worship and discipleship requires such humility. Otherwise the powerful images constructed for our viewing become idolatrous substitutes for the sovereign Lord, and tyrants rule.

If this is so, then how God's messengers reach us through the seeing of things and creatures, events and people, is very important. We need these angels to stand beside us in the fires of cultural adversity lit by hubris, to shield us from the flames of tyranny. Let us learn, as creatures made in God's likeness, how to interrogate the myriad images that strike the eye, so we will not be led into idolatry, but rather find affinity with the whole creation, and together offer praise for the Creator.

Natural and artificial visualizations need not become idolatrous. They can become icons through which we give and receive God's gift of light. They can be means of grace. A heap of stones may be an altar for human sacrifice or a ladder of ascent to God. Mountains need not be the abode of demons, but platforms for God's moral law. Temples need not house fertility rites and ritual prostitutes. They can be sanctuaries, where God and human creatures meet. Art need not deify the artist, but can glorify the Almighty and the creation.

Throughout the centuries, however, the community of faith has not found it easy to distinguish between idol and icon. What should be a means becomes an end. The Eastern Church early adopted the practice of stipulating specially designed artifacts as holy icons, true windows onto the eternal. Prayers are said to go *through, not to* these designated holy objects. These icons continue to be reverenced by Orthodox Christian churches. After the fall of Rome, Western Christians vacillated on the subject, on the one hand fearing "graven images" forbidden by the Mosaic law, on the other hand facing a need to teach the Gospel to masses of illiterate people—to reach their eyes with the Word of God. They drifted into the second option, and sacred pictures and statuary became ritually as well as educationally commonplace. Roman Catholicism, too, sought to distinguish between an object worshiped and one through which one worships. Accordingly, Christ, Mary, the apostles, the saints, and biblical scenes were pictured in mosaics, frescoes, carvings, and statuary, all across the medieval landscape. Church buildings became themselves holy objects to be viewed with veneration. As the church became more hierarchical it sought to control iconoclastic viewing by officially designated artifacts. The natural order got bypassed for iconoclastic consideration by this bureaucratic approach.

The "iconoclastic issue" became a political football, unfortunately, with charges of idolatry hurled about. Islam attracted adherents partly because some people thought the Church had compromised Sinaitic law and had become idolatrous. Various reform movements subsequently, including the Protestant Reformation, gave prophetic challenge to the abuse of religious symbols. Puritan soldiers took potshots at altarpieces, for example, during the English Reformation. Protestants considered that the Church had compromised the Gospel and had substituted idolatry (disguised in religious form) for obedient service to the Almighty. Dramatic depictions also fell in disfavor, with Puritans disdaining Christmas ornaments and celebrations as unworthy accommodations to pagan culture. For most Protestants only the eucharist remained as an approved sensuous ritual depicting spiritual meanings. Word pictures of Christ seemed more appropriate to Puritans than paintings, and logically stated concepts more important than stylized Gospel imagery. Direct visualization returned to Protestant churches, however, in the form of stained glass windows. Symbolic visualization reappeared in the architecture of the buildings, crosses, steeples, and spires, and engravings on altars and pulpits. In the revivalist era, especially among less affluent groups, in unpretentious buildings (transitory "tabernacles" rather than "temples") theater became a substitute for visual artistry. For such religious theater Aimee Semple McPherson was the consummate artist although dramatic flair has characterized many evangelists, including, for example, Robert Schuller performing for God in his "glass cathedral." This edifice, interestingly enough, was designed to let the outside into the worship experience. Drama is itself iconic, and with the development of motion pictures, has offered the church a diversity of visualization, some of this appearing ecumenically on religious television networks, or through symbolic banners on the walls of meetinghouses.

To prevent icons from becoming idols requires continual spiritual discipline by the whole community of faith. Anyone who has felt uncomfortable viewing visualizations of Jesus in drama or film will testify to this. To give special objects holy status indeed may detract from the sacramental character of the creation itself, and lead to "Babylonian" idols in modern culture. Religious idolatry may lurk within religious rituals, as well as in pictures and religious artifacts.

In all probability Christian devotion is threatened more now from modern equivalents to Nebuchadnezzar's golden image, given immense clout by the media industry, than from traditional religious artifacts, such as stations of the cross or pictures of Jesus and the children on a bedroom wall, or movies portraying Jesus and the Gospel story. In the news images seen nightly on television the factor of selectivity is even more significant than in written history, where time permits greater inclusiveness. Think for example, of how much prime-time exposure was given to the war in Bosnia compared to Angola, where the human suffering was even more severe (there a thousand persons a day were killed compared to a few dozen). My point is not to excuse atrocities anywhere, but only to suggest that a thoughtful person will have to seek out a balance in the images seen, and will have to put television viewing into perspective along with other media. Book reading continues, in spite of television. One reason surely is that people want better control of the images that instruct their minds and tug at their hearts.

Seeing is so much a part of our lives we seldom ponder the act itself. Given the power of the image, we should do so. Ask how the eye can be a gate through which God's messengers come and go. Beware idolatry. Discern how the eye can be single to God's glory so that your body may be full of light. Such reflection upon sight may be informed usefully by noting first what happens when we see, and then how sight functions personally and socially.

The physical stimulus required to experience "sight" is a photon of visible light. The light that we perceive is a very small band of frequencies in the middle of a continuum with high energy gamma rays and X-rays at one end and low energy microwaves and radio waves at the other. Within this narrow band of visible light lies the spectrum of colors. As in sound, light is perceived as a combination of frequency and wavelength. The colors we see are distinguished by their frequencies (the highest is indigo, the lowest is red). Color perception is the most complex of the five main components that make up the phenomenon of sight. The other components are photosensitivity in general, movement discrimination, form discrimination, binocular vision and depth perception.

Before we begin to examine the functions of the visual system, we must explain the physical process of light detection, perception, and cognition. Light enters the eye through its clear outer covering, or cornea, and through the lens. The amount of light that gets through is regulated by the iris, a reflexive, circular muscle that can expand or contract to make the pupil (area of the lens) bigger or smaller, depending on the intensity of the light stimulus. The lens is flexible and is held in place by muscles that expand and contract to give the lens the ability to focus light on the back of the eye, or the retina.

The retina is lined with photoreceptors and the nerve cells that carry their message. There are two types of photoreceptors—rods and cones. Rods, numbering well over 100 million, are located around the outer edges of the retina. Rods detect the presence of light and many rods converge onto one nerve cell that then carries that singular message up the optic nerve. Since many rods converge on one intermediate cell, sensitivity to the presence or absence of light is very high, but acuity (what we think of as focus or clarity of image) is poor. Cones are concentrated in a very small area at the center of the retina (around the optic nerve) and number only about six to eight million. Cones are the receptors for color and each cone has its own nerve cell converge upon it, so even subtle neural information is carried to the brain. Acuity is very high.

The retina is actually derived from brain tissue during early embryonic development. The central nervous system develops on an axial gradient from anterior to posterior, the olfactory starts first, then the eyes, and later the otic vesicles; some have tried to make evolutionary sense out of this developmental order. The eyes start as an evagination of the forebrain (same major part that gives rise to the cerebrum) that grows to the embryonic skin and then recoils forming an optic cup. The optic nerve grows back from the neural retina through the optic stalk to connect to the forebrain. Thus eyes (i.e. retinas) are brain tissue—"windows of the brain." This also helps explain why eyes cannot be transplanted, regenerated, or the retina restored. Of course we can surgically manipulate the cornea and lens since they are derived from non-nervous tissue, embryonic skin.

The axons of the innumerable nerve cells carrying the information of the rods and cones make up the optic nerve that leads out through the center of the retina. This creates a small blind spot in the field of perception because the photoreceptors do not actually face the lens, but point away from it, with the axons that make up the optic nerve being the first outer layer. This configuration is probably exactly backward from the typical conception; however, the rods and cones remain fully functional through this organization.

Photosensitivity, then, occurs when rods and cones are exposed to a quantity of light. The mechanism by which light energy is translated to a neural impulse is through pigmented molecules contained in the rods and cones themselves. In rods, these molecules are called rhodopsin; in cones, they are molecules that are maximally sensitive only to the frequency of red, green, or blue.

Photoreceptors are constantly charged in their resting state. When a quantity of light hits the retina, it causes the components of the rhodopsin molecules to split apart and a bleaching effect occurs. This creates the energy for an impulse to be sent along the intermediary nerve cells and to the visual cortex of the brain.

In a current theory of color perception, various cones are maximally receptive to the frequencies of red, green, or blue and minimally sensitive to the other two colors. From this pattern, all color combinations can be perceived. Taking the theory one step further, some cones are maximally sensitive to opponent combinations of red and green, yellow and blue (yellow is a certain combination of red and green), and black and white. Hence a red spot surrounded by green triggers one cone to fire. This creates a neural impulse. This action inhibits the cone that responds to a green spot surrounded by red. Information about brightness and saturation, or color purity, along with the pattern of cone responses, gives the brain the means to process and understand color in our environment.

We perceive movement and decipher forms in space in a number of different ways. Lateral motion is detected by the stimulation of photoreceptors at different locations on the retina with the same image, or when the image is held relatively stationary on the retina, but the eye (head, neck) moves instead, as in tracking the movement of a running animal or vehicular traffic. The increase or decrease of the size of an image on the retina leads to the perception of forward or backward motion and to clues about the relative distance between objects.

As experience grows, the brain establishes rules for the probable outcome of perceived events, including motion. However, as anyone who enjoys 3-D movies and 3-D poster art will tell you, the mind is easily fooled by optical illusions and does not maintain a realistic interpretation of motion as it actually occurs in the environment. The technology of virtual reality, in both commercial and recreational simulation, depends upon the creation of these kinds of illusion.

Another important aspect of gleaning meaningful information about shapes and motion through sight is that we have binocular vision, or two eyes at different locations. The images on each retina of the eye will be slightly different from each other because they are two or three inches apart. This is called binocular disparity, and the brain can reliably use it to create the perception of depth. Coupled with certain learned protocols about shape, size, perspective, and color, binocular information helps create a representative of the dimensional world we live in.[5]

How Sight Functions

Each of the five senses provides access to the world. Each has unique functions and appropriate symbols for memory and communication. But the eye offers the most complex sensory participation in reality. The eye basically gathers light from the spectrum. As one scientist has said, "Color doesn't occur in the world, but in the mind."[6] Color is how we code differences of light. Scientists have observed the phenomenon of *synesthesia*, in which the senses merge, sometimes to the point of driving people mad. This is beyond occasional synoptic associations of smell and color. Sensory overload such as this can also be induced by drugs such as mescaline.[7] Seventy percent of the body's sense receptors are lodged in the eye. The eye is so much involved in making sense out of things that when puzzling scenes are encountered the eye often puts them into a picture (schema, or mind-set) of what it has already programmed. Visual acuity enables us to perceive and interact with the world, to interrogate its meaning, and to share it.

Through our eyes we perceive the world about us and to a large measure determine whether propositions formed in our mind by processed impressions correspond with reality. In conjunction with touch we act upon these perceptions; we share our experiences symbolically through language, create artistic representations of reality, design and build useful things, engage in work and play. Think of the intricacies of eye-touch coordination next time you drive a golf ball or gauge the distance needed to overtake another car safely, or even to bring food to your mouth. Our eyes provide visualizations vital to logical inference and intuited meanings. Analogy occurs when we "see" parallels between one type of experience and another, between outward impressions and inner convictions, between vistas and visions.

As it is with the other senses, objects of sight may be grouped conveniently into natural, social, artificial, and linguistic experiences. Obviously, many experiences interact. By viewing the natural world we locate ourselves in it. Seeing enhances mobility; we can walk without stumbling, and increase the scope of persons, places, and things experienced. Our viewing of the natural world may be practical, such as getting to places safely and accomplishing tasks responsibly. Or it may be purely aesthetic—enjoying things. Scientific viewing uses instruments to enhance vision and thus enables us to see farther out or farther in. Whatever the case, the phrase "I see" is voiced when visual perception elicits understanding. Practically speaking, this metaphoric term has become loosened from its perceptual base. It is a synonym for "understanding." In all usage, it means that the inner has interrogated the outer self and provided lenses for cognition.

In the parlance of our chapter, Plato "cast a jaundiced eye" upon sensory perception. Not just because the senses can be fooled, but because, he thought, ideas are the true form of reality. In Platonic thinking, a painting is twice removed from reality. It is a picture of a picture. The tree painted on canvas represents a physical tree, and the physical tree represents the pure, eternal, forms that it transitorily embodies, forms expressed by words such as symmetry. For him perceptions were epiphenomenal to concepts. Plato's student, Aristotle, disagreed. He gave material greater metaphysical standing than did his mentor. The rift in the West between mystical and scientific modes of understanding is in some ways a partisan continuation of this philosophic quibble over the relationship between mind and matter. Given Plato's influence, and the Old Testament warnings against idolatry, it is no wonder Christians had difficulty deciding whether (or when) the senses become traps for the soul or serve as messengers from God.

Good seeing extends the observed landscape beyond the horizon of cultural expectations. "Truth dawns" is an idiomatic expression used when inductive evidence or logical deduction yield valid conclusions about things seen by our eyes. By using analogy, the mind magnifies perception—seeing one thing well fosters clear inferences about other things. By reflective imaging we transform ordinary visual events into new configurations of reality. Thus disciplined, we paint pictures, write poems, invent machines, design houses, and reconstruct organizations according to an envisioned pattern.

The phrase "flashes of insight" describes the process by which we draw into a unifying circle of coherence surveyed objects and occasions, and claim mental title to them. Intuition grasps reality at the very edge of, or even beyond, the horizon of direct observation and logical entailment. Dub it tacit knowledge or co-naturality, or faith. Intuition grasps reality greater whole than in the sum of perceived parts. Intuition sees beyond descriptions and explanations. It "gets the whole picture." Intuition grasps the significance of persons, things, and events. Faith, hope, and love are the attributes of personal attention requisite to effective intuition. These disciplines enable eyes to penetrate reality, but in a manner marked by humility, not pride, by an awareness that in this life knowledge is partial, and remains to be completed. As the apostle Paul said, "Now we see but a poor reflection as in a mirror; then we shall see face to face. Now I know in part; then I shall know fully, even as I am fully known." (1 Cor. 13:12 NIV)

As exemplified above, our idioms give us the clue: Physical light is intertwined with perception. Light offers both a physical and a metaphoric base for interpretation and communication of reality experienced. Visitors touring underground caverns typically are exposed to a few minutes of heavy darkness that reinforces feelings of dependence upon the primacy of light. Psychology classes use light deprivation exercises to teach social interdependency. Despots use light deprivation to break the will of victims. As energy, light provides life through the sun. As illumination, light provides place and identity. Without light we lose direction, we become disoriented. Recipient of energy and illumination, our eyes receive, refract, and transmit light. Reason in turn transmits what light reveals and intuition conveys the signification of such revelation.

For seeing to be an instrument of righteousness instead of unrighteousness we ought to give faithful attention to light and God who made light. As the psalmist says in a hymn of praise to the Almighty, "For with you is the fountain of life; in your light we see light." (Ps. 36:9) Light/ dark metaphors are favorites with Isaiah as metaphors for God's presence/ absence. A Gospel writer uses Light as a messianic name for God incarnate historically in Jesus Christ (John 1). This writer also quotes Jesus as saying, "I am the light of the world. Whoever follows me will never walk in darkness but will have the light of life." (John 8:12) To walk in light one must be sensitive to light, in all its meanings. Having eyes, let us see.

How does the natural world strike our eyes? What is our usual visual landscape? The sky, obviously, vegetation, grass, trees, mountains, fields and farms, trees in the parking strip. Planters in the apartment window, parks, birds and animals. Household people, family, loved ones, neighbors, co-workers and their clothes, cars, pets, gardens and assorted accouterments. The artificial vistas include our habitations and cities and all the manufactured things that have become important accessories to our lives.

Our eyes offer an immediate sensory grid for such interaction and provide the most significant set of interpretative secondary symbols— language. There are many kinds of secondary symbols: paintings, pictures, cartoons, architectural drawings, icons, hieroglyphics, ideograms, sculptures, stylized motion (games, dancing, skating), uniforms, rituals civil or religious, or the more abstracted linguistic alphabets (such as the type you are now reading). These visual symbols offer enduring representations of sensory perception. Through language we communicate symbolically what the eye sees, and in an infinitely rich way. How incredible is human language, enabling us to send and receive images that strike us from without and well up from within!

The biblical promise in Psalm 1 that the righteous shall be "like a tree, planted by streams of water," is understood because we have seen trees and streams with our eyes, our mind has processed certain character-istics of healthy plantings, and our spirit intuits the analogies. The scope of visualization staggers the mind. Our concern is not to be comprehen-sive but to ask how the sense of seeing can come under spiritual discipline, how seeing can join us with the earth, with God, and with each other.

Consider the deficiencies related to seeing. The first, obviously, is to be born blind, to experience light tactily through the skin, but not to be visually informed through it. Another deficiency is color blindness, the inability to refract the light into colors. Various limitations impair eye-sight. We have natural boundaries. For example, our vision is not as acute as an eagle's. To an extent we can remedy certain deficiencies, such as be-ing nearsighted or farsighted, astigmatic, dyslexic, or suffering from a de-tached retina or cataracts. To cure tunnel vision is a harder problem!

Tunnel vision is a term often used to describe persons who don't have good peripheral vision; they see just what is right in front of them, and presumably, seldom turn their heads to the right or to the left. A culture with limited or slow communication contributes to such limitation. So may an overdependence upon linear print, for the neurological muscles need for peripheral vision may not be sufficiently exercised in young chil-dren for them to become good observers at the periphery. Tunnel vision metaphorically refers to persons who stubbornly stick to a narrow, paro-chial view of the world, and in consequence often hold hostile or preju-diced opinions about what lies outside the range of their narrow vision. Tunnel vision, however, may extend in the horizontal mode as well as the vertical, especially in a culture that has wide access, mobility, and rapid communication. In the first instance some people see just their own nar-row social tradition and refuse to perceive the values of other coexisting cultures.

Ingrained ethnicity is one form such tunnel vision takes. In the sec-ond instance people visualize life along a narrow band on the horizontal spectrum, viewing only what contemporary society shows them (how to be "with it" socially or how to be "politically correct"), rather than gain-ing wisdom by looking to the past or envisioning the future. Avant garde modernity partakes of this form of tunnel vision. The first type of tunnel vision lacks breadth, the second, depth, of perspective.

Consider now the different categories of seeing and how these kinds of seeing may be vehicles for the Holy Spirit rather than occasions for seduction to evil.

Passive Seeing

Passive seeing means receiving visual stimuli neutrally, unburdened by a need for conscious moral or categorical judgment. At this level attention is selective but not self-consciously so. Such passivity does not connote lackadaisical interest, but rather a low-level receptivity of visual stimulus, a response to the optics about us, a quiet feeding of the visual appetite. We let the landscape flow across our line of vision—trees bending in the wind, cars winding down the highway, waves crashing on the beach, children playing in the yard. (Impaired persons are aided in visual perception by eyeglasses, lens replacement, and cataract surgery.) Simple aesthetic joy is a basic, uncritical attitude of accepting ourselves as creatures bearing the image of God.

There are benefits to the nurture of passive seeing. We keep our eyes open to simple aesthetics, like letting a sunset bathe the eyes, unconcerned whether that brilliance comes from too much dust in the air, not worried about how best to photograph or sketch the scene. Passive seeing is unconcerned whether the beauty of the neighboring hill is threatened by condominium development, or the tumbling stream by pollution. Sensuous ecstasy shivers the spine just by observing how fog swirls down a river valley on a fall morning, or how a howling wind sculpts the snow gracefully on a cold winter day. The earth daily puts on a show for us and we have been given a life pass to view the performance.

Passive seeing pertains to seeing artificial objects, too, at a primal level, enjoying the dynamic flow of a new fighter jet, for example, without worrying over its purpose. Urbanites can wax rhapsodic watching from a central apartment tower a steady stream of red taillights flowing along the freeway to the airport or the suburbs. For others, the social landscape offers especially prized visual images, such as the fluidity of motion and beauty of body observed in professional basketball or in the intricacy of ice dancing, the concert-like efficiency of a well-served meal, or the evocative power of dramatic performance. The beautiful may become enemy of the good if social irresponsibility accompanies such envisioning. But in itself this way of seeing affirms what the ancient writer of Genesis said of God's creation, that it is good.

Conditioned Seeing

Conditioned seeing means that prevailing culture portrays reality for people. More than we care to admit, the way we see is programmed by culture, sometimes for good, often for evil. Cultural biases skew how we see. For example, for many people the sight of black-jacketed motorcycle riders on the highway conjures up images of thugs or drug users. These observers do not "see" the utility of this clothing for persons exposed to the elements. They don't see members of the group as individuals. Instead they see stereotypically, charging the whole class with the excesses of a few Hell's Angels. Persons of color understand such prejudice; they have experienced the effects of this unfortunate characteristic of ethnicity. So do all who visit or live in a culture other than their own.

Television has a positive force in widening cultural understanding and breaking down petty ethnicity. But it has an awesome power to condition attitudes and behaviors. On January 11, 1994, Ted Koppel was reporting a special conversation with President Clinton in Brussels, where Clinton was meeting with heads of European nations. They were discussing Progress for Peace proposals and the future of the North Atlantic Treaty Organization. The President had flown to Brussels immediately following the funeral of his mother, and viewers were aware of his emotional burden. The well-conducted interview dealt with serious and important issues, but the program was interrupted by commercial breaks which featured advertisements for: 1) a laxative, 2) a toilet bowl cleaner, and 3) a rinse for bad breath. A grieving President, working hard for a peaceful Europe, and an astute commentator enter and leave our living rooms at the will of powerful patrons brashly unconcerned over visual discontinuity within the homes of the viewers. Visually, the advertisements (product value aside) trivialized the program. It was tacky, like garbage strewn about a national park, like graffiti on the courthouse.

Television advertisements may be technically superior pictures. But in substance and even in style often they are rude interruptions of serious presentations. Commercial patrons use elevated noise and overstated visual buffoonery to keep our eyes attuned to their commercial pitch. Store employees would be fired for sticking out tongues at shoppers, or mincing like streetwalkers, or burbling like bug-eyed simpletons. On commercial television such salespersons are more highly paid than the clerks on the mall. What is the implication for psychological closure? That advertisements, not programs, are the more important pictures for us to see. Such a barrage of images trivializes our common life. Now politics must be sensationalized in order to get on the news, as venders vie with each other for sales. Patronage has corrupted art and distorted truth.

The stark contrast of that Koppel-Clinton interview made me feel like a nonentity whose feelings about visual order are unimportant and can be trampled upon. I wonder, did Koppel and Clinton feel the same way? I'll guess they did.

In our culture the television set is the most potent cultural conditioner of the eye. It is sad to watch children lose their natural visual appetite for dandelions and toads and rocks and become fixated upon moving images thrown at them from a television screen every day of the year. Their view of reality, and their range of choice become inexorably molded by televised images. Children often do not distinguish readily between program and promotion. It is silly for producers of dangerous or addictive products to try to disclaim the appeal of their images to children. Simple logic suggests that advertisers would not continue to pay huge sums of money to sponsor programs unless their investment paid off in sales.

This is true for adult viewers, also. We are all subject to the strong visual and auditory images projected by advertisements. Our capacity for judgment is trivialized by flattering invitations to distinguish between a former product and a new and improved one, or between nearly similar products. Unlikely associations are forced upon us and weaken our ability to draw logical inferences. We are led to associate beer beach parties with sexual sophistication or athletic endorsement with product quality. Such advertisements dull the mind by letting us view lazily differences that have no significant distinction. They pander to sloth by giving the commercial image priority over programmatic ones. Or by requiring scriptwriters to include car crashes and murders every half hour in prime time because marketing experts insist the viewing of violence is necessary to achieve good ratings. As a result of such opportunistic management we have become serfs living on a huge commercial estate, dependent upon wealthy patrons for what we see, how we understand, and how we choose. The whole commercial sight-producing industry surfeits the eye with a continuous stream of artificial images. The result is linguistic and cultural deprivation.

In our culture television is an entertainment mode of communication. Efforts by religious broadcasters to offer worship via television have not succeeded well, despite some notable efforts to make presentations serious as well as dramatic and eye-catching. The medium is too weak for conveying true worship ("in spirit and in truth"), which needs a special place, a gathered people, and a shared inner vision in order to achieve communicative power. The imagery of the church as the body of Christ is poorly conveyed via impersonal electronic ties. Dissonance occurs whether televised worship is high or low in liturgy, whether theologically liberal or conservative. To camera pan someone's countenance wrapped in prayer and bring that image to me electronically a dozen feet away in my living room offers a different and inferior sense of spatial reality from what I experience when standing in a house of worship with my neighbors a dozen feet away, bowed in prayer, or together singing "Holy, Holy, Holy, Lord God, Almighty!" As a forum for discussion, a theater for evangelism, or a market tool to collect funds for the needy, television is somewhat more effective, mostly because there can be greater use of those dramatic features that mark entertainment.[8]

Once during the five years Terry Waite, an Anglican intermediary, was imprisoned in Beirut, often chained, alone, and cut off from the outside world, his captors brought him a video. It turned out to be an American hit-'em-up movie. The thing sickened him and he asked his captors next time to bring him a book instead. He found it obscene that violence could be thus glorified and, with mutilation and death, marketed for entertainment. Suffering yields certain perspectives about the power of visualization. We ought to receive these perspectives thoughtfully.[9]

Aristotle's notion that drama offers viewers therapeutic purgation does not apply to the violent movies cranked out for the market today. They offer an illusionary escape from reality and a beguiling seduction into irrational and destructive behavior.

Adults, at least, may be building up resistance to visual manipulation by television. This I infer from the increase of stupid and surreal images, and from the more sensationalizing of newscasts. How desperate advertisers must be to do a hundred stupid things to hold our eyes to the commercial. It's called "in your face" advertising. If our children acted this way they would be sent to their rooms for time out. A store clerk, or even a door-to-door salesperson would get fired for such shenanigans. And to think we pay these advertisers to be so boorish. Of course, they are driven to desperate measures by the high cost of time. They have our eyes so briefly they want to grab them, even at the cost of being considered obnoxious. And how rude it is for television programmers to tease us with an important visual image—a fire, or tragedy, a monumental political treaty—and then snatch it away so that we can see violent clips from a forthcoming movie or TV series. Or to interrupt a momentous public event by picturing the agony of an upset stomach or constipation. Or to pay criminals for interviews about titillating scandals.

In all cultures beauty is given preference in any assessment of the good. Sometimes this just speaks of a need for what is harmonious, a preference for what unifies form and function. But there is a down side. The beautiful people get unfair advantage; plain and awkward people are put to disadvantage despite laws enacted to assure equality. In an entrepreneurial society the down side is accented. The eye tends to process information with a quantitative bias. Quality judgments are skewed by quantity assessments. Thus tall people are assumed to be better leaders, bigger books are better ones, bigger boxes hold better products.[10] That merchants accept this bias and exploit it was brought home to me when I ordered a specialty software program for my computer. The colorful cardboard box was larger than a book, but all it contained was one disk, shirt pocket sized. It could have been mailed in an attractive small envelope, but in the minds of the marketing agents image considerations triumphed over common sense and any concern for energy efficiency.

Conditioned seeing is more than television, obviously. It occurs through home patterning, through educational models, through the books we read and the things we choose to see, as well as by general expectations embedded in culture. There is even in America an intercorporate Color Marketing Board, which selects colors of the year. In 1995 green and purple were "in," browns and greys were "out." This process keeps products variously hued, manipulating the consumer yen for change in the direction of market profitability. (My last green suit was in 1940, when I graduated from high school. I will not buy another, whatever CMB says!)

Perhaps an awareness of television's impact can help us reexamine *how* we see within our culture. For communities of faith it may mean reexamining the visualizations through which transcultural values are conveyed from one generation to the next. These visualizations, whether through ritual, art, drama, book, or artifact should not be in the form of counter propaganda, but creative, skilled efforts to liberate the eye to be a more open gate for the Spirit.

Egocentric Seeing

Egocentric seeing refers to the world from a perspective of personal gain. Egocentricity isn't quite the same as egoism, which indicates preoccupation with personal gain at the expense of others and connotes vanity and selfishness. All our experiences and volitions are funneled through the self. We cannot really stand outside ourselves, cannot become completely dispassionate, cannot be fully objective. Such is the egocentric predicament. We can be egocentric, however, without becoming egotistical. But it isn't easy! On the one hand, if we aren't completely programmed, we usually know our own mind better than others know it. We do have "privileged access" to our own understandings. We are not a social construct, we are human beings. The acceptance of such freedom leads to sturdy convincements, social accountability, and a proper self-respect. Babies can watch a mobile with excitement. Toddlers can stare up grandpa's nose and scrutinize the hairs, unhindered by conventions of politeness. Small children find bugs fascinating, and bits of wood and stone, too. Such investigative visual activity reflects the natural curiosity of the ego and claims the world as its own unhampered by social conventions that later may preclude close scrutiny. In matters of business or professional work adults interpret data from their own cognitive base. We seek to enhance our capabilities, to see better what is the condition of the world and to modify our response to it in the light of personal knowledge. Sometimes this is called "enlightened self-interest," with the implication that if everyone acted in this way all would benefit.

On the other hand egocentricity can lead to prejudice, greed, covetousness, and arrogance. Or to pigheaded obstinacy. Experience indicates that the self selects enlightenment skewed toward personal advantage. Selfish persons shove God and others off stage. "Having eyes they don't see." Egoists view persons, creatures, inanimate things, and manufactured goods as objects to be used primarily or exclusively for one's own purposes. What they collect or latch on to becomes a shield against God's light. Against truth. Whether their view of reality is mercenary or aesthetic their working hypothesis is: "What's in it for me?" Such seeing is basically predatory. Egoists look for prey to carry home to the nest whether these be sexual triumphs, athletic trophies, professional recognition, or art collections. Egoists view life as an opportunity to acquire, to control, to consume. They "look out for number one." A biblical writer characterizes them as *experts in greed*, "With eyes full of adultery, they never stop sinning; they seduce the unstable; they are experts in greed...!" (2 Pet. 2:14 NIV) Another pinpoints the source for such selfishness as "the lust of the eye." (1 John 2:16 NIV)

Experts in greed, lust of the eye. What striking characterizations! God's judgment on selfishness has been made graphic in biblical history. Here's one example. At a sumptuous banquet while he was drinking wine from stolen temple vessels, Balshazzar saw before his eyes a hand writing on a wall. "You have been weighed on the scales and found wanting," was the judging note scrawled by an angelic messenger before the eyes of the idolatrous king (Dan. 5:27). The drunken tyrant had little time to repent—he was assassinated the same night. Consider another vivid vision, from the New Testament. God arrested Paul from his self-appointed vendetta against the Messiah, blinding him with light on the road to Damascus. The one who thought he saw how things were was blinded until he saw things God's way. In this case judgment on egoistic behavior resulted in an amendment of ways, a dramatic personal course correction. It is one of the world's great conversion stories. To be converted means to re-envision the world, beginning with oneself.

Somewhat different, but equally compelling are images contained in the book of Revelation. Cryptic visions sent by the Almighty to John on the island of Patmos, gave beleaguered believers bright hope for a future during dark and deadly times. The striking, almost surrealistic, word pictures from this book continue to illuminate readers today, projecting images of the coming garden-city of God, the New Jerusalem, in which righteousness prevails over a violent and dysfunctional "Babylon." Here is a dazzling vision of a future when the cosmos itself will be reconstituted by God's creative and redemptive word after humanity is healed and chaos yields to divine order.

Consider then the bright side of egocentric seeing. Some kinds of seeing are self-fulfilling as well as humbling. They honor God as creator and ourselves as co-creators. Anticipate the world's future. Disciplined seeing gives focus to bright hope of a personal value in a purposive cosmos. Here are some disciplinary exhortations for the eye to be a gate for the Holy One.

1) Look closely at things. Consecrated to godly purposes, the scientific method is an acceptable form of sacrifice. That is, it enhances the worth-ship of what God has created by discovering greater characteristics of form and function in the physical universe. To discover secrets in ordinary things and make them socially beneficial portends the City of God, in which the trees, as depicted symbolically in the Revelation, stand for the healing of the nations. Technology greatly strengthens sight. Our power to know is enhanced by instruments as diverse as eyeglasses and microscopes and telescopes. Microtechnology enables us to see farther into reality than ever before, and macrotechnology to see farther out to reality than ever before. New planets are discovered outside the solar system. Neurological patterns in the brain are scanned for abnormalities. X-rays and other scanning devices offer images useful for treatment. Now in standard medical practice, heartbeat can be heard not only by a stethoscope, but can be translated as visual patterns by special machinery. An-

giograms allow both cardiologist and patient to view arteries in the heart. Technology offers many tools for enhanced vision, the objects of which are adapted to ordinary sense perception, appearing as numbers, graphs, photographs, enlargements, or computer simulations. We are so used to these things now that we take them for granted and often fail to appreciate the wonder of it all.

Not all scientific seeing aims at exploiting things for human health and comfort. Or for war and discomfort! Some of it widens our appreciation for the world outside us and lets us learn from the earth and its other creatures. Good photography of flowers or butterflies or incense cedars or polar bears or prairie dogs heightens our respect for them and for the Creator. Careful analysis lets us see the symbiotic relationships we have with other life forms. Unless imprisoned by a restrictive social environment or addicted to manufactured stimuli, we want to see what's there, whether it is the other side of the mountain, an artery in the heart, the terrain of Mars, or microorganisms in the sea. The psalmist found the heavens both awesome and humbling, "The heavens declare the glory of God; the skies proclaim the work of his hands." (Ps. 19:1) So should we! It is not ignorance but knowledge of complexity that elicits wonder and reverence. Once in a church I attended, a carpenter prayed one morning, "God bless my tools!" Would that more scientists could thus dedicate their tools to the Almighty and commit themselves to constructive service to humanity!

2) Let things reveal their natural significance to the eye. I have tipped my hat to technology for the way it can enhance our seeing. Now I offer a word of caution. Too much reliance upon technological imaging dulls our sense of seeing, whether the images are commercial advertisements, photographs, art objects or CAT scans. We can become too dependent upon secondary viewing, and thus become less sensitive to natural things and natural persons. We can become less sensuous than we should be, and consequently more susceptible to sensual exploitation, especially from commercial images. When the boundaries of our ordinary visual field get blurred the soul lacks clarity of vision.

A few years ago an avid photographer was visiting the scenic Pacific coast, near where I live. Preoccupied with proper camera focus on a spectacular rocky setting, he failed to watch the incoming tide and was swept out to sea. Fortunately, not all dependence upon secondary images is that life-threatening. But the story illustrates the importance of direct visual discipline. That is why direct viewing of things in their natural state is important. Gardening is a sensuous experience—sight and touch blend harmoniously. Nature study, hiking, bird-watching, woodworking, painting, these activities similarly recharge dull senses because they combine them at a level of primary perception. That is why camping and outdoor schools are important to children, whose natural curiosity is thus abetted by adults who teach them what and how to see, and provide them natural settings in which to do so. One good look at the flora and fauna along a forest trail can heal a mind overly imprinted with Saturday morning cartoons and arcade video games. An afternoon at the tide pools, or hiking in the mountains can heal an adult mind overly imprinted with editorial page columns, cartoons, and computer graphics. The current generation of youth and young adults has been brought up in a culture which not only tolerates gambling but turns it into a public enterprise, often using receipts to fund economic or educational projects. It's a new form of regressive taxation. Many people are being seduced by gambling. This seduction is a powerful sensory stimulant, involving both seeing and touching. We should not underestimate its addictive force. Gambling, like other addictions, causes chemical changes in the brain. It competes with drugs in its intoxicating effects. Negative technical imaging must be offset by opportunities for natural visualizations.

3) Discern the appropriate use of things seen. To offset impressions foisted upon us commercially, it may be important to visualize how things function, so that the desirability of an anticipated purchase is a product of its functionality and not its commercial hype. How will the tool work? How will the jacket look on me? How will the house suit the needs of the family? Here the old adage applies: Let form follow function.

4) Retain images appropriately in narrative, art, and in the memory. One does not have to be wealthy to enjoy visually satisfying paintings on the walls, or artistic decor of the home. Well-arranged books, calligraphy, pottery, poetry, photography, sculptures, wall hangings, floral arrangements, craft work—these and more objects of human fashioning offer aesthetically pleasing visualizations of the world about us. Take time to look at them. Savor them. Look at the piece of the earth under your control. Look at your lawn, your garden, your fields, your trees and shrubs. Utility and aesthetic pleasure can coincide in your stewardship of the earth. I know an architect who has turned down attractive commissions because he would not do tawdry work—he would not use inferior materials or pander to conspicuous waste by gold plating the plumbing. His artistic vision was enlightened by social responsibility. Persons who view the world with such eyes do not cheapen what they interact with visually. They do not demean themselves with shoddy merchandise, or misuse of

the creation. They curtail egoistic desires. Such people may not always be overtly thankful to God, but their demonstrated respect for the creation and for work done with integrity constitutes acted praise.

Empathetic Seeing

Empathetic seeing means actively engaging the mind with the visualizations of others. Empathy means seeing objects, persons, animals, plants, the earth, artifacts, as possessing inherent worth, dignity, beauty, design.

Given the opacity of reality and human finitude, it is no wonder we use words like "vision" to describe our quest for common guidance. We want to see our goals and visualize progress toward their realization. Institutions use "envisioning" conferences for this end. Their leaders try to *see the future* in order to plan more wisely for it. To see the future involves looking through the eyes of others. These futurists are trying to do what prophets, and *seers* (note the word) have done historically—to see the world as it is and how it might become a better sentient community. If experience is a guide, the unexpected (the chaotic eruption of evil or serendipitous triumph of the good) will negate or severely skew such envisioning unless God's judgments and God's grace form a respected context for all human probability assessments.

Here are some means of disciplined seeing that are marked by a concern for others.

1) See others as persons not things. Kibitzing the work of others can be a way to honor creativity, not just an opportunity to criticize. To observe the work of others empathetically means accepting their labors as a testament to humanity made in God's image. Find the glory in a new visual landscape that possesses social utility or aesthetic worth, whether that work is the laying of an asphalt road, the building of a bridge, the making of a quilt, the landscaping of a lot, or the preparation of a field for sowing. Offer a prayer of thanks to God for the workers who have achieved such a visual field.

My dentist has rooms that look out onto an enclosed garden, with shrubs and flowers, and birds. It makes us both appreciate our position, not as professional and patient, but as people who require a context of natural beauty for our eyes while we are engaged in stressful work. We are both reminded that we are creatures of God and that God called the creation good. An effective workplace requires some natural beauty, and not just artificial beauty.

2) See other persons whole not in part. There are many biological and cultural compulsions to see people partially. Egoistic desires for control

and ethnic pride often combine to produce tunnel vision. We tend to see only body shape, or sexual configuration, or skin color, or size, fluidity of motion, or clothing style. Habits of looking at others begin in the home, so parents need to teach their children to look at others as whole people, visually to measure people not against some mannequin-like model of the human persona dictated by manipulators of culture as the true type of model human physique, but as children of God with many variations. To see beauty in many forms, not just as measured by models. Because the human quest for aesthetics forces us all to make gradations of beauty, it is important to help children see more than one standard of perfection. Is someone's nose unusually long? Look at the skin texture. Is someone's body broken by disease or age? See the beauty of a gentle face. See in the wrinkles and scars evidence of a courageous life. Above all, look deeply into the eyes of another and see beauty of soul. To see others as whole persons made in the image of God is a major challenge if we would accept the bodies of others as temples of the Holy Spirit.

3) See persons as they can become. This is an especially important axiom for adults who must overcome symbolic appearances to see their developing children and grandchildren. Look at these gangly, queerly dressed adolescents, lolling about at the edge of a school campus, sucking on cigarettes, or skateboarding on the church parking lot. Their penchant for bizarre attire and behavior reflects an uncertainty about who they are and who they may become. Look through their eyes at the dangers lurking about them, at dysfunctional homes, at a peer group both alluring and alarming, at commercially promoted anti-hero role models. Peer beneath the pathos painted on their empty faces and look for what will give them hope, instead of fear, joy instead of sadness. See them as seekers whom God would gather in to the company of the faithful. How will divine light enter the gate of their eyes? Is there a way you could be one of God's messengers on their behalf? Can you find better vistas for their eyes than MTV and parking lots?

To see another as that person can become by the grace of God lays upon you a burden to act rationally on the one you see before you. Whether that person is a hungry child, a lonesome senior citizen, a harried working parent, a close loved one, to see empathetically is to accept the burdens as well as the joys of the other one. This is seeing through the eyes of Jesus. To see the world simply as it is leads to cynicism. To see the world only as it may become is idealism. To see the world both as it is and as it can become is godly realism.

4) Try to see through the eyes of other creatures. We may not be on the same linguistic level as the creatures of the earth, but we share a common visual field. Animals, at least, can look at us. How do they see us? As food sources, as friends? As a child I liked to look into the eyes of our cows. They were more than blobs of protoplasm, more than milk containers. No one visiting the goats at the fair can doubt the power of eye-to-eye contact with the creatures. Our pets, especially, give us visual feedback. They look into our eyes, and sometimes, it seems, into our souls. Whether plants sense our presence in any rational way is doubtful, although animists, feeling a kinship with the flora of the earth, claim to find spirit present. Perhaps touch is the key sense, here. In any case, to the extent we gain empathy with creatures that relationship will make better, more responsible persons.

5) Accept reciprocity. There is a difference between *looking at* and *being looked at* by another person. Sympathy involves seeing another person as distressed or needing help. Empathy, however, is reciprocal. It involves letting the others see us as openly as we see them. For professional caregivers this is difficult, for in their profession they are the ones doing the thoughtful looking; the patient is the one being looked at. They have many needy persons to see after, not just one. They require dispassionate objectivity for emotional stability. But if the doctor or the nurse or the social worker can allow the other to see them honestly, to minister to them by their own personality, then some of the emotional weight is lifted. Gifts of self have been exchanged, not just money and services. Caregivers can be conned by hypochondriacs, but they can also be ministered to by those they serve, and will be the richer for it. We cannot fully overcome professional distance, but we can accept a wholesome reciprocity of persons who see each other in a time of need.

6) Identify with the feelings of others. We can let their sorrows and joys reach us. Our eyes can discern what is going on with them. It is a biblical teaching that in bearing one another's burdens we are fulfilling the law of Christ (Gal. 6:2). To do so requires that we be literally sensitive. Other persons, known and unknown, are our brothers and sisters, our children, our mothers and fathers, our uncles and aunts, our grandparents and grandchildren. In a rather unorthodox fashion Walt Whitman celebrated this unity of humankind in his "Song of Myself," offering a long and rambling litany about the comings and goings of ordinary people, with whom he linked his own being. In one word picture he wrote: "I am the mashed fireman with breastbone broken/Tumbling walls buried me in their debris."[11] This poet took seriously that humanity is of one blood.

Godly Seeing

Godly seeing means using one's eyes as instruments of God. "Interrogating" their meanings, to use Augustine's phrase, we see persons, animals, plants, the earth, and artificial things in the context of God's ordering. Such is the eye single and full of Light. Focused for the long view, we see the human community as God's kingdom, the Church as Christ's body, the heavens and the earth as God's handiwork. Focused on the short view we see persons as they are and not simply as a member of a class or special ethnic group. Focused on the long view we see the cosmos and all its creatures as they will become when redeemed by God's grace and fitted for eternity.

Godly seeing means seeing God's presence in the world to the fullest extent possible in this life. Here we go beyond using our eyes in a right and godly manner to letting sight draw us metaphorically into divine presence—to see God. I wrote earlier that most of us do not often experience theophanies. We hear others tell of special dreams, or visitations, but do not experience such ourselves. For us God's presence is a combination of faith and logical inference, mediated through ordinary things and events. Sometimes God's presence is warmly felt, at other times just rationally acknowledged. But occasionally we do experience luminous encounters with God. Then the divine presence becomes an overwhelming experience, a cloud of glory enveloping us beyond our capacity to anticipate or to describe.

Such ecstatic visions draw us to consider what Moses experienced on Sinai and Peter on the mountain of Transfiguration. Can we gain insights from their experiences? I think so. As reported in the Bible, Moses achieved an unusual intimacy with the Lord. A curious, but instructive, dialogue is reported in the book of Exodus, a more upbeat scenario than that depicted in a gloomy modern play, *Waiting for Godot* (where God is a no-show). Here is the account of that dialogue between Moses and God:

> Then Moses said, "Now show me your glory." And the LORD said, "I will cause all my goodness to pass in front of you, and I will proclaim my name, the LORD, in your presence. I will have mercy on whom I will have mercy, and I will have compassion on whom I will have compassion. But," he said, "you cannot see my face, for no one may see me and live." Then the LORD said, "There is a place near me where you may stand on a rock. When my glory passes by, I will put you in a cleft in the rock and cover you with my hand until I have passed by. Then I will remove my

hand and you will see my back; but my face must not be seen."
(Ex. 33:18-23 NIV)

To glimpse God fleetingly is as much ecstasy as one can stand. It is enough for us to see God as a luminous trail of glory *after*, not before, or during, the moment of truth. I guess that is why faith is so vital. Moses learned these truths. So did Job. When the old patriarch came through his ordeal with the powers of darkness and light it was the affirming presence of God, not theological answers, that satisfied him. And it came after Job demonstrated true faith, after he had endured the trial, with his integrity intact. Chaos yielded to purpose, despair to hope, silence to song, sorrow to joy. Mystery deepened, but not darkness. Job exclaimed, "My ears had heard of you but now my eyes have seen you. Therefore I despise myself and repent in dust and ashes." (Job 42:5-6 NIV) Job got a glimpse of God in passing and it was enough. And so it can be for us.

What is the lesson in spiritual discipline? The great vision came to Moses after he saw the goodness of God, and to Job after he had dared question the Almighty about disorder and injustice in the world. God honors those who struggle to interpret what their senses have received about the world. These persons become true ministers of God's truth and grace. Significantly, God chose Job, his unflinching interrogator, to be the priestly intercessor for those unctuous friends, who were more concerned for God's reputation than for truth. From Job, the "first dissident," in William Safire's words, we learn that "As a basis for worship, awe is better than fear, and the need to engage is best of all."[12]

How do our eyes see God? Not as object, but as subject interacting with subject on a common path of vision. Sight is a two-way street. God uses our eyes to look at us. God parades the creatures of the earth, including humanity, before our eyes. The eyes of earth's creatures reflect the light of God. Gaze without bias into the eyes of another person, or creature, and what do I see? I see myself there reflected, mirrored in their pains, their hopes, their yearnings for trust and love. And I see God there, whom we love because he first loved us.

No, we do not see God as object, but we can "see God" imaged in events, things, and persons about us. Having one's eye fixed singly on the good enables us to see God as subject. To look at the world about us with pure intention is to see, if not God's face, at least God's back, to see where the Almighty has been and where God is going. And that will suffice.

"Blessed are the pure in heart," promised Jesus, "for they will see God." (Matt. 5:8) That promise was echoed by the apostle Paul, who had experienced a dramatic vision on the road to Damascus. The zealous persecutor of Christians, after his conversion, became their strong advocate. Through this ecstatic experience Paul saw where God was going, so to speak, in time and space. He saw God's universal Light to humanity demonstrated in Christ, whereas previously he saw Jesus as a threat to Israel's witness to the nations. Another early follower of Jesus wrote, "Dear friends, now we are children of God, and what we will be has not yet been made known. But we know that when he appears, we shall be like him, for we shall see him as he is." (1 John 3:2 NIV)

The discipline for seeing God is not some posture, no special litany or words, no iconic representation. It is rather that stance of the soul exhorted by the writer of the book of Hebrews, "Let us fix our eyes on Jesus, the author and perfecter of our faith, who for the joy set before him endured the cross, scorning its shame, and sat down at the right hand of the throne of God." (Heb. 12:2 NIV)

Hope is a God-given virtue that directs the will toward seeing ourselves, others, and God in ways not yet evidenced. Our hope is quickened by fleeting, serendipitous glimpses of God that come our way. These glimpses are images, if we have eyes to see, of angelic messengers flowing along the rods and cones, firing these photoreceptors with meaning: perception, conceptualization, logical entailment, general implications, personal application, significance. Our powers of vision thus enable us to interact rationally, emotionally, and volitionally with the Creator along a network of the Spirit. Hope expects an even greater visualization of the Holy Presence in the life to come. The Spirit within us, this wondrous gift from God, enables us to hold fast to that hope. The Spirit is our earnest money on the Kingdom, come and coming.

It is no surprise
that some I meet
in this place
or that street
have loved so hard
that they assert—
in glances met—
that love can hurt.

It is no surprise
to see such care
in shadows—
which I share—

and to realize
a mutual mirroring
of pain
within our eyes. [13]

Notes

1. Michael Crichton, *Jurassic Park* (New York: Knopf, 1990).

2. On the replacement of memory by reference works, see an article by Milton J. Coalter, Jr., "Imperfect Tailors," *Theology Today* (Oct. 1993), p. 391. Coalter contrasts the richness of memory stored in minds in other eras, through memorization of Scripture, songs, prayers, for example, and laments our dependence upon books and commentaries. Too much dependence upon archival material or official books and Bible versions cripples Christians who must transpose the Gospel into new cultural forms. Memories make transitions to new cultural modes better because the old (the transcultural) is not lost in transition.

3. Stephen L. Carter, *The Culture of Disbelief* (New York: Harper, 1993) has helped me understand more fully the bankruptcy of the post-Enlightenment era, and its effect on our culture. Carter shows how hope has dimmed that the moral authority of human reason could replace divine authority. He speaks of a prevailing liberal (Enlightenment) bias against people who call upon the authority of God in respect to social issues. He says the voice of religion is not heard in the public square; it is trivialized, even though lip service is given to piety in public pronouncements. See particularly pp. 223ff.

4. Cited from *The Witness of William Penn*, edited by Frederick B. Tolles and E. Gordon Alderfer (New York: The Macmillan Company, 1957), p. 111. Another essay by William Penn, whose 350th birthday was celebrated in 1994, is his *Essay Toward the Present and Future Peace of Europe*, which was remarkably prescient in showing how cooperation works better for justice, and hence for peace, than war.

5. See Chapter One, "Thinking about the Senses," note 10, and the bibliography for authors whose books provided useful background for data used.

6. Diane Ackerman, *A Natural History of the Senses* (New York: Random House, 1990), p. 254.

7. Ibid. pp. 259ff, and p. 230.

8. This judgment about religion on television was influenced by Neil Postman's book, *Amusing Ourselves to Death* (New York: Penguin, 1984), pp. 116ff.

9. Terry Waite, *Taken on Trust* (New York: Harcourt Brace, 1993), p. 171.

10. This has been demonstrated empirically. See Robert A. Josephs, R. Brian Giesler, and David H. Silvera, "Judgment by Quantity," *Journal of Experimental Psychology: General* (March 1994), pp. 55-60.

11. Stanza 33. I have cited the verse from the collection, *Major American Poets*, ed. Oscar Williams and Edwin Hong (New York: New American Library, 1962).

12. William Safire, *The First Dissident* (New York: Random House, 1992), p. 88. Safire states further, "Job refused to quit protesting until he was permitted to see—that is, to get a quick peek, a metaphysical teaser, at a corner of all he is yet to learn. God may take offense at disrespect, and if he chooses to reveal himself you'll soon know that, but he is more profoundly offended at phony piety....You may or may not find the answer by demanding to know, but you will surely never find the answer by fearing to ask."

13. Arthur O. Roberts, *Sunrise and Shadow* (Newberg, OR: Barclay Press, 1985), p. 45.

CHAPTER FOUR

SMELLING

*For we are the aroma of Christ to God
among those who are being saved
and among those who are perishing.*
—Paul (2 Cor. 2:15)

In this chapter we consider how the olfactory sense is connected with spirituality. If our bodies are indeed temples of the Holy Spirit, then we must ask how our noses can interrogate incoming messages and find divine truth and personal empowerment. But first, a story. I'll entitle it "Nose to the Wind." We shift our minds to analogical mode and do theology in narrative style.

Nose to the Wind

Riding in the car beside me, Charlie puts his nose to the open window aquiver with delight. I can only guess at what aromatic smells flow across his nostrils. My nose lacks his sensitivity. For me bad odors repel, good ones please, but vaguely so and in a diffused way that must puzzle him. *Why did God make my master so stupid?* he muses. (Actually I, the wordy one, muse thus on behalf of one of God's more instinctive, less reflective, creatures.)

"Charlie," I say to him, "my nose may not be as good as yours, but I've got a more sophisticated ear. You hear sirens sooner than I do, and you howl at them nose heavenward fairly synchronously, but as a connoisseur of sophisticated sounds, such as symphonies, I've got you beat a mile!"

Charlie wags his tail affectionately, and lays his nose on my leg, glad for pleasant sounds even though they don't carry any specific instructions, pleasant or otherwise. To borrow a word from my mouth, Charlie has no taste in sounds; I have no taste in smells.

After a spell of driving we park the car at a pleasant spot for a break. Immediately Charlie cases out the place with prolonged sniffing and marks numerous spots whose significance escapes me. Then, satisfied by his olfactory perambulations, he curls up beside me against a warm tree trunk, content to let me ponder what he processes by instinct.

Why did God give human creatures such poor acuity in smelling, I wonder? Have we allowed our olfactory system to atrophy because we can cope easily enough without it? Or have we closed our nose to the world carelessly, and missed something important in doing so? It was a warm afternoon, and my reflections slipped into sleep, I guess, for what followed partook more of dream than of wakeful reflection. Suddenly a visitor stood there, startling me. "Well, good afternoon," I said, introducing myself, "I didn't see you come."

"Sorry to have startled you," he replied, "but I smelled you from across the field and came over to get acquainted." *Smelled me?* I thought, *who is this weirdo?* But I held my peace and asked, "Oh...where are you from?"

"I've been traveling around the earth on a special mission."

"Oh," I said, "with the government or an oil company? Or the CIA, maybe?" (You never know about that bunch.)

"Oh, no," he said, "no, not that at all. I am an agent of sorts, though. I am God's agent, an angel."

Well, I'd never met an angel before. My experiences with extraterrestrials had been limited to science fiction movies. Was this some kind of kook? I decided to keep the guy talking. "So," I said as politely as I could manage, "you're an angel. What's your job?"

"Olfactory detail: I monitor smell," he replied. Suddenly I thought of Charlie who remained sound asleep beside me, nostrils twitching slightly. I wondered why he didn't check out this guy who seemed more up his alley, so to speak, than mine. But Charlie was no help, dozing away contentedly, so I resumed the conversation. "Why does your boss want you to check out smells?"

Well, that got him started, just like a college professor who plunges deftly into the smallest conversational space. It took me a while to get back into the conversation.

"Smell," he said, "offers a good socio-theological index to a culture; it yields important data, although it is difficult to gather. Smell has to borrow heavily from eye and ear languages, for example. You people borrow from sound to rhapsodize over baked bread and from sight to versify the fragrance of a nicely perfumed person. And then, too, some cultures are olfactory deprived. Ancient cultures didn't like what smells told them about their world, so they used spices and perfumery to cover it up. Western culture seems interested mostly in masking bad odors with sprays and stuff. From your television I learn that contemporary human persons consider a smelly armpit worse than adultery, and that more is spent on cosmetics to hide the smell of sweat than what the World Health Organization spends to abolish children's diseases."

"Your particular culture," he continued, "approves of giving, number one, admiring glances, number two, flattering speech, number three, affectionate touch, and number four, convivial tasting. But it frowns upon rapturous sniffing. Dogs sniff, people look."

"Well, of course," I exclaimed, "it's gross to go around sniffing people."

"Why?" he asked. That stumped me for a bit, so I stared across the meadow and scratched my head above my left ear (I do that when I'm flustered).

"I know," I said finally, "that the word *olfactory* literally means to make a smell, but this, ah, sniffs slightly scatological, to use your jargon. After all, we wouldn't say to someone, 'I smell you.'"

"Oh, why not?"

"It just isn't done!" I retorted impatiently. "Saying that implies the other person has bad body odor. It's a put down! It isn't like saying 'I hear you,' or 'I see you.' The transitive verb 'to smell' lacks transitive meaning in the grammar of our culture."

"What a shame," he retorted. "You miss so much by limiting your language of smell, it seems to me. In my report I will state categorically that contemporary earth culture is woefully undereducated smell-wise. There are courses in spelling but none in smelling. There are taboos and very intricate rituals for touching but mostly just taboos for smelling. Musical performances are popular for the ear, and quite sophisticated with their intricate notation systems, their well-trained performers, and their truly incredible artificial memory banks. Speech gets high billing, too. The words of great leaders such as Abraham Lincoln can be read in books and those of Martin Luther King, Jr., can not only be heard every year on the radio but recalled visually on television. How remarkable! You have great eye literature, all kinds of books and magazines for prose and poetry, and art galleries to enrapture the eye.

"But where are the repositories for smell? I would think a memory bank entitled 'Great Battle Smells' would be instructive to school children, and evocative on Memorial Day. Even by metaphor your great literature bridges meanings mainly from touch to sound to sight. One poem I read has a line: 'this is the forest primeval, the murmuring pines and the hemlocks.' Why not 'this is the forest primeval, the vaporous marsh and the humus, smelling all fecund and fertile'?"

This lecture was making me nervous. What trump card did this strange fellow have up his sleeve? So I muttered crossly, "Don't you realize that we hide smells that are, ah, ugly to the nose, just as we clean our houses to get rid of dirt that is repugnant to the eye, not healthy to the mouth, and dangerous to the skin? What's the big deal?"

"Oh, you misunderstand me," he replied. "It's not that we're against being clean and tidy. It's only that your civilization has a way of masking smells rather than learning from them. Having noses you smell not. It's like, what's that expression, 'sweeping dirt under the rug.' Although it must borrow the languages of the other senses, smells can provide significant whiffs of the divine or the demonic. In the old Hebrew culture, for example, incense and burnt offerings were part of worship. These pungent offerings were more than burned meat and smoky candles. They signified praise to God, and submission to holy purpose. And...[Here he waxed emphatic] and when their worship was hypocritical the Almighty thundered at these covenant people and said those votive smells were a stench in the divine nostrils!"

That was the punch line, all right. I got the message. Quick as a sneeze I jumped in. "Actually, we have a slang phrase that conveys a residual human memory: We say 'It stinks to high heaven' when you smell political corruption a mile away, and 'It's a rotten deal' when you get the short end of the stick on some supposedly mutual business venture. Slang remembers!"

The rhetorical space following my exclamation gave the agent his cue to complete his lecture. Which he did. "The nose," concluded my visiting lecturer, "as an instrument of the body, can be used either for righteousness or unrighteousness. Whether your nose receives God's message or not depends upon how the inner self interrogates the smells that drift across it. The nose is a good monitor, if you let it be one."

At that point something cold touched my face and broke my reverie. It was Charlie's nose. He was awake, barking, and raring to go. "Okay, Charlie," I called, "let's hit the road again, noses to the Wind."

WHAT HAPPENS WHEN NOSES SMELL

How can human noses catch the wind of God? Obviously, we haven't the acuity of creatures like dogs, these "smell engineers" who are so useful in locating missing persons or sniffing out contraband. Our skills pale beside that of the ant, attracted to a smudge of sugar left on the kitchen counter, or sea creatures like sharks, which can smell blood a mile away. The male moth can detect and find a female moth over seven miles away! Smell may be an ancient scent, rendered less important to human survival than the other senses, although crucial to other creatures. But it is a significant route for the messengers of God. Aromas and scents may play a larger role in our lives than superficial reflection would indicate. That it is so becomes evident when we consider the importance of trade in aromatic substances, including perfumery.

To appreciate the significance of this sense we first describe what happens physically in olfactory sensation, then show how smell functions individually and socially, and finally elaborate the categories of smell.

It may be instructive to acknowledge that as long as we are breathing we are smelling things. We can't just close off smell as we do sound on TV, or shut our eyes from an unwelcomed scene. We can move away from a smell in space and time, but memory retains the residue in a primal fashion, in a special part of the brain, the residue becoming an associational marker.

Olfactory receptors are bipolar neurons having an axon and a dendritic process with a unique capacity for reproduction and replacement. The average olfactory receptor has a life span of two months, after which time it is replaced by a previously undifferentiated basal cell. Olfactory receptor cells typically number in the area of 10,000,000, and are unique in another way. They receive sensory information from cilia embedded in the mucus layer that are dendritic projections of the receptor cell itself. Thus the receptor cell receives sensory information and transduces it as one unit to the surrounding olfactory nerve fibers, without the need of a relaying intermediary.

The stimulus required to perceive an odor or "smell" is a molecule in the air we breathe that is both water and lipid (fat) soluble.

It must come in contact with and be dissolved into the mucus membrane of the olfactory bulb. This bulb is located high in the nasal cavity above a series of bones and spaces. In a real sense we do not smell with our "nose" at all. When air is inhaled, molecules dissolve into the mucus layer in which the olfactory receptors are located, creating a chemical condition that inspires the receptors to activity.

Apparently, the more prevalent and pervasive the dissolved molecules, the more activity among the receptor cells. Intense stimuli tend to produce strong electrical responses that persist over time, and the more molecules involved, the more receptors involved in their detection. It is harder to account for odor quality and discrimination.

Despite speculation about encoding odor quality, nothing has been concretely proven. Researchers believe that various receptor cells respond to molecules in a set behavior, and an analysis of the aggregate of many receptor cell responses will indicate that different patterns exist for different smells. While there is scientific evidence to back such claim, it would be premature to give it credibility.

From the olfactory nerves, fed directly by the receptor cells, impulses go through two sets of cells, mitral and tufted, and their helper interneurons. The axons of the mi-

tral and tufted neurons feed directly up into the olfactory cortex, made up of five ascending areas that variously involve such things as olfactory discrimination and the limbic system. People can distinguish approximately 10,000 olfactions.

The olfactory sense has been called the most primitive sense. Many feel that the sense of smell is obsolete, as it is not needed to procure food or a mate as is the case for some of the lower animals. However, there is speculation that olfaction provides human beings with valuable information about things and other persons through the chemical con-tent of the air, and studies of chemical communication between individuals through "pheromones" is continuing. One investigation has to do with gender specific body odors that relate to sexual stimulation.

Some scientists think there is a sixth sense that accounts for a function our culture generally treats as smell. We refer to certain aspects of sexual attraction.[1] Scientists have experimented with a bundle of nerves halfway up our noses, which they think may be a wholly different sense. The waxy area between cheek and nose indicates cells loaded with pheromones. They call it the vomeronasal organ (VNO). Apparently this skin organ is susceptible to chemical reactions. Part of our skin, but near the nose, it is a signal mechanism for sexuality, they claim, a philter, if you please. Perhaps it serves for human beings like tail glands serve dogs. Scientists debate whether this organ emits true pheromones, whether it is vestigial or functional. They are convinced male and female noses respond differently to stimuli through this organ. Lacking a working verb for this activity they say people "VNO" each other. When people kiss, or rub noses, this erogenous zone is stimulated. The closing of the eyes reinforces the intimacy found through such sensory experiences.

Whether VNO is a sixth sense, or even a physical characteristic, will continue to be debated. Let us just say it illustrates the co-mingling of the senses, in this case smell and touch, from which we may infer that the whole of sensual experience is greater than the sum of its parts. It also illustrates how intermixed are physiological and cultural factors in human behavior.

By smell we locate ourselves within the world, even if olfactory markers are not as strong as other sensory ones. By smell we know where we are in respect to many objects, persons, and circumstances. We define our territory by scent, often unreflectively. There are natural smells and artificial ones. Sniffing forms the basis for various sorts of ethical and aesthetic judgments. We go or stay, act or refrain from actions in accordance with messages relayed by our noses. The nose is an educator. We learn about the forest from ozone in the air, about the sea from salt smell carried by the breeze.

Our society is quite conscious of the needs of hearing, sight, and physically impaired individuals, providing special services to them such as hearing aids, guide dogs, and wheelchair-accessible buildings. Society is less aware of the special needs of another group, smelling impaired persons. Officially labeled Multiple Chemical Sensitivity-Environmental Illness (MCS-EI), this disability impairs the ability of its sufferers to function well in an urban culture dependent upon chemical products and processes. Carpets, smog, perfumes, certain cleansers, electrical appliances, and host of other things in everyday use for most of us, seem to induce asthma-like reactions in some people. Is the condition psychologically induced? Many professionals once thought so, and psychological factors may be present in some cases. But now it's generally considered that the sensory system of some people can't easily cope well with the many chemical agents present in our environment. Unless checked the malady seems to get progressively worse for these people, as one bad whiff triggers an olfactory chain episode to which the brain overreacts. Special housing, diet, clothing, and social environment may be required for the worst sufferers.

Most of us are only mildly irritated by chemical agents that bother others. A bout of sneezing, for example, may be triggered simply by walking down "detergent alley" in the grocery store. So we make our selection and hurry along.

Our olfactory sense helps us smell danger or trouble. The nose is a responsible guardian, usually, and not a paranoid alarmist. We sniff the air for the smell of smoke, and check around the house to see if the odor has blown in on the wind from a distance or has sprung from a fire on our property. By smelling the exhaust, a mechanic may find clues to a malfunctioning engine. The nose is a tool for nurses and physicians. Smells can signify fear or disease. Sometimes the message our nostrils send to the brain is clear and unambiguous. Something stinks! Sometimes the message isn't all that clear, but after a few bad episodes we have learned to heed the prudent counsel of our olfactory system. "This food doesn't smell right," we say, and dump it into the garbage, uncertain whether we wasted money or preserved health, but grateful for an alert sentry that guards an important gate of the body.

The psalmist had the poetic way of portraying idolatry: Idols have noses but smell not. (Ps. 115:6) By inference people who have noses but don't used them to scent out truth are idolatrous. The nose, too, is an important temple door—a route for angelic messengers. To use that door appropriately is an objective of spiritual discipline, thus we now consider smell within the several sensory categories.

Passive Smelling

What are some of the smells received passively? Well, there is the vegetation around you, whether that flora be flowers and carrots in your garden, alfalfa in your field, or the grass and trees in your yard. Our Creator has drenched the world with a multitude of pleasant smells. They inform us the earth is good. We can walk about on any fine morning and let the Spirit lead us through a gloriously scented world. Spring blossoms and fall leaves promise God's providence and renewal.

Passive smelling receives as well the myriad smells of human habitation, that aromatic intermix of familiar persons, household goods, pets, and manufactured things. Often we are unaware of a particular set of chemical molecules that makes home until we move, or visit a different culture. It may be a good thing for us to open our nostrils to the ordinary odors about us. To smell anew the woodwork, the kitchen aromas, the shop, the office, the lotions and perfumes in bathroom cabinets and on our bodies. To savor the smells of life and activity. We are called to be sensuous, to receive these aromas as angels from the Creator, not as idols or toys.

Conditioned Smelling

Once a child showed me her new book. "Scratch each picture," she said, "and you get its smell." And so it was. A banana, a slice of bread, each yielded an artificial approximation of its natural odor. I wondered then, could this be an incentive for the non-reader to get his nose into a book? Or is this simple, childish thing an ominous sign about the future of media? Will Joe Cool signs exude the smell of tobacco and overworn basketball shoes? Maybe in a few years the popcorn smell may move from the theater lobby to the film itself. Turn on the projector and you get a "smellie" not just a "movie." Odors will be scored for the film by Hollywood olfactory engineers. Get a whiff of the process. First, smell will be grouped into chemical ideograms, then into a completely abstract chemical alphabet with smell symbols correlated to the script. Imagine it. Love scenes will spread perfume and VNO pheromones around the house; horse sweat and manure will add pungent reality to westerns. Discovery channels will add smells to the sights and sounds of the beluga whale and the tiger. Late night shows will heighten scatological ratings by odoriferous additions to the script, and the public outrage at the ultimate in crudity will make protest of the "F" word seem mild.

I am for posting smell as a protected preserve, a place of primitive perception below the level of conceptualized language. Fortunately, television has not yet incorporated smells in its programming, and scratch-and-smell books or advertising gimmicks in women's magazines are too frivolous to influence our judgments. So our noses are not as badly preempted by entrepreneurs as our ears and our eyes have been. Not yet. But there are forms of conditioned smelling that do have significant cultural influence, both beneficial and injurious. These conditioned smells range from the simple use of exhaust fans that waft bakery smells down the street to more complex and subtle forms of olfactory promotion, such as expensively advertised perfume products and wine tasting rituals. The sensual character of our culture is conveyed by labels used to sell odors. People with good noses and a scientific knowledge of perfumery engineer aromatic packaging for all sorts of personal and household items. Names such as "Brute" and "Intimate" and "Sin" hype skin lotions and perfumes. Thus our noses are conditioned to associate smell with sensuality, or at least with personal body functions, and to depend upon the market for their education.

Our culture has learned many ways to mask bad smells and enhance good ones, but it needs to become more adept in teaching our noses to interrogate smells for their social significance and to become more sensitive to receiving God's revelations of judgment and redemption.

There are some general ways, however, in which the nose is a pretty effective, sensuous, monitor of truth and value in this and any culture. When the wind is right, the nose detects God's judgment upon sin. The olfactory sense is a messenger of God to prevent the world from crushing us into an evil mold. Nudged by the Holy Spirit, the Wind of God, one's nose is an alert prophet, warning of neglect, exploitation, excess, injustice, poverty, and disease and holding us accountable for them. When one walks into a nursing home to visit an aged friend or relative does not the nose ask questions about accountability? If a stench of senility assails the nostrils, the practices and principles of the management and one's own accountability is put in question. And if this stench is barely masked by scented spray a cover-up of shoddy health care services is suspected. Our olfactory system imprints "neglect" or "exploitation" upon the mind before the eyes and the ears can articulate their judgments. The nose knows.

The nose can sniff out injustice in the open sewers that leach out the pride of the poor along with their excrement in shack towns that ring third world cities swollen by peasants uprooted from the soil they once tilled. On a drive in the countryside on a quiet evening, the nose interrogates the air. Does it smell of pesticide blended with urea? The nostrils label the smell agribusiness and warn of political trouble ahead. Will it be a bloody and destructive or a bloodless and constructive revolution? The answer depends upon how well and by whom these odors are interrogated. Does the Wind waft the common good or selfish interest?

Uncollected garbage in the inner city reeks of economic frustration and the death of hope as well as the putrefaction of cabbage. Alcoholic vomit rises putrid from the curb to curse the demons in advertising agencies and distilleries and conglomerates. If we inhale that odor prayerfully we may sense God's judgment upon persons who spray themselves with corporate anonymity (along with perfume and after-shave lotion) and through visual media offer public diversion (as well as divestment) from accountability, through images of well-tailored clothes and athletic prowess. The smell of tobacco at side entrances to office buildings, hospitals, and high school campuses, testifies to addictions meticulously nurtured, cultivated, and exploited.

To use deodorant is to be considerate of others; but it is no substitute for good diet. Chemical factory scrubbers are socially beneficial, but they are no substitute for more appropriate technology. The judgment of God can be smelled in the cancer wards of veteran's hospitals. Remember all the free cigarettes to our soldiers? Evil can be smelled in rat-infested hotel rooms reeking with exhaust fumes, musty rugs, stale body odors, and tears of futility. Society finds it easier to train dogs to scent out "the criminal element" than to interrogate and remedy rot in the city.

As you approach the city where you live pay attention to what your nose reports about hydrocarbon smog. Savor the earth in travail awaiting the redemption of its designated caretakers. Then drive to where the air is clean and breathe again, prayerfully, until the green grass and the fragrant trees put you on to the scent of God. Let the aroma of the Spirit, heady with hope for Jerusalem the golden, the garden city, healer of nations, the Eden of the future, intoxicate you. Smell the Kingdom come and coming! Follow doggedly in thought and action where this divine aroma leads.

God's messengers come to us through the gate of smell. Our acts as stewards of the earth and our words as witnesses to the Gospel become our aromatic offerings to God. As Paul wrote (2 Cor. 2:14-15), "...thanks be to God, who always leads us in triumphal procession in Christ and through us spreads everywhere the fragrance of the knowledge of him. For we are to God the aroma of Christ among those who are being saved and those who are perishing."

We are called to be living sacrifices, the "aroma of Christ"! Such is the programming of the Spirit.

Egocentric Smelling

The sense of smell is a gift from the Lord. It is right and holy that the body, as God's temple, should receive the scented world with joy. But first one must resist selfishness, resist the need for conspicuous consumption of peddled odors. Olfactory beauty is more than slapping on aftershave lotion and exotic perfumes, more than incense burned to make the bathroom smell better.

Smells come to us as gifts of God, not only for safety in avoiding noxious fumes and bad food, but for the enjoyment of creation. We find God aromatic in the ozone of the forest and in the vegetative odors flowing invisible above meadow grasses. Within the mosses of the rain forest, the alpine pool, the marshlands, the tide flats, the estuaries are these gifts found. We are invited a Sabbath rest in the cool, dark basement of God's creation. Even the occasional smell of death in the forest is enveloped in stronger smells of life. Thus our nostrils breathe divine drama with its promise of resurrection. The aroma of the Logos rises from garden humus, in odoriferous vegetables displayed at the grocery store, and in kitchens everywhere that good food is cooked and served. We have but to breathe deeply to express gratitude to God for persons whose feet and hands and backs bear the brunt of toil that enables us to smell the flowers and enjoy earth's harvest.

Disciplined by maturity, memory can enrich the present moment with accessible associations of smell. The smell of varnish on the benches of the old meetinghouse in which I worshiped as a child enriches my present moment. So does the smell of my father as he came in to lunch after a morning of heavy farm work among the animals and the hay, and the redolence of green grass—laced with wild onions—upon which we lolled at recess. I can summon to consciousness a certain aromatic bouquet from milking time when I sat on a three-legged stool, head tight against the flank of a cow, a steam of fresh milk mixing its aroma with others and swirling about my nostrils.

One of my winter farm chores was to spread manure from the strawed cattle lot into a wagon, to be strewn upon the frozen alfalfa fields. Alone, warmly clothed against the wind, I forked rotted, nutrient manure into the spreader. At each forkful steam lifted into the frosty air and with the steam a pungent libation. It was an unveiling of hope, light out of darkness, birth from decay, green life from brown death. It didn't smell bad to me, although it might have to an urbanite. Using the verb intransitively, I *smelled* like cow manure when I came in from work. Transitively, I smelled well. My nose taught me an understanding of, and active participation in, certain rhythms of life. My nose located me in reality.

I remember the offensive smell of the floral arrangement at my father's funeral. Visual order came at the expense of olfactory disorder. At least so it seemed to me at sixteen. The artist latent in me longed for olfactory design.

I remember from my youth a heady olfactory mix of asphalt, metal, rubber, and petroleum. The ecstasy of power is how my nostrils interrogated those odors, an eager youth lured to challenge inventively the limits of the world received. What he cannot customize he will crush, unless and until the Lord becomes his partner and power is used creatively and constructively.

Other persons have similar olfactory memories easily retrieved, memories of Thanksgiving dinners, the mudpots at Yellowstone Park, tennis doubles, intimacy and love. These memories reach family members now deceased, and to houses once lived in.

Consider the smells of health. To keep the body healthy is spiritually important. The Spirit dwells here. The temple of the Lord is the whole person, body, soul, and spirit. It is good to let smell monitor health. A clean, healthy baby is a good smell to the Lord. So also is a perspiring worker laying sewer pipe from the house to the main line. So is one's own body after a good bath, and fed with good food. The smell of good food is an offering unto the Almighty, an offering of praise to the Lord of sowing and harvest.

Empathetic Smelling

How can smelling be used for the good of others? In many ways. Keeping noxious odors away is one. Perfume is another, either worn or given. One empathetic discipline for workplaces means acknowledging that sexual pheromones are subtle and powerful and vowing to use them responsibly rather than exploitively.

In general, though, smells enhance friendship by sensory linkage of life with life. Other cultures may be more richly aromatic than is American culture.[2] Symbols of sensuous friendship may be coffee and fresh baked pastry shared at a cafe, or at the kitchen table. Aromatic incense or pleasant-smelling plants can be part of home courtesy for guests. The familiar smelled presence of a loved person in the room is a gentle affirmation of how much we depend upon each other. So are sweet scents and spices for sick persons and those shut in day after day. For some poor children a day at the beach or in the mountains offers a bouquet of unaccustomed scents. An old adage reads, "Perfume and incense bring joy to the heart, and the pleasantness of one's friend springs from his earnest counsel." (Prov. 27:9)

All churches include scent in worship, usually flowers. Some include incense. Why not? Aromas reach persons of all ages and education levels without discrimination in the community of worship. Sweet smells offer joy to the Creator. Frankincense and myrrh matched gold as worthy gifts offered by the Magi to the Christ Child. Aromatic offerings for religious purposes is an ancient practice. Today, people in our culture use flowers and worship folders for the eyes, sermons and music for the ears, wafers and juice for the palate, and the laying on of hands for ceremonial touch, so why not incense for the nose? The more liturgical churches do so. Such rituals symbolize the sacramental character of sensory experiences that greet us routinely. Rituals aren't ends in themselves, they are merely signs pointing to the greater reality of God imbedded in the creation and incarnate in the church as the witnessing community of faith.

Sometimes these rituals become hindrances rather than helps; they indulge our inclination to limit spirituality to settings abstracted from ordinary life. Through them we pay our dues to religion, so to speak, without accepting disciplined spirituality. The senses serve best when sacral rather than liturgical. Common things carry divine grace, to senses open to these carriers. A delicatessen heady with the aroma of pickles and pasta, or a family celebration, or a tea party in a third floor flat may become holy ground. A wood-carver's shop may be a covenant tent of meeting, a place where cedar, pine, maple, locust, sagebrush, cherry, black walnut, teak, and apple wood enters the nostrils as beautiful votive offerings of praise to God. Here God's presence is wafted on the air as shavings curl and fall to the floor. Wood is a word of God in form and fiber. God shares the tree with us, and each smell of a planed board reveals something of divine presence in form and function. As a messenger of God smell invites us to blend what is given to us in creation with what we can shape for ourselves. The good smells of earth constitute a metaphor of all the offerings we lift to God. Smell calls us to reverence, to praise, to prayer. As the psalmist says, "May my prayer be set before you like incense; may the lifting up of my hands be like the evening sacrifice." (Ps. 141:2)

Godly Smelling

A seventeenth-century Quaker leader, George Fox, reported in his journal that upon conversion to Christ "the whole creation had a new smell." Not only did the Spirit sensitize him to see the world more clearly, both its evil and its good, but the Spirit sensitized his nose to receive the scent of the earth and receive it as God's revelation to him. He gained insight about how Christ's redemption impacts the created world. I was ecstatic when I first read that account in a college class. A few years earlier, I had dedicated my life to Christ at a youth camp on Payette Lakes, in Idaho. I had walked along the lakeshore that night, my spiritual epiphany enhanced by a pungent odor of pine. The association of smell and spiritual experience remains strong nearly six decades later. This conversion experience released my body from the prison of guilt, fear, and the confines of dull routine. Similar releases have occurred subsequently, of course, but a part of my spiritual discipline has been to relax the senses and let them receive the world afresh—to let odors waft across the nose, to receive the world as it is and relish its pungency. Such incense offerings are pleasing to the Lord.

The discipline of godly smelling, in sum, means letting our noses inform us about the world of creation and culture, so that we can more fully enter into and enjoy its rhythms and patterns, and more wisely avoid evils that would trap us. It means training the mind more closely to interrogate odors for prophetic messages about righteousness and unrighteousness. The nose forces us to acknowledge responsibility as stewards of the earth and as keepers of our brothers and sisters. Good smelling enhances the enjoyment of the creation, enabling us to share in the ecstasy of the created order. When we are spiritually disciplined, the common odors of life yield sacramental significance. They provide a metaphor for the offering of our lives as the sweet savor of Christ in service to the world.

Notes

1. This has been reported in newspaper articles. It may be overstated in respect to scientific analysis. I read about VNO in the Eugene, Oregon, *Register-Guard* (5/16/94). David Berliner is noted as a major researcher. See also sources cited in Chapter One.

2. Diane Ackerman indicates this in her 1995 NOVA television series, *The Mystery of the Senses* (The Corporation of Public Broadcasting and WETA). See also her book cited earlier, *A Natural History of the Senses.*

CHAPTER FIVE

TASTING

O taste and see that the LORD is good;
happy are those who take refuge in him.
—Psalm 34:8

Savory Memories

Taste is a gratifying sensory experience immediately, in anticipation, and
in memory. For example, we eat a well-seasoned baked potato or a piece
of crumbly apple pie, after mouthwatering anticipation, and then we savor these delectables pleasurably. Later, when we are hungry again, we anticipate that renewed pleasure, and subsequently savor favorite food
items. The "flavor" of foods derives mostly from a combination of smell
and taste but is influenced by tactile sensations such as mild pain in "hot"
foods, and by visual and auditory associations—such as decor, ambiance,
and atmosphere .

Early taste experiences shape eating habits for life, providing a scale
for measuring pleasure derived from sensations of food and drink. Tastes
linger long in the corridors of memory. Some gustatory memories lurk in
sensory shadows outside the door of conscious interrogation, an amalgam
of smell and taste and touch and sight. These sensory ghosts from the
dawn of consciousness arise unbidden from time to time, haunting us
with poignant intimations of fetal and infant feelings.

What are some long-standing taste memories? Perhaps the vanilla
flavoring used in cake making or ice cream churning? Or less pleasant
memories of bitter medicine, like cod liver oil, spooned into unwilling

young mouths? Often smell and taste so co-mingle that some foods (certain cheeses, for example) are rejected because of the smell, not the taste. Some ingested things disappoint the palate: they don't taste as good as they smell.

When I was a lad my friend and I got a cigar at a wedding party. Its aroma conjured up associations of masculinity wrapped in the allure of the forbidden. Previously we had unearthed an Indian clay pipe, so we carefully unwrapped the cigar and crumbled the tobacco into that pipe, just as we had done with burdock, corn silk, and mullen. Then we lit up. The tobacco didn't taste as good as we expected, and after coughing and choking on the burning stuff for a while, we doused the pipe and headed home. Faced with the prospect of arriving there smelling like a pool hall, we hit upon the notion of masking the cigar odor by eating wild onions, which grew in abundance thereabouts. Drive out one weed with another! So we thought. Accordingly we indulged the sharp tangy taste of onions until our stomachs signaled enough; then we trudged home. Alas, our parents' uncontaminated noses readily detected the whole silly business. A bellyache and a firm warning from parents was punishment enough; we didn't try that dumb trick again. Nor did tobacco seem appealing anymore. We had a lesson in tasting, and it called for greater skill in judging messages from the palate and the nose. Sensory skills require the discipline of many years. The dissonance we experienced that day between taste and smell illustrates a lifetime struggle to interpret and rightly act upon our sensations.

Perhaps considering how taste can serve as God's message-bearer may provide a context for interpreting the disparity in the modern world between the stuffed and the starved and aid us in choosing appropriate disciplines for the palate. Some people are hungry while others are sated. Unequal distribution of food and clean water is a major world problem, a difficult one to solve, one which we can't fully address here.

For purposes of reflective judgment it may be useful to make an inventory of the stimuli that reach the palate. For convenience we group them in these categories: passive tasting, conditioned tasting, egocentric tasting, and empathetic tasting. In each of these categories we will suggest how taste can be a medium for the divine rather than the demonic. We will suggest how the mind can understand these sensations in order to discern and act upon the will of God. Finally we will adduce appropriate disciplines for taste, so that through this sense the body may become a better temple of the Holy Spirit.

But first we describe what happens physically from sensation to cognition, and then how taste functions individually and socially.

WHAT HAPPENS IN THE SENSATIONS OF TASTE

The sense of taste (gustation) and the sense of smell (olfaction) are similar in many ways, and intrinsically related. Physiologically speaking, both are chemically based senses, in that they rely on a chemical substance to initiate a response from receptor cells. With taste, a substance must be dissolved into a solution of saliva before it can be detected. Both taste buds and olfactory receptors are in a constant state of replacing old receptors with new ones (the life span of a taste receptor is 10 days), formed from surrounding, undifferentiated basal cells.

Taste buds are clustered on the walls of papillae and number about 10,000 in various states of longevity. They are predominately located on the tongue, but do exist in smaller concentration on the inside of the cheek, throat, and soft palate. Taste buds are recessed in a small pit, with the taste receptors, the microvilli, extending out into the pit. When the microvilli come in contact with molecules dissolved in saliva a chemical reaction is created through the cell body and to the connecting sensory nerve fibers of the facial nerve system (chorda tympani branch) and to the glossopharyngeal nerves of the tongue and throat.

Functionally speaking, the senses of taste and smell work in tandem to help make important choices in food acquisition and consumption. Research has verified what common experience indicates, that scent functions to improve and enhance the quality of taste sensation and that an inability to smell often renders food tasteless.

While taste discrimination has been found to be a partial function of location on the tongue, no such findings exist for olfaction. However, an aggregate processing pattern appears to be a viable explanation for scent discrimination.

Taste qualities can be broken down into four categories: sweet, salty, sour, and bitter. Some evidence, not yet endorsed by those who study sensation, supports a primary metallic taste as well.[1] Each of these "tastes" has a certain area on the tongue where reception is best. For example, sweet is best detected on the tip of the tongue, salty about a quarter of the way back, sour about three quarters of the way back. The bitter taste buds are sited on the base of the tongue. This is thought to have some significance because many toxins have a bitter taste and thus it may linger on the back of the tongue warning us about its nature. Sensations of saltiness and sourness seem to coordinate with a concern for environmental quality and safety, whereas sweetness and bitterness relate more to detecting nutritional value or toxicity in foods. In the human experience, however, all these tastes function in unity to create, in part, the sensation of flavor. Children have a more acute sense of gustation than adults—i.e. taste buds do disappear not to be replaced. Children also have more sweet taste buds than adults. Adults often enjoy sour/bitter salad dressings (e.g. blue cheese) rather than the sweet dressings (e.g. French) of their youth. Taste buds differ by gender, and are habituated through cultural experience. The taste buds are cleansed by saliva (1-1.5 liters/day) so that they are sensitive to continued stimuli and bacterial growth is minimized. Saliva does have antibodies that neutralize some antigens. Saliva also has enzymes that convert carbohydrates to simpler forms.

Flavor is not merely an interaction of the four primary tastes, but a medley of texture, temperature, aroma, and environment. Flavor induces "hedonic judgment" of pleasant versus unpleasant, based on many variables in the eating experience. Although physiological need of a nutrient or mineral is sometimes the basis for craving a particular food, it is more likely that these feelings arise from the complex social and psychological framework surrounding it.

How Taste Functions

The first function of taste is basic and personal, it whets the appetite and thus promotes nutritious eating and bodily health. Taste is one of the body's important regulating mechanisms. It is like a thermostat, calling for fuel when energy levels fall, and cutting out when they rise. The habituated "settings" of that thermostat seem to operate even beyond the actual nutritional qualities of the foodstuffs themselves.

A second function of taste is more complex. Because we are social creatures, factors other than the chemical reactions of our taste buds influence this primary body function. Eating figures importantly in social intercourse. Under favorable conditions conviviality fosters good nutrition and social order. New tastes are acquired by learning from others and supported by social conventions. Standards of taste arise from shared experiences. The interchange is catalytic; eating habits lead to further social interactions, and lend mythic force to culture. When the social order is supportive and non-threatening, conversation and laughter reinforce eating habits. They aid in food digestion and support good health. Rituals arise from such festive occasions. These rituals become acculturated and reinforced by traditions and social civility is enhanced. Such civility is transmitted from one generation to the next most readily when early eating habits have been nourished within loving homes and safe communities. Friendship and intimacy whet the appetite. Eating rituals define people in relationship to others by degrees of intimacy, from sharing adjoining booths in a restaurant, to sharing the same table in a house, to drinking with separate straws from the same cola, to eating popcorn with a loved one by the fire of an evening. By sharing food together we demonstrate community. We are interdependent, together drawing nourishment from the earth.

Consider the interpersonal significance of family meals, of the interactions that occur in restaurants. Reflect upon the symbolic meanings of certain shared meals: nonaggression pacts, business negotiations, the cementing of professional solidarity, the nurturing of romance. "To break bread together" has enormous social significance, and is manifest culturally in many ways.

There is a third important way that taste functions socially. Taste provides a basic metaphor by which to communicate meanings relating to personal and social fulfillment, to declare our "hungers and thirsts." No wonder Jesus' statement about being the bread of life draws so powerfully. Hunger and thirst are foundational yearnings of the body, and as such archetypical for less tangible desires. The body offers language for the soul. The eye and the ear are capable of greater linguistic complexity, but they learn their symbolic ABC's from the taste buds.

The language of taste has spread throughout our culture in ordinary ways, diffusing its analogical force to secondary and tertiary levels of interpretation. At these levels the metaphoric source is largely forgotten as taste terms become part of the mother tongue. To scan the idiomatic periphery can, however, lead us to refocus at the center. In the days of my youth people would say of an unreliable worker or of a suspicious stranger "he is an unsavory character." Or of a neighbor whose house was poorly arranged, "she lacks taste." Or, conversely, about a well-dressed person, "she has good taste," or to describe a room, "it is tastefully decorated." Many linguistic expressions employ metaphors based upon taste buds and the savoring of food and drink to articulate a wide range of human emotions and experience.

Such expressions are borrowed, of course, from the physical sensation of tasting. So important to life and well-being is taste that its linguistic signs lend themselves metaphorically to expressions about ethical, aesthetic, and spiritual matters. We rightly say that taste "gets jaded" when the senses have been honed too often on the grindstone of gourmet gratification. By analogy we discern that our tastes (in music, clothing, architecture, not just food) are often acquired through the dominance of others rather than by our own studied consent. When confusing sensory signals overload neural circuitry and the will surrenders to despair, this situation can be communicated by metaphors of the mouth: Life becomes tasteless, vapid, bland, flat, we say. Or, conversely, our high moments of spiritual ecstasy are offered heavenward in terms of the palate: "How sweet are your words to my taste, sweeter than honey to my mouth!" (Ps. 119:103 NIV)

In the Gospels' account of the desert temptation, Jesus rebuked Satan for seeking to derail his mission by materialism, using an eating metaphor to do so: "we do not live by bread alone!" Food is necessary, but it is not sufficient to satisfy the good life. Beyond physical sustenance we seek the word from God that nourishes us. We hunger for the Bread of Life. And so we use taste language to express in words these haunting quests for meaning, for assurance, for affirmation, for redemption, for achieving a coherence of the finite with the infinite.

Passive Tasting

Passive taste refers to routine daily gustatory sensations to which little reflective thought is given. Bodily regulation of taste is often taken for granted, especially if we don't have to worry where the next meal is coming from, and we have good health and time to savor what we eat and drink. Under such benign circumstances we can enjoy coffee and a breakfast roll, or oatmeal and a side of crisp bacon along with perusal of the morning paper, devotional reflection, and rituals of family parting. Under such routine circumstances we cherish quick snacks and sit-down dinners, we relish "going out to eat," and munching popcorn and apples on an evening. On a hot day a cold drink "hits the spot," but on a cold day hot tea tastes just right!

Tastes are both natural and acquired, and vary with age and bodily needs. If one is very hungry from hard work or very thirsty from long exposure to the hot sun then a slice of bread or cold water satisfy. Tastes are reinforced by memories. Experiences of hard work create conditions for savoring simple, nourishing food. My long-term memories make corn bread (or better yet, fried cornmeal mush) spread with honey a continued delight. The taste of fresh garden peas is a pleasant one, but the taste of overcooked canned peas is not; it brings back childhood memories of bland, pasty, overcooked vegetables.

Some persons lack satisfying memories, or they lack the discipline to draw upon them. If a person is frustrated, unable to let banks of past experiences and future hopes contain the flow of present sensations, then cravings for food and drink are not easily or healthfully satisfied. These persons become vulnerable to addictions, such as to junk foods or to drugs, including tobacco, and alcohol.

Ordinarily taste buds develop as children grow, and, as their exposure to new foods occurs, tastes become more sophisticated and discriminating. Maturity leads to gustatory experiences beyond the simple sensations of salt and sugar. If mealtimes have been relatively stress free while children are growing up then bad associations are transcended and the child comes to appreciate a varied and healthful diet, gradually accommodating to new or available foods and being properly nourished and aesthetically pleased by them.

It is good now and then to be reflective about our passive taste experiences. These queries may offer a useful discipline for that reflection:

1) Is my taste "thermostat" calibrated to energy and nutritional needs?

2) Are my taste buds whetted by good exercise and healthy habits?

3) Do my meals abet conviviality and affirm community?

4) Do my tastes provide apt metaphors for the heart's deep longings?

Conditioned Tasting

Conditioned tasting refers to the power society exerts to manipulate cravings for food and drink. Greed and market competition makes the manipulation of taste inevitable, with fortunate and unfortunate consequences. The industries catering to our tastes are enormous and corporately influential. In some cases tobacco and food vendors are joined in marketing conglomerates, competing to gain our money in exchange for servicing our tastes. Given the human propensity for sloth and greed, the natural correlation between taste and nutrition generally gets skewed to favor taste over nutritional value, even if taste is artificially engendered. But public concern and market competition have joined forces to correct this tendency. Recently, for example, the public has become irritated at having its tastes manipulated through advertisements charged to us at the cost of reduced nutrition. So label laws now give consumers more understanding of ingredients, and better choices. "Fat free" labels appear on packages of cookies as a bid for consumers wanting to reduce cholesterol levels. Competition and label laws have resulted in new designs in taste satisfaction, as producers seek to cater both to taste and to nutrition.

Consumers may be grateful, also, for efforts to prevent contamination of processed food. They now recognize that in a complex, industrialized society, in which many persons handle foodstuffs, vigilance is in order. Fortunately, technology can make changes quickly. We should be grateful that science has enabled us to live healthily in an interdependent society. And we should hope, and pray, that the benefits of technology can accrue to the benefit of all without harm to the earth. We should commend those who govern for their continued attention to health and well-being in respect to foodstuffs. And we should be willing as citizens to pay taxes for adequate surveillance of food production and delivery and for careful husbandry of the earth and sea sources from which food comes. To maintain an ecological balance in the face of increased human consumption is a difficult task. Pessimists abound, Malthusian or otherwise, and it requires creative hope to overcome their fears.

Because our commercialized culture honors celebrities more than heroes, the rituals of eating and drinking are subject to enormous entrepreneurial manipulation. The liquor industry is heavily involved in that manipulation, perhaps to overcome negative aspects of drinking—for example, its addictive force. Alcohol has been awarded cultic status in many different societies, our own included. Thus society ensures a continuity of alcohol consumption and justifies its role through community rituals, despite the serious social costs of alcohol abuse. This cultic role is reinforced in literature. To read some novels one wonders how the principals could ever drive home, or even function, after all the liquor consumed page after page!

On one level the cult of beer drinking is fostered visually by showing youthful devotees cavorting on the beach, associating alcohol and the good life. On another level, one finds a sophisticated cult of wine tasting, supported heavily by television advertisement, by "news" about the latest vineyard competition, by highway signs, by wine tasting events, and by full-page spreads in national magazines. The drumbeat of all such patronage is aimed at teaching us to feel good about ourselves through the taste of alcoholic beverages. We are flattered, in effect, for making minor distinctions in taste—to the point of absurdity. Young adults horsing around on the beach in happy sex play is subtly editorialized as tolerated rites of passage. But such rites are commercially contrived for the conditioning of children. Recent increase in drunkenness by college men and women, especially disastrous binge drinking, shows the consequences of such entrepreneurial indoctrination. Knowing the statistics of death and violence induced by drunkenness, concerned people do well to heed an ancient admonition: "Wine is a mocker and beer a brawler; whoever is led astray by them is not wise." (Prov. 20:1 NIV)

It should be acknowledged that nonalcoholic drinks are promoted vigorously, also, along with fast food products, and are winning their own way into received patterns of acceptable taste. These promotions use celebrity status and colorful advertising to show that the good life correlates with taste buds in a nonintoxicating manner. The trend to offer truth in advertising is bound to work in favor of sobriety and nutrition, to the extent that people make rational choices about what flows past their taste buds. The bad requires heavier promotion than the good. The social and personal cost of drunkenness is such that moderation or abstinence of alcoholic beverages is bound to become a more normative lifestyle. The bottling of nonalcoholic wine in fancy bottles, promoted for festive occasions, may be a sign of the times.

How can one avoid having the corridor of taste become a road of exploitation? How can the gustatory route be protected from invasion by others. How can it be kept open for the messengers of God? Here are a few suggestions:

1) Let the eye and the ear help the taste buds. These strong siblings must help the weaker one. Let taste buds learn from the eye to avoid the bright lights of the manipulator, from the ear to shut out the siren call of

sensory seduction. Let the senses together tell the brain not to be taken in by blandishments of greed. With these reinforcements taste will be protected from assault and will be able to keep its neurotransmitters open to the angels of the Lord.

2) Take advantage of the new truth-in-packaging provisions by finding foods that satisfy the taste and provide good nutrition. Teach this in the schools, let its truths guide school lunch programs and church social functions.

3) Find social substitutes for the rituals of alcohol, drugs, and junk food so that food habits symbolize again our unity with each other, the creation, and God.

Egoistic Tasting

Egoistic tasting means letting our need for food and drink become personally satisfying throughout life. Once we had a puppy whose needs for chewing required daily practice. So to protect the furniture we bought him a few leather "bones." He enjoyed them greatly, tossing them about, gnawing on them, and eventually eating them. Several months later he had graduated to real bones. And when, one day, we found a half-eaten leather "bone" behind the sofa, we thought he might be interested. But no, he sniffed this once-enticing pacifier briefly, then looked up at us as if to say, "Who wants such kid stuff, anyway?"

So it is with us human creatures. Physical and social maturity changes our eating and drinking habits. Our taste buds become more sophisticated. The palate learns and stores new information in the memory. Peanut butter, hot dogs, and milkshakes no longer suffice for adult ego satisfaction. The range of delectable foods increases proportionately with greater geographic mobility and wider social contacts. We learn to enjoy unaccustomed fruits and vegetables, differently prepared protein dishes. We discover and delight in diverse drinks, condiments, and spices. We find new ways to prepare standard food items such as potatoes and rice. The taste of soft white store bread sans crusts no longer excites adults who have discovered the gustatory delights of pumpernickel, rye and multi-grain varieties, or the superior taste and nutrition of home-baked bread.

Because of easier global travel and transportation, people find their taste enriched by ethnic cuisine different from that of their own subculture—for example, Eskimo muktuk and Italian pasta. Maturity brings new powers to discriminate among savory variations. This sophistication is often healthful—making a varied diet appealing, and, hopefully, nutritious, without unnecessary resort to food supplements. Such maturity also adds taste to other aesthetic aspects of the sensuous life. To eat well becomes as gratifying to the ego as to wander the corridors of a good art gallery, or to listen to symphonies recorded and played on good sound systems.

But ego satisfaction has an evil underside. Just as the eye can see beauty and be ennobled, or leer at beauty and become depraved, so it is with taste. Gustatory habits ennoble or deprave. The topside suggests delightful savoring; the underside, gluttony. To satisfy the ego "tastefully" two desires intertwine: having nourishment needs met, and taking pleasure in it. In an affluent society temptations to cheat are mostly at the second level, taking inordinate pleasure in a superfluity of food and drink. To take pleasure in good food and drink is one thing, to become entrapped in sin by it is another. When does the aesthetic good become the enemy of the moral good? When the ego becomes god and the meal becomes a ritual adoration of the self. When the table becomes an altar upon which the foodstuffs of the earth and the labor of others are offered in worship of the ego instead of God. When the consequences of one's eating are construed only in terms of personal pleasure rather than in terms of the human community. In a curious transvaluation of values, the philosophic principle of human contentment fostered by the ancient Greek philosopher Epicurus flipped over from an exaltation of simple pleasures and pain avoidance to an espousal of indulgent gratification. The adjective "epicurean" now connotes indulgence of the appetites, not discipline of mind, body, and spirit. This is typical of movements toward the simplification of design in human living whenever God gets replaced by ego. Similarly, though they cite the homeless, wandering, Jesus as their leader, some Christian groups justify upward social mobility by glorifying excess. They are prosperity cults, with slogans such as "the King's kids deserve only the best."

Gluttony, then, is a qualitative as well as a quantitative abuse of gustatory desire, a subtle, beguiling sin of affluent cultures. Gorging on food is neither healthy for the body, considerate of others, nor kind to the earth. Historians have recorded the excesses of the Roman rich at the beginning of the Christian era: all-night banquets featuring ostrich wings, flamingo tongues, goose livers, as well as rare fish, fowl, and fruit, all devoured (and sometimes upchucked to make room for more) by an elite class of people contemptuous of the poor, who survived on vegetables, fruits, and grains. Today the social classes may not be so diverse, but the temptation for the rich to flaunt power through food remains and constitutes a snob culture of cuisine and liquor consumption.

Thorstein Veblen's theory of conspicuous consumption by the leisure class is verified when it comes to taste: Social status is demonstrated by a conspicuous waste of food. For every egocentric individual wishing to elevate the self to a godlike power and standing, ten entrepreneurs hustle to supply the means for that conspicuous consumption. Whether the appetite be for exotic meals in a posh hotel or diamonds on every finger, or reindeer horns ground into powder for aphrodisiacs, suppliers will arise, willing to exploit human labor and to rape the earth, if necessary, in order to sustain the greed of the glutton. On balance, if not case by case, the true costs for gluttony are borne by the earth's poor. Energy that could be more wisely expended on wider social benefits is conspicuously wasted in catering to the tastes of the few. One may argue that the values of ornate cathedrals, castles, great art collections, and literature accessible to a leisured and wealthy elite, achieve over time a sort of social equity. An aesthetic legacy remains for poor and rich alike to enjoy. But this is not so with gluttony, except as wasted food is salvaged by beggars, fed to hogs, or made beneficial to physicians and clinics whose skills are required to repair damage to the body done by gluttonous waste.

A glutton gremlin, which wants taste to be titillating, not just pleasurable and filling, resides in each of us. We like being filled with food, but we also crave tasty food, and the ego abets this craving with the subtle appeal to the exotic, the expensive, and the culturally fashionable. If such sophistication occurs before habits of discipline awaken our capacity for savoring good food, uneducated appetites may continue, only just more expensively sustained, with reliance upon larger quantities of ordinary food and drink. Beer guzzling and greasy fast food consumption may characterize unhealthy habits of common folk. But gluttony by sophisticated people is still gluttony, and perhaps more reprehensible. To feast on pigeon tongues (or modern exotic and expensive equivalents thereof) or to become fixated on aged and rare wines may not fatten the waistline as much as low brow eating, but it is still an example of conspicuous waste.

About those elite Romans who reached the ultimate in exotics, a contemporary critic wrote: "Their destiny is destruction, their god is their stomach, and their glory is in their shame." (Phil. 3:19 NIV) Perhaps we should ponder that indictment.

Medieval Christians called gluttony one of the seven deadly (or root) sins—a bodily proclivity to be brought under discipline lest it, like covetousness, lust, envy, anger, sloth, and pride destroy the soul. Ascetic practices to secure that discipline, to "keep the body under," included fasting, plain foods, and extreme austerity, even to the point of inducing ill health. If a person was anorexic it was for the glory of God, not for the glory of the ego. The Reformation era returned to a more fulsome view of physicality: the creation was good and under God's grace was to be received joyfully. Holiness belonged to the hearth not the cloister. God's grace was sufficient for the sins of the body. More attention should be given the disciplines of the mind and the spirit.

The spiritual discipline needed to cope with gluttony, however, is neither monastic austerity nor antinomian disregard, but the right use of what God has given. Asceticism refuses the divine offer of sufficient sustenance, to be received gratefully; gluttony presumes upon that sufficiency greedily. Paul elaborated thus upon Jesus' principle of disciplined simplicity:

> But godliness with contentment is great gain. For we brought nothing into the world, and we can take nothing out of it. But if we have food and clothing, we will be content with that. People who want to get rich fall into temptation and a trap and into many foolish and harmful desires that plunge men into ruin and destruction. For the love of money is a root of all kinds of evil. Some people, eager for money, have wandered from the faith and pierced themselves with many griefs. But you, man of God, flee from all this, and pursue righteousness, godliness, faith, love, endurance and gentleness. (1 Tim. 6:6-11 NIV)

How can our taste buds yield to the work of the Spirit in a temperate way, so that our bodies may indeed, be God's temple? Here are some suggestions useful to achieve personal discipline in respect to food and drink.

1) Learn to savor foods. Awaken your taste buds for a full savoring of ordinary, nourishing foods, rather than a quick gratification from sugary and salty condiments.

2) Search for variety within the major food groups, and from other food cultures than your own, rather than from expensive exotics.

3) In purchasing, give priority to those foods that move efficiently between producer and consumer, rewarding both fairly. Avoid food and drink that squander energy by diminished nutritional blending, by superfluous packaging, and by exorbitant promotional costs.

4) Create a pleasant atmosphere for eating and drinking, with meal arrangements as tasteful, and complementary as the food itself, thus curbing the desire to gorge oneself.

5) Trade at stores that accommodate to your tastes.

6) Find the "golden mean" between asceticism and gluttony. Satisfy your ego with achievements and friendships, by an easy trust in God, by confidence in yourself, not by starving or stuffing yourself.

Empathetic Tasting

Empathetic tasting means uniting emotionally with other persons through shared food and drink. Such experiences involve multiple sensations, of course, but taste is the sensuous catalyst. A person who selflessly serves others hosts the Spirit among the guests. And a thoughtful guest demonstrates graciously that to receive a gift from another is to honor God. On several occasions Jesus demonstrated the high privilege of serving. "The Son of man," he said, "came not to be served but to serve." (Mark 10:45) Serving others, even enemies, rather than lording it over them, marks godly spirituality. Even defeat in war is redeemed to some extent by the victor sharing food with the vanquished. The Marshall Plan after World War II illustrates the redemptive power of even a pragmatic political application of this principle.

Service takes many forms, of course, but a major and symbolic service is to provide food for another. To "put food on the table" occupies the time and energy of parents everywhere, directly and indirectly. When because of civil strife or natural catastrophe countries of the world need food or potable water, other peoples respond to these needs with relief programs, flooding the needy country with plane loads of basic foods and clean drinking water. Many relief programs are motivated by spiritual concern. To feed the hungry is to offer love to God. This, too, is putting food on the table. At times the needs are so tragically compelling, so overwhelming, that those who serve, those who receive, and those who give, all lose perspective. Providing food becomes a grim task acted on a tragic stage. But underlying such service is a foundational principle: To break bread with the hungry anywhere and everywhere is to love one's neighbor as one's self.

Beyond altruistic service, with or without a specific host, with family or with strangers, the sharing of food and drink demonstrates community. Eating together bonds humanity whether the occasion is dinner at home, lunch at school or work, catered celebrations, restaurant dining, church potluck dinners, Kiwanis picnics, or relief packages tossed from the tailgate of a truck. Whether with friends or with strangers, eating bonds us to the rest of humanity. Even dining alone involves human interdependence. Few persons anywhere are self-subsistent.

Sensuous tasting has been central to much of worship. Feasting is a major feature of religious festivals. It is a way to celebrate the work of the Spirit within the lives of covenanting people. Community is reinforced, faith is restored, hope is sustained. This use of food in symbolic ways is evident from reading the Old Testament, with its accounts of various feasts, some of which continue to be a significant part of Jewish and Christian tradition. Especially the Feast of the Passover, which celebrates God's deliverance of Israel from Egyptian bondage under the leadership of Moses. At the last supper before the Passover preceding his betrayal and crucifixion, Jesus turned the breaking of bread and the pouring of the wine into symbols of his impending saving sacrifice. Henceforth, this historic festival will celebrate deliverance by this new prophet, the Messiah. A greater than Moses will lead people from universal bondage. "Do this in remembrance of me," said Jesus at the meal with his disciples (Luke 22:19).

After Pentecost the beleaguered but inspired followers of Jesus reinforced each other's faith at shared meals. From these experiences and remembrances the common meal became a symbolic sign of Christ's presence with the church, the new covenant community. As the church became more priestly, and reached further into the Gentile community, liturgical ritual gradually replaced the simpler symbolic meal, and became distanced from its Jewish festival roots.

For Christians, deliverance from the bondage of sin found significant symbols in sensuous tasting. Over time this ritual use of food took various forms, and its use ranged from daily to occasional liturgical festivals. The Roman Catholic mass became the central ceremony of public worship, with central theological significance (the bloodless repetition of Christ's sacrifice). It became a necessary means of grace for the believer, served by a specially ordained priesthood. For Protestant Christians the ceremony evolved into a memorial of God's saving grace in Christ, celebrated within a wide liturgical range. The followers of John Wesley used love feasts as annual ceremonies for mutual forgiveness and humility before the common Lord. Quakers and some other groups abandoned liturgy as a hindrance to the inward sacramental, nourishing, presence of Christ in the common ventures of life, and particularly in the awesome act of worship itself, with the risen and living Christ meeting with the church to teach them directly. For Messianic Jews the Passover offers a high and historic occasion for remembering Jesus' sacrifice, and the fulfilling of the Law.

Despite the variant practices, for Christians the sharing of food for the body signifies the meaning of Christ as the bread of life, body and soul of the community of faith nurtured together. Such sharing, as signified by the bitter herbs of Passover, acknowledges that we live, body, mind, and spirit, by the pain and death of others, even by divine suffering. As one New Testament writer declared: "...we see Jesus, who was made a little lower than the angels, now crowned with glory and honor because he suffered death, so that by the grace of God he might taste death for everyone." (Heb. 2:9 NIV)

Godly Tasting

Godly tasting acknowledges the role of food and drink in providing disciplines for the spirit, directly through bodily consumption, and metaphorically by satisfying hungers of the heart. To eat the flesh and drink the blood of Christ brings about submission to the will of God and attention to the needs of others. In the biblical account of the trek from Egypt to the Promised Land, the covenant people of God were for a time fed miraculously by manna. It was fresh every morning. At first this handout was welcomed. Any food tastes good when you are hungry! But soon crankiness accompanied saliva. The trekkers "mouthed off." They complained of a monotonous diet, bland compared to the spicy foods of Egypt. The belly grumbled to the mind. Taste had become a channel for the Adversary, not for the Lord.

Terrified by the desert about us, like these ancient pioneers of faith, we too easily forget how sweet the bread of heaven is, even after a harrowing escape from an enslaving past. Manna becomes bland to ungrateful people, and remembered exotic tastes can make us forget even the horrors of entrapment. Isn't there a parable here about the interplay of food for the body and food for the soul?

Critics often use the term *secular* to describe a current cultural drift away from purpose; but the condition might better be described as "sensate." A sensate culture lacks spirituality because it makes the body the temple of the ego, not the temple of the Spirit. Gluttony and conspicuous consumption of food and drink mark that culture. They induce spiritual stupor.

We often try to satisfy inner yearnings for holiness and beauty with food and drink when we really need other and better nourishment, when stimuli from other senses ought to be called upon to answer those yearnings. Not further gustatory indulgence, but a godly interrogation of sensory experiences is what is really called for. Let the angels of God arrive via the palate as well as through the avenues of sight, sound, smell, and touch. Drunkenness, illness, and obesity are sensate markers for wrongheadedly assigning to the mouth the whole burden for answering all hunger signals. Let us discipline the palate to be a monitor of sensory fulfillment, guiding us to right not wrong choices, affirming good stewardship of the earth not its abuse. Through sobriety, health, simplicity of taste, and physical fitness the body unites harmoniously with the whole creation. When the palate conforms to divine order, health and wholeness occur. Biblical injunctions based upon metaphoric implications gain analogic force. One who accepts tasting of food and drink as an angelic summons is in a spiritual position to receive the gracious invitation, "O taste and see that the Lord is good." (Ps. 34:8) Such a one is prepared to heed the words of Jesus, "Blessed are those who hunger and thirst for righteousness, for they will be filled." (Matt. 5:6)

There are certain spiritual disciplines useful to keep the taste buds sensitive to the Holy Spirit. Here are some disciplines of a sensuous spirituality involving taste:

1) Saying grace at meals acknowledges gratitude for daily bread. It's a minimal spiritual discipline. Whether voiced aloud or silently, by a prayer of grace we reverence the Creator, the creation, and acknowledge all whose labor provides our food. We respect not only the family food preparer and the wage earners, but also the farmers, the field-workers, the packagers, the shippers, the store managers and clerks, and those who cheerfully carry the bags to the car. Many persons are involved in the food we consume in a single day! Saying grace acknowledges how much we all need each other to sustain life and to make it palatable. In a prayer of grace we ask God to sanctify our taste buds, to set them apart as ready messengers of the divine will. We ask God to instruct us about the creation, that we may partake of its bounty wisely and in deference to the needs of other persons and other creatures.

By this prayer, also, we signify gratitude to God for the gift of spiritual rebirth through the death and resurrection of Jesus Christ. Let every meal symbolize the saving nourishment God has provided, through Christ, the Bread of Life, leading us out of sin's bondage, through freedom's fierce desert, to a secure home.

2) Disciplines for eating can be spiritually instructive. Indulgence is a mark of our food culture. So some restraint is called for, some denial, some way of asserting that we do not live by bread alone but by that divine word that nourishes, that instructs, that heals. For some persons fasting accomplishes a needed bodily discipline.[2] There is a long religious tradition for fasting as a means of opening the self to clearer perceptions and to godly direction of life.

3) For some persons vegetarianism is a useful discipline. The rationale for the vegetarian lifestyle often includes pragmatic concerns for more prudent use of the world's food supply. But there are other reasons. Some vegetarians are not comfortable with the sacrifice of other creatures, especially if they consider such sacrifice to be unnecessary nutritionally. They believe that the killing of animals induces a callous, rather than reverent, attitude toward life. To critics this position is needlessly legalistic. Most of us, nonvegetarians, accept with humble gratitude the sacrifice of animal life for human nourishment, considering this to be a part of the world's order, useful in the larger scheme of things, provisionally justified in the world as it is now. But the conscience of the vegetarian ought to be respected.

The monastic movements have emphasized bodily discipline in regard to taste. Accordingly, food deprivation has been part of their spiritual discipline. We need not join a monastic order, however, to practice periodic fasting or to follow a regimen of good, simple nutrition. We can acknowledge that some restraint to food consumption "mortifies the flesh," to use monastic terms, and strengthens the soul. Thus indulgence is checked, the ego is restrained, the self is identified with the creation and the Creator. As Brenda Meehan notes, "the practices of mortification and prayer are practices of cleansing and communion."[3]

The good life, not just nourishment, is what we yearn for when we pray, "give us this day our daily bread." Such yearnings are best satisfied, not by stuffing ourselves with food and drink, or by titillating taste buds by exotic food and drink, but by acknowledging the body as God's temple and eating in ways nourishing, aesthetically pleasing, and disciplined.

The apostle Peter, who had tasted the bitterness of failure and the wonder of forgiveness, wrote of having "tasted that the Lord is gracious." Perhaps it was the broiled fish by the sea that Jesus prepared and shared with the disciples after the resurrection, that remained in Peter's memory. May our gustatory memories be that enriching! Then our yearning for a word from the Lord will be as sweet as honey. Mystical writers such as Fénelon and Guyon used taste as an appropriate metaphor for meditation, urging their readers to savor Gospel passages or the writings of the saints like candy held in the mouth until it melts. Spoken or unspoken, whether interrogated directly from sensory experience, analogically by the mind, or metaphorically through intuition, the word arising from our deep hunger is "Lord, fill me now!"

Notes

1. Linda M. Bartoshuk, "Sensory Factors in Eating Behavior," *Bulletin of the Psychonomic Society* (1991), p. 251. For this information on the sensations of tasting we have used sources cited in the chapter "Thinking about the Senses," note 10.

2. On the subject of spiritual disciplines, Richard Foster's books have been of great help to many people. On the disciplines of fasting and service, see *Celebration of Discipline* (New York: Harper & Row, 1978), chapters 5 and 9.

3. *Holy Women of Russia* (New York: HarperSanFrancisco, 1994). Meehan believes that these practices "help effect an interior personal transformation from the solipsistic bubble of our phony and anxious selves to a true, trusting inner self. This authentic self, liberated from sham and posturing, is capable of real, loving encounters with others and with God." p. 148.

CHAPTER SIX

TOUCHING

People were bringing little children to him {Jesus}
in order that he might touch them.
—Mark 10:13

Introduction

What a wealth of meanings flow from the simple declaration "I am touched!" When spoken sincerely, or even sarcastically, the phrase refers to sensations internal as well as external, ranging from primal physical and emotional reactions to spiritual ecstasy. From actual experiences of physical touch, our words convey certain values and underscore them through sight and hearing to the brain. The alphabetized languages of vision and sound communicate through symbols what touch senses directly. These formal languages also encompass tacit knowledge arising largely from tactile perception. Touch is a vital mechanism—and thus an apt metaphor—for connecting and communing with oneself, with other persons, with fellow creatures, with inanimate creation, with the earth itself, and with the Creator. Touch is the most complex of the senses, psychologically as well as physiologically. Accordingly, it is difficult fully to measure or to explain. Touch is multidirectional, open to subjective interpretations, and clothed with intuited spirituality.

Currently, within modern society tactile conventions have become ambiguous, and consequently confusing, conflicting, and frequently in cultural disarray. Why do our eyes beg our hands to do what is immoral or inappropriate? When is it right to touch, when is it wrong? When is touch violent, when is it healing? We're all playing a cosmic skin game, it seems. The cells that form the boundaries of the body constitute a communication system linking us with the world inside and outside of us. Perhaps only when one suffers pain—like an aching tooth knifing into our consciousness from ear to chin, or nagging arthritic spasms—does the sense of touch become burdensome. Only when such pain is prolonged, with no ready relief, and for no apparent reason in the scheme of things human or divine (as dramatized so poignantly in Job), does pain threaten the spirit.

But what hurts also protects. Not long ago the news featured the experiences of a small child who felt no physical pain. The multiple fractures and bruises experienced, with consequent trauma to the family, revealed a different tactile burden, a rare sort of sensory deprivation in which pain fails its function as bodyguard, and the self is vulnerable to dangers from the environment. Fortunately, few persons are so afflicted.

In this chapter we consider how touch is a messenger of God so that our bodies may be fit temples of the Spirit. To offer the body as an instrument of righteousness is no easy matter, given the many temptations to sin entering from without or arising from within. We offer first a few scenarios about touch, then descriptions of tactile sensing in psychological and physiological terms, then an overview of how touch functions for the individual and for society. Following these presentations, touch will be considered more specifically in the selected categories of our inquiry— passive, conditioned, egoistic, and empathetic touching—with concluding attention given to certain spiritual disciplines that mark the godly life.

Scenarios about Touch

STORY ONE: FIVE STRONG STEEDS In the twelfth century Alan of Lille wrote an epic poem, *Anticlaudianus,* about the quest for the good life. Included was an allegory depicting the senses as five horses. The first (sight), a progeny of the sun, soars swiftly through the air. The second (hearing) flows musically with the wind. The third (smell) stands beautifully adorned with flowers, and the fourth (taste) nourishes the rest. The fifth (touch), perfect in form but lowly in comparison with the others, keeps eyes to the ground, concerned with earthly things. This allegory was dramatized in various medieval scenarios. Its lesson: The senses exist in a hierarchy of values, each perfect in its own right. Like horses, "strong, willful and unruly" the senses must be tamed. Controlled by Reason, they bring their treasures on the chariot of Liberal Arts to the Mind, and the

Mind extends the journey to the very house of God.[1] Spirituality may be the goal of body and mind, but to reach that goal touch—the earthy steed with eyes to the ground—must be brought under mental rein.

STORY TWO: TIGER THE CAT Tiger, the outdoor cat, crouches in the bushes by the door, waiting for someone to enter or exit. Whenever the door opens to family or stranger, he streaks through it and hides quickly behind the couch or under the bed, tail twitching excitedly—inviting pursuit. If ignored, Tiger dashes for another cover, peering out to make sure he is seen, and followed. When the master's hands seize him, initially he resists arrest, digging claws into the carpet, but then pleads no contest. It's a quick surrender prompted by certain prospects of shared affection. Climbing on his friend's shoulder he purrs loudly, touching nose to ear, and flexes his claws playfully into the host's shoulder. The human friend reciprocates by stroking Tiger's back and under his chin while speaking loving words. Thus joined, they march ritually about the house for a while. The game ends with Tiger outside again, where Missy, the grey cat, who has been sunning herself contentedly, greets her more adventurous friend by arching up against him. Then Missy finds the dog Sally and rubs up against her. Pretty soon the trio walk about the territory, checking the other creatures, including the cows who stand in the shade of an oak tree, grooming each other with their tongues and switching tails to keep the flies away. Meanwhile the human friend, affirmed by touch, curls up with a good book.

STORY THREE: A LOVE-DEPRIVED GIRL At the church office a woman seeks counsel from the pastor. Her home situation is not good. In sociological terms it's dysfunctional. The current husband is an alcoholic. The woman's face is drawn and anxious as she pours out her troubles, fidgeting as she speaks. The woman's small daughter, meanwhile, hugs the legs of the pastor, trying to move herself from periphery to the center of attention. Her needs are as urgent as the mother's, but she lacks words to express them. She is, however, no less sensitive to pain, no less hungry for loving touch.

STORY FOUR: A LOVE-DEPRIVED BOY On his daily walk, a retired gentleman pauses to talk to boys who are kicking stones to each other and idling on the asphalt parking lot. New playground equipment recently installed by volunteers has been mutilated already. The man notices and is concerned about it. He's also troubled that one lad, barely into his teens, is smoking cigarettes. So he attempts conversation with them, talking about the new equipment and how much the smaller children like to play on it. When it seems appropriate he warns about the health risks of smoking. This advice isn't well received, although the smoker, having begun at the age of ten, admits he's hooked and would like to stop, but can't. His mother accepts his habit and buys him smokes, he says. In leaving the youngsters the man puts a hand on the shoulder of the smallest boy, as a gesture of friendship, much as he would a grandson of the same age. "Don't touch me!" snarls the lad, flinging off the elder's hand. Taken aback the man asks why. The answer? A shrug and a mumbled, "I dunno, I just don't like to be touched." Rebuffed and bewildered, the man trudges home. And along multiple neuron networks on bodies young and old sorrowful angels retrace their steps to the Source and ponder Calvary.

STORY FIVE: HOSPITAL BED The patient lies on the hospital bed. It has been several days since surgery, and she is sicker from an unexplained pancreatitis attack than first acknowledged. The doctors don't seem very encouraging; she feels herself hovering in the shadows of death. Exhaustion, pain, and drained emotions mark her condition. But every day a Hispanic nurse's aide serves as God's angel, holding the sick woman's hand, and saying in broken English, "You I pray for each day. I burn candle in church. You get well!" Together the two women experience that life is precious, and that it is often preserved by caring hands, loving presence, and comforting words.

STORY SIX: ANGIOGRAM The patient lies on a hospital bed after an angiogram has been completed. To prevent arterial bleeding from the procedure, a nurse positions a cotton compress tightly against the insertion point at the groin, holding the pad steadily in place for two hours, without wavering, ignoring tautness of muscles and back strain, until danger of rupture is over. Few words are spoken, but the two men experience together that life is precious, and that it is often preserved for one by the caring hands of another.

STORY SEVEN: HANDS ACROSS TIME The old mother has lost touch with the normal affairs. Her life is ebbing away and soon will be over. She remembers events seventy years ago but doesn't know where she is now. Her adult son, remembering the hands that long ago soothed his fevered brow, now brushes his mother's hair to take out the tangles and gently strokes her gnarled hands. Few words pass, but many emotions do. They are bonded by a touch that holds their love together in this difficult time of passing.

STORY EIGHT: HOBBIT TRAIL The Hobbit Trail is hard to spot from Highway 101, just a small parking space, and an identifying sign pointing to the beach. But the couple who stop there know where it is.

They get out of the car and walk eagerly into the thick forest, putting feet onto spongy ground and breathing fecund air. The trail leads through rhododendrons towering twenty feet high, down to a sandy beach. He grasps a walking stick fashioned to fit his hand. She takes his other hand to steady her when the path gets steep near the shore. Soon they emerge onto the beach, enjoying its warmth, still walking hand in hand, for love's sake, listening to the roar of the surf, searching for tidal treasures. After a while they climb back up the trail, pausing to puff a bit enroute, before easing their bodies into the car for a return home.

STORY NINE: TURF TROUBLES Dick and Jane are seated at the family table. They are five and seven, respectively. Because they have been bickering, mother has "zoned" the table to achieve a truce in hostilities. Jane lays her arm as close to the line as possible. Dick does the same, but he lacks sufficient eye/hand coordination and diplomatic skill. Or he is a crafty trespasser. In any case, Jane wails "Momma, he touched me!" The truce has been broken. The endless struggle to adjudicate personal space resumes.

STORY TEN: TOUCHING IS BELIEVING After Jesus' crucifixion people were confused. Amid the grief, hope loomed; the faithful said the Master had risen from the dead. Was this so, or only wishful thinking? A disciple, Thomas, wanted tangible proof, hard evidence. Then one day Jesus appeared to the group and said, "Thomas, put your finger in my hand, and your hands in my side, and be not faithless but believing." Thomas did so, and immediately resurrection reality surged like electricity from Lord to disciple. Thomas's senses became the messengers of God. Many persons subsequently believed on the basis of his testimony, and that of others present. But they also believed on the basis of an inner touch by the risen Christ. Thirteen centuries later, an earnest believer became so emotionally caught up in the passion of Christ that nail prints appeared in his own hands. Stigmata. Did this strange event occur because Francis of Assisi had an acute, dedicated, sense of touch? Probably.

THE PHYSIOLOGY OF TOUCH

In the world of sensation, the sense of touch has taken a backseat to the senses of sight and sound. The skin is the largest and most important sensory organ, but its tactile importance has been taken for granted. While the capacity for detecting pain and the extremes of heat and cold are clearly essential survival mechanisms, the capacity for pleasure through touch is more a quality-of-life issue. Tactile stimulus is perceived differently by each person, and although the physical structures are quite similar in most of us, possibilities exist for the human body to learn unique preferences and over time to seek out those preferences through choice, not just through trauma avoidance.

The mechanics of touch are poorly understood empirically, but some general structural guidelines can be acknowledged with a degree of certainty. The skin performs many vital physiological tasks. It protects the body's internal organs from dehydration, it keeps bodily fluids in and external fluids out, it protects the internal organs from ultraviolet radiation and helps maintain homeostasis of body temperature.

Our skin has two classifications. "Glabrous" skin is hairless, and is found on fingertips, hands, feet, lips, and mucous membranes. "Hairy" skin covers most other parts of our body, even including the fine, blond, fuzzy hair on our ears! The skin is composed of many layers. The outermost layers of skin are actually dead-skin cells that act as a protective barrier and are sloughed off continuously. The epidermis is a layer of living skin cells with many free nerve endings embedded in it. Under the epidermis lies the dermis, which supports the epidermis with a web of connective tissue and fat. Embedded in the dermis are hair follicles, sweat glands, oil glands, more free nerve endings and specialized neurons that aid in the sensation of touch.

The sense of touch encompasses mechanical (pressure) and thermal (heat and cold) sensations. It also encompasses the sensation of pain. The mode of reception of these sensations is unclear. Unlike hair cells in the inner ear or the rods and cones of the eye, the receptors involved in the sense of touch cannot be isolated and differentiated. They appear to work in concert, some providing a baseline or summation experience, others in highly specialized functions. Receptor cells, moreover, are not evenly distributed in the skin. High concentrations exist in such places as the fingertips, lips, and genitals, and more sparsely on the limbs and torso areas. Sensitivity to a stimulus can vary not only from person to person, but from one area to another on the same person.

There are also some indications of the existence of special receptors in the skin that respond to dangers such as tissue damage from pain, extreme heat or cold, or excessive pressure. These receptors are probably free nerve endings. They are nerves whose neurons terminate directly in the skin, internal organs, muscles, and joints without the intermediation of a specialized receptor structure.

Most of us probably associate touch with the sensation of pressure. The skin is elastic and malleable and its manipulation in and out of shape triggers sensation in the surrounding receptive fields. Some receptors respond to the vibrations in the surrounding skin as a reaction to pressure. Others respond to the presence of texture or the delineation of sharp edges. Pressure sensitivity is adaptable; applying constant pressure without movement to a receptive field can diminish the sensation of touch.

Stimulation of the receptors in the skin sends messages along a neu-ral network to a specific area of the brain called the homunculus. In the homunculus, specific areas correspond to specific areas on the skin. For example, the lips and mouth have a high concentration of receptors and the forearm a low concentration. In the homunculus, the actual area of space devoted to processing information from the lips and mouth is much greater than that devoted to the forearm.

Another important function of pressure sensitivity has to do with the haptic system. The haptic system of the body combines information received tactilely by the skin and information received from free nerve endings in the muscles and joints to create an accurate representation of the way we move in the world, interact with other objects and persons, and perceive space and dimension.

Like pressure sensitivity, thermal sensations are adaptive in nature. The detection of sensations of heat and cold occurs because the skin keeps a summary reading of the body's temperature at all times. It was once thought that there were separate receptors in the skin for hot and cold sensation respectively; however it is now believed that one mechanism provides perception of both. Scientists speculate that hot and cold sensation may come from neurons in the walls of blood vessels that record the reflexive contraction or expansion when presented with thermal stimuli. This theory has not had adequate study to provide concrete validity.

Pain is generally considered a subjective term, involving emotional and cognitive roles as well as physical ones. Pain can be acute or chronic. It can stem from physical trauma or disease or it can be psychosomatic. Curiously, the very organ that gives us the perception of pain—the brain—has no pain receptors; thus surgical procedures on it can be done while the patient is awake. Pain receptors are probably the free nerve endings that proliferate in the skin, muscles, joints, and internal organs of the body.

The most promising theory of pain, the gate-control theory, supposes that two types of nerve fibers supply the brain with information about pain. One type, long and fast conducting, conveys sharp or intense pain sensations. The other type, short and poorly conducting, conveys dull pain sensations. In the gate-control theory, stimulation of long nerve fibers sends messages to a structure in the spinal column that inhibits transmission of the impulse, in essence closing the gate to the brain. Stimulation of the long nerve fibers also inhibits the short nerve fibers. Conversely, if the short nerve fibers are stimulated, they send messages to the spinal column to keep the gate open. It is the combination of the messages received from the long and short nerve fibers at a given time that determines whether the gate is open, open partway, or closed.

Another factor in pain perception includes the body's production of natural "painkillers" called endorphins and enkephalins. These chemicals are generally produced in times of stress, such as in a fight-or-flight response, or to override the body's pain information to the brain much as synthetic drugs are used to do. The condition known as a "runner's high" illustrates this phenomenon.

Much of what is known and written about the sense of touch is speculative and anecdotal. However, research continues in hopes of unraveling the mysteries of the body's most essential and aesthetic sense.

The Social Functions of Touching and Being Touched

Our idiomatic expressions accent the significance of touch. Consider phrases such as "she is out of touch," "I'm just a soft touch," "be careful, he's touchy," "he's lost his touch, I'm afraid," "it's a touchy situation," "you have to be thick-skinned on this job," "some things just get under my skin," "it's only skin deep," and "she has a touch of class." The acquisition of tactile knowledge is so elemental we take it for granted—until some deprivation occurs such as a broken wrist. If we are to query the angelic messengers that travel the pathways of our muscles and nerves, it may be useful to reflect upon how this sense functions.

So important is the hand as a tactile instrument that many expressions convey its centrality: "real handy around the house," "walk hand in hand," "hands across the sea," even "handicap." The word *manufacture* literally means "make by hand." Consider the symbolism in verbal or artistic communication of clasped or folded hands; outstretched hands; upraised hands; the hand of blessing; finger signs for victory, direction, or for insult; and clenched fists.

For most of us sighted people touching and seeing, and to a lesser degree, hearing, fire the neurons of the brain into a rhythmic dance. We look and then we touch, or we touch and then we scrutinize. In situations where dexterity is required, we touch and look and hear at the same time. The achievement of eye-hand coordination is a major skill acquired in infancy and childhood. Sight and touch team up to define the self on a scale of size. Bugs and viruses are obviously smaller than we are, elephants and solar systems manifestly larger. Any of the senses can trigger touch to act. Intimacy, however, requires that the others, and especially the eyes, defer to touch for heightening sensuous immediacy and for experiencing ecstasy. This occurs most significantly in sexual intercourse and in prayer.

Touch has a natural language communicated mostly by the body's appendages. With hands and feet we probe our environment. Is it safe to walk here? Will this structure support our weight? Which way is the wind blowing? How far can I lean without falling? Is it hot, cold, dry, wet, sticky, firm, or soft enough? By touch we test our tasks, and accomplish them. How much effort over how much time is required to lift this load, to use this tool, to activate this program? Through touch we adapt to forces of gravity, to pressures of the earth's terrain, and to wind and water. Touch establishes our place in space relative to other persons and other things, and enables us to move efficiently among them. Touch monitors the involuntary actions of our body organs on a scale of pain to pleasure, warning us when we've eaten the wrong foods or overstressed our legs.

The natural language of touch includes an enormous range of activities employed in myriad ways. Many of these activities involve the hands and the feet. Here are some of them: crawling, walking, running, hopping, hobbling, limping, tapping, dancing, jumping, skipping, kicking, scuffing, climbing, kneading, bending, twisting, turning, kneeling, sprawling, curling, flexing, drumming, pointing, pulling, pushing, pounding, prying, probing, pressing, wiping, shaking, tossing, grasping, releasing, digging, lifting, shoving, stroking, grooming, caressing, beckoning, scratching, tickling, throwing, catching, signing, and manipulating objects.

Body language occurs apart from hands and feet. The torso itself twists and turns and shoves and performs gyrations of all kinds. Kissing and sexual intercourse constitute intimate forms of tactile speech. An older phrase for orgasmic sexuality, "carnal knowledge," aptly coined the communicative power arising from physical coupling.

Kinesthetic experience is sometimes considered separately—as a sixth sense. We treat it here, however, as a part of touch. Kinesthetic refers to sensory experiences mediated by nerves from the muscles, tendons, bones, and organs of the body. Sensory feedback from touch reaches our brain through skin and bones and muscles and body organs, signaling degrees of pain or pleasure, comfort or discomfort, danger or safety, success or failure in coping with our environment. Such tactile experiences enable us to be individuals within an intersecting and cosmic system of selves and things. Thus we live self-consciously as particular beings and yet belong to the whole. Unit and unity cohere. We are not an island, to use Donne's metaphor, but part of the continent. Kinesthetically we locate ourselves in the creation. Tactile communications, then, flow along electro-chemical pathways of the nervous system and signify meanings to ourselves and to other persons and creatures. Touch interprets how we use and are used by the earth and creatures and things we share it with. That the emissaries of God use these pathways should come as no surprise.

When I was a child, having heard that the earth wobbled a bit on its orbit, I lay prone on the grass one quiet summer day to test that hypothesis. I imagined I could feel the wobble! Maybe in some way brain acquiesced to will and allowed this child to experience physical reality as a pulse.

The universe (our persons included) can be analyzed mechanistically into units of material and energy, but it can also be perceived organically—as a living cosmos. A theistic worldview encompasses both perspectives, a concept some modern materialists and neo-animists find difficult to grasp. "In God we live and move and have our being," announced Paul when he would convince the pagans about the Gospel story. God is both transcendent and immanent, both "out there" and "in here," which means that material stuff is not inert. Nor is it deity diffused. The cosmos is within us as well as outside us. The circuitry for the Spirit is located within the intricate neuron network of the body as well as within the immense network of the cosmos. In all the permutations of physical motion the hand of God may be discerned, sometimes rationally, more often veiled in mystery. God is both transcendent—outside of time/space—and immanent—within time/space. Every religious story of epiphany is also an account of theophany—every occasion of personal spiritual ecstasy is an answering response to the call of divine revelation. All truth is ultimately revealed.

So whatever it means metaphysically for angels to exist, in whatever mode of reality they appear, whether as living persons, material things, or disembodied concepts, these messengers from God must travel our sensory routes and fire our sensory perceptors in order to do their work. Our own reality is defined in different modes. When we examine the body as a cluster of things we do not deny its reality as person and concept. We can accept variant forms for godly presence.

The skin is a God-given mantle enabling creatures to exist as individuals autonomously within natural and social communities. Burn victims understand the terrible importance of this mantle. Skin provides a sensory edge to the body; it is a cambium layer of flesh for the human tree of life. It is a wall protecting the castle of the soul. Skin variations in color and design that enrich humanity unfortunately give occasion for sinful prejudice. In conjunction with God's second mantle, clothing, skin provides a persona for the soul, to convey to ourselves and to others who we are, or who we would become. The nude body is beautiful, especially when it is young and unblemished, but most of us value the second skin for how it enhances our appearance. We would rather present a clothed than an unclothed persona to the public. Most persons are "naked and unashamed" only before those with whom they share intimacy without feeling personally diminished. By clothing and by other constructed walls of the human habitat we co-create the self that is viewed through the eyes of others (the social self), and also the self seen through eyes of self-consciousness (the autonomous self). Clothing achieves more than enhanced appearance. By clothing we achieve a comfort level in variable temperatures. We are shielded from hostile environments, including that of human predation. Besides, clothing provides handy portable bags in which to stuff, or hang, assorted objects, useful and ornamental!

Touch has its conventional language. That is, the natural language of touch becomes modified by the social order and regulated into certain routine behaviors. Thus society gives touch conventional boundaries in respect to various kinds of skin-to-skin contact such as shaking hands, kissing, stroking, petting, hugging, wrestling, dancing, as well as by rituals of sexuality. Conventional signs include putting on and taking off different kinds of clothing and other adornment, being seated, gesticulating, clapping, bowing, beckoning, reading Braille, acting.

Tactile languages are often ritualized in games and performances, such as basketball, ice-skating, and drama. Many tactile signs are reciprocal. These include greeting rituals such as handshakes, hugging, and kissing. Others are unidirectional. When a parent marches a naughty child into the house clearly one is the sender, the other the receiver of touch. From the cradle to the grave touch binds people together and gives security.[2] Touch provides a reality base for linguistic metaphors. Tactile experiences assert and defend the social order along a qualitative and quantitative scale of dominance and subjection.

Because of sin what is good by creation becomes evil in social experience. The sense of touch is a major route for violence. Beatings and rape breach the victim's skin; they assail the wall that protects the castle, and, of course, they violate the dignity and wholeness of the person.

In contrast, when bodies are committed to righteousness touch constitutes a major language for love. Good touch raises the drawbridge to the interior castle and lets love in. Through touch temples of the Holy Spirit accommodate to shared space.

We now elaborate some of the ways touch occurs and how these experiences can be rightly sensuous.

Passive Touching

Passive touching means unreflective tactile sensations ordinarily experienced. Such tactile sensations are so much a part of our lives we don't think much about them, but if we did we would be overwhelmed by the act of accounting—like the centipede pondering how its legs function synchronously. Impaired persons find technical assistance through crutches, specially equipped vehicles, and various tactile prostheses. But most of us give little thought to ordinary tactile experiences. A few reflections may suffice to show how passive touch offers sensuous satisfaction.

Most of us are a long way removed from the time when squeezing the toothpaste tube was an intriguing eye-hand-taste-smell experience. We have programmed into memory the motor functions involved in this and other health routines. Motor responses have become habituated. For the very young, however, the world is new. Ordinary things fascinate and beckon to be touched. The mind yearns to explore its body and its encompassing environment. Daily activities have not yet been organized, prioritized, and reduced to routine. Just being alive is exciting! So babies play with their toes, suck their thumbs, probe their body parts, pull grandpa's beard, pound spoons on the table, poke into the dog's ears, stir cereal with their fingers, or fling it on the floor. Small children collect pebbles and sticks from the beach and tramp in mud puddles. They run around in circles, fall down and roll over, and scribble on walls. And, yes, occasionally they stick beans up their noses!

Turning boards over to catch bugs squirming beneath may be fun for young children, as is curling up in a cardboard box, catching raindrops on one's tongue, racing with the wind, climbing fences and trees, swinging one's legs from a church pew, or pulling the sides of one's mouth into different shapes to make faces. An older child delights in kicking a rock down the road for half a mile while another happily spends the afternoon digging in the sand. Older siblings explore all the body parts, tan the skin, squeeze pimples, endure braces, feel each other's biceps, and festoon their firm young bodies with bizarre clothing and assorted gadgets.

It is by touch that each generation checks out their environment. The sound of an advising adult voice or the restraint of an adult hand is not enough. Cradles and playpens do not long provide protective custody. First crawling, then walking, then running—and the world gets wider fast for a child. In the process of inquiry, of course, some children get hurt, despite efforts to make things safe for them. If it isn't sticking a tongue on frozen metal it is touching a finger to a hot stove. If it isn't falling from a tree, it is getting a head stuck on the sticky fly catcher. Some young investigators, however, whose curiosity has been channeled constructively by good parenting, fortunate trial and error experiences, and exciting education, become scientists who refine their eye-hand coordination with skilled use of instruments, abetted by logic and acquired knowledge of the natural world. But it all starts by touching, and being touched by, ordinary things and probing their meaning.

Children investigate the world, starting with what is within reach. Sight and touch often work together. To widen tactile competence we provide swimming pools, jungle gyms, beach walks, wood chopping at summer camps, travel to distant places, craft classes, hands-on zoos, household chores, and formal or informal apprenticeship programs. Kids learn to work. To provide guidance in how the mind interprets what the hand reaches for, parents teach what is socially acceptable touch. Municipalities enact ordinances to protect curious children against "attractive nuisances" such as abandoned refrigerators. In many ways society enhances the prospects that touch will be used for good not evil, and with fulfilling, not tragic consequences.

When persons get older, with joints that ache every morning, exercise programs notwithstanding, they reawaken to life's passive tactile values. Some of this comes about because of an increased awareness of the body through its infirmities. For aged or physically impaired persons it may be a small triumph to move one's legs from one end of the house to another, or to step onto public transportation, or to arrange flowers on the table, or to prepare a meal for guests. For some impaired persons even to write a letter, to comb one's hair, or to brush one's teeth becomes a studied task. Such persons understand the complexities of passive touch and appreciate its wonders all the more.

For older persons an appreciation for elemental touch is heightened by the recognition that life is no longer an endless romp but a rapidly diminishing journey through time. The world is not exactly an unexplored wilderness to retirees. Their feet have walked many places, their hands have touched many things. Their bodies have been buffeted by viruses and accidents, socialized by marriage, and shaped by cultural pressures as surely as their shoulders have been stooped by gravity. But these persons have lived long enough to know how vast and varied the world is, especially the natural world. They long to lay hands on different objects and walk across new terrain, to put their bodies in different locales and circumstances. They would feel the sun and the wind and the rain in different climes while they have time and strength. So with the help of travel agencies the more affluent give their feet new paths to walk on, whether these be the streets of Vienna, the mountains of Tibet, or the golf courses of Arizona. Those who want intellectual stimulus, or a respectable rationale for roaming about, attend Elderhostel conferences in exotic places. They tread where the Amish or the Tlinkit walk, they handle dinosaur bones in Utah or explore the ruins of ancient cities. Those who cannot afford to travel, or dislike the hassle of strange places and different beds, find a world of tactile wonder in what is close at hand (acres of diamonds, as it were). They sculpt wood or they make quilts. They paint pictures or they garden. They build houses for Habitat for Humanity.

What do the travelers and the stay-at-homes have in common? A recovery of early tactile enjoyments. These senior adults do not need to stomp in a mud puddle to recover childlike wonder. They have found other and better ways to touch the earth and be touched by it. Hands and feet that have handled the hard challenges of life are capable of a deeper curiosity than tots who try out their limbs at the start of life's journey, and youth who flex their muscles and tan their firm young skin on the beach.

Between times, however, during the long middle years of life, when a quickened social pace locks our feet and hands into restrictive obligation, when our bodies move here and there within boundaries of employment, then passive touch is pretty much autonomic and not very reflexive. During these years the sense of touch has been impressed into service to others and harnessed to ego enhancement. Touch has been mortgaged to The Cause. We no longer have time or inclination to kick a rock down the road half a mile or to climb trees. We brush our teeth to prevent cavities not for the sheer fun of squeezing toothpaste from a tube. If we are healthy, the body functions more or less without maintenance other than morning calisthenics, tennis on weekends, and a medical checkup now and then. Life is busy, so we routinize primary sense perceptions to make conscious room for important vocational and social agendas. We are no longer happy little innocents playing on a dirt pile. We are adults. Our hands are engaged in strenuous daily commutes by car or public transport, between which times they are devoted to job skills—drilling teeth, toting up columns of figures, typing, repairing motors, surveying land, mining ore, cutting out cancer cells, manufacturing computer chips, building houses, cooking meals, filling shelves, selling things, scrubbing things, digging things, sawing things, driving things, and cultivating fields. Our feet give us standing on the job, a fulcrum for our muscles. Our feet have no time for random strolls through the woods, they are for walking about at the office or the store or factory or school or the farm. They are busy stepping on this or that lever, or propped up on this or that desk. Morning to evening we surrender our sense of touch to the mind for its purposes, how to achieve this or that labor, how to make more money for the firm, to sell more products, to secure tenure, to win political approval, to make influential friends, to keep the family fed and reasonably content, to give leadership to the service club or the church, praying for moral strength not to dip into the till or to swipe an item from the store (or sophisticated equivalents thereof). We would travel a straight line, from here to there, hand on the steering wheel, foot on the accelerator and sometimes on the brake.

For those in the hardworking middle years, particularly, but for the rest of us as well, the implication is clear: Let's keep in touch with ordinary things. Feel again the rain on your face as a friend, not as an annoyance. Spread your coat to the wind and be pushed along happily like a child. As the sun warms your skin one fine day acknowledge it as a gift from God. Let your body signal to you about kinesthetic needs—for stretching your neck, for relaxing taut leg and arm muscles—for carefree exercise—not just a call for aspirin and business as usual. Enjoy feeling the flex of feet as you climb steps, the dexterity of your hands as you drive to work. When you go to bed don't hold your body up with the cares of the day. Yield to gravity, relax your feet and your hands and your head, and go to sleep, grateful for the comfort of covers and an easy conscience. And in the morning wiggle your toes, grateful to be alive in a new day of creation.

Each day let the earth touch your feet with its variegated surfaces, soft, spongy, hard, rocky. Interrogate these mute messengers. Let your hands intersect with trees, feeling their trunks, needles, and leaves. Receive as a free and loving massage the cat's tail pushing against your friendly hand. Heft stones and let them instruct you about shape and texture.

Montaigne, I read somewhere, called scratching where one itches one of nature's sweetest gratifications, and the one nearest to hand. Any child knows this to be the case. Let's put it in a more comprehensive, biblical context. Maybe it isn't such a puzzling saying, after all, this word from Jesus, "I tell you the truth, unless you change and become like little children, you will never enter the kingdom of heaven." (Matt. 18:3 NIV) We are walking a path toward the kingdom when in joyous praise to the Creator we touch earth's ordinary things with an attitude of praise! At day's end let everyone exclaim, "I am touched!"

Conditioned Touching

Conditioned touching refers to socio-cultural dominion exercised over persons by the manipulation of their bodies or the physical environment. This sort of touch may be exerted directly by one body in some manner physically touching another body, or indirectly through objects. Such touch may enhance or demean the self. A culture is sensuous when it does the former, sensate when it does the latter. Thus we can hug another's body in friendship, or we can design automobiles that hold a body snugly and safely within. We can strike with a fist directly, or hit with a missile indirectly. Technological society offers an *enormous* range of instruments for touching people indirectly, "at second hand." This technical capability has good consequences, such as an increased capacity through our tools to provide food, clothing, habitat, and health care, and to provide machinery that spares the human body from backbreaking and dangerous toil. Technology also has bad consequences, such as using machine surrogates to marginalize, demean, torture, or destroy other persons at a distance without the messy, risky, business of direct body-on-body contact. To be violent at a distance, whether that distance be across the street with a handgun or across the ocean with a bomb offers depersonalized invasion of another's space.

Technology offers objectivity, with good and bad consequences. Medical personnel touch patients' bodies with scalpels to heal; military personnel, with bullets to destroy enemies. In typical euphemisms used to distance the attention of the general public from the direct physical impact of warfare (witnessed at first hand by ambulance crews and hospital personnel), civilian casualties are called "collateral damage," and an effective bombing raid is called "a surgical strike." Such expressions imply that the opposing aggregation of individuals is a single organism—a body—from which diseased parts can be cut out for the social good. There is, however, an ironic significance to our technological revolution, for although instruments provide personal distance from public enemies, this same technology enables opposing peoples to see and hear what is happening. Thus they are brought closer to each other. Interdependence in trade also cancels out the distancing effect of technology. We all live in a neighborhood now and must confront its violence as events occurring on our turf, and its benefits as entitlements to be received equitably.

The Force of Will

In considering how tactile responses are conditioned it may be helpful to consider the force of will one person or group lays upon another. Will combined with physical or technological strength to impose it, sends tactile messages to another's brain soliciting, eliciting, or demanding response by the recipient. This response may be consensual or begrudged or compelled. Our bodies are employed in the service of others, willingly or unwillingly, with or without equitable and reciprocal service. Society offers corporate methods for regulating the interacting forces of personal and group will. Control may be imposed by the more powerful persons upon the less powerful, or it may be agreed to by individuals willing to subordinate their wishes to the corporate good through contract or constitution. Democracy is such a contract. To avoid confusion and moral anarchy society creates a corporate person, through which interests of the group exceed those of individual constituents.

Politically, this corporate person is the state. We refer to the "violence of the magistrate" wherein force is applied under legal sanction. But human order provides other corporate powers in varying and competing hierarchies too—a truth fervent nationalists often forget. These use various kinds of force. Secondary circles exist within primary circles of affinity. These alternate social entities may, and often do, challenge the state for the primary allegiance of persons. These circles include the family, the tribe (or the club/gang), the business corporation, the professional guild, and the religious fellowship. Martyrs are persons who resist to the death political preempting of ultimate authority over their bodies. They would rather be burned at the stake by imperial decree than to disobey the Almighty God or compromise their faith.

Force has varying intensities. From the most to least invasive to the self, the kinds of force are these: violence, coercion, restraint, intimidation, inducement, persuasion, example, and prayer. These are the means whereby one person or group gets another person or group to act in conformity to its will. The cultural powers using these means include the family, school, government, business, and religion.

To this list of cultural powers I would add media. Although intertwined, as are other affinity circles, media has acquired a distinct corporate persona. How we see and hear regulates our motions. And the physical motion produced by television skews natural and conventional perceptions of such activity. Media has increasingly modeled behavior—often to the dismay of the family, the school, business, and religion. Because commercial time is so expensive, advertisements and programs accelerate conventional motions of bodies in time/space, whether these programs be talk shows, entertainment, or news reports. Everything has to occur rapidly and in short duration. Events that occur over hours or days are telescoped by television and other electronic programs such as video games into sequences only seconds or minutes long. Violent action fits into this econo-technical need to accelerate time—the powerful fist to the jaw, the fiery car crash, the drawn gun—these offer a quick solution to problems. Tempo is adjusted to the pocketbooks of commercial patrons. Much of the social impact is hypnotic and destructive. Children adapt to that pattern of telescoped physical motion. Consequently, they have difficulty comprehending duration of activity in the processes of learning, working, and socializing. They are programmed for instant gratification. Their desires multiply more rapidly than their moral understanding. Some children become sexually active at a very young age, some commit heinous crimes. Others become addicted to material acquisitions, or to incessant motion, or to drugs. One reason for increased television coverage of golf may be the respite offered adult viewers from the usual television fare of frenetic motion. Quietly to watch a golfer line up a putt provides the viewer a welcomed relief from a continual and noisy barrage of images in accelerated motion.

Apostle Paul said that Christ had triumphed over the "principalities and powers." (See Eph. 1:21-23.) For the early community of Christians this meant that the Cross signaled a divine triumph over a tyrannical empire which might imprison the body but never the spirit. Can we provide our youth with the wisdom and the courage necessary to overcome media "powers" that shape, control, and exploit their bodies, and may destroy their souls?

These social powers all put certain boundaries around the lives of creatures within their circles, either to enhance freedom of action or to hinder it, to expand or to diminish the self, to shatter the group or to solidify it. To be a member of the group implies some consent to be governed by its rules and/or to be subordinate to its collective will and purpose. The very shape and appearance of the human body, its health and well-being, and the symbolics of its tactile experiences and interpretations are influenced by group affinity. Touch in the Islamic world differs from that of the Christian world, and both differ from touch in the secular world. For one who believes in God, the ultimate circle is God's Kingdom. Here is the locus of authority for individuals and their social groups. To recover this insight is important, for anarchy threatens to override order and cause freedom to fail.

Controlling Access to Nature

Consider nature as the reality that stands outside human manipulation. How has our culture conditioned our access to nature? First, the technological revolution has increased the distancing of nature from most people. The industrial revolution initiated a process that the technological revolution has accelerated. The hands and feet of most of us are not principally involved in husbandry. Our backs do not bear the burden of heavy loads. A relatively few workers spare us direct physical contact with the soil and food production. Some of these toil in stoop labor but others use machines. The same can be said about the clothes we wear, the vehicles that transport us from one place to the other, and the houses we live in. We are almost wholly dependent upon the expertise of others. Consider a favorite scenario of science fiction writers, coping with a complete break-down of the industrial infrastructure because of nuclear war, or other disaster. How would *most of us* manage if we had to secure our own food and water directly from the earth, make and maintain our own transportation, make our own clothes, and build our own houses?

There is a bright side to this techno-culture that makes the individual dependent upon the whole for access to nature. A larger population can be fed, clothed, and housed than if we were all tribal hunters and gatherers, all scrounging for logs to build our cabins in the forest. I for one am grateful for the creative genius and skilled work that bring us a healthy diet, clean water, comfortable houses, and automobiles that carry us about safely and without breaking down. *Our lives are in the hands of others*; society has caught us all in a network of inderdependence; we are conditioned by this highly industrial/technological society. Every minor war demonstrates the fragility of the human network. Therefore it behooves us to find equitable and peaceful ways to interchange knowledge and skills, so that some persons are not marginalized to enhance the luxury of others.

The dark side of techno-culture is a significant loss of that sensuous spirituality afforded persons whose bodies interact with the earth directly, and who offer praise to the Creator through their work with natural objects. As we become more and more urbanized, nature too readily becomes just a collective term for resources to be harvested by strangers for our food and shelter, save for aesthetic set-asides such as parks and zoos. People who handle the earth for food and habitat in a primary way may be more keenly aware that the earth is the Lord's than those who only derive benefits at a distance.[3] In the little medieval story at the head of this chapter it was the horse "Touch" whose feet were most firmly planted on the ground.

Another way our culture has conditioned access to nature is by political systems of entitlement. Private and public lands establish conditions for use. Streams and fields and forests are not open to all comers. Legal title authorizes access and control. Such ownership usefully sustains social order, but it hinders the kind of freedom enjoyed in sparsely settled places, or by tribal peoples who often think of the land as a common home to be used for all within the affinity circle.

A third way technological culture conditions access to nature is by clustering people within artificially constructed locations, in megacities. As technology increases, fewer and fewer farmers are required. This condition forces rural people into cities. The major cities of the world are ringed with ghettos of the poor who have left their villages to seek new economic security in the cities. As space for urban dwellers becomes more expensive, the amount of space allotted for homes gets smaller and smaller. Many new bedroom subdivisions and apartment complexes are not even framed with grass. To afford these houses both spouses must work, and they haven't time for gardening. Thus their hands and feet are further distanced from the earth. The landscaping is designed to please the eye not the foot and the hand. Jogging paths must suffice aesthetically for the foot and indoor gyms for the hand.

In some cities the little neighborhood parks required of developers have become dangerous places, resulting in the proliferation of substitute indoor spaces for recreation, complete with artificial cliffs to scale and artificial trails to run on. Rooftops become the playing fields for children in crowded cities of the world. These commercial substitutes cater to wealthier citizens. The poor, pulled by economic necessity from the villages of the world, must play on hot streets or in gutted apartment buildings. To reach national parks, open beaches, and wilderness areas, thoughtfully reserved against enormous commercial pressure, requires extensive travel for many people. These places are essentially out of reach for many poor children except through outdoor school and camps operated by religious agencies.

Unavailable for direct primary sensation, the outdoors is now offered vicariously, through Discovery channel and other televised programs. The zoom lens has added enriching detail for eyes, but nothing for our feet. The eye may be satisfied by seeing birds soaring over rocky outcroppings, or fish wriggling up streams, or polar bears trudging on Arctic ice, but the feet would like to trod mossy trails to the beach. Hands would like to feel sparkling stream water flow over them, accompanied by the sound of fir trees soughing and wild birds singing, and the smell of salt spray.

To liberate touch from these narrowing boundaries of an artificial world requires close attention. Some effort, financial or otherwise, is necessary to keep our bodies from losing direct sensuous touch with the earth. Here are some suggestion:

1) Maintain contact with some arable soil, whether it be a garden or flower plot, so that your hands feel the humus of the soil and engage in some husbandry of the earth and its fruits.

2) Take some time each day to feel unpaved earth beneath your feet.

3) Use vacation time not just to look at but to feel natural things. Try letting your hands and feet provide the mind with memories of places visited.

4) Teach children how to handle trees and streams, rocks and grass in a way that respects the integrity of these natural things, so that little fingers feel differences in pine needles and oak leaves, and discern the intricate textures of sand and stone.

5) Enhance natural objects, such as rocks and driftwood as art objects for the hands, objects for touch as well as sight, such as agates or polished wood.

6) Make sure that sufficient lands are kept open to the public for direct tactile experiences, so that generations of children will have a chance to run along forest paths or on ocean beaches, to climb trees, to splash in mountain streams, and thus literally to keep in touch with the earth.

Touch and the Artificial World

In affirming the value of the natural world must we deny the value of the artificial world? Not at all! Human beings are creatures of the earth, as much as are animals and trees. Obviously our powers to reshape the elements of the earth are significantly greater than that of other entities, and can severely disturb the social and natural orders. Tools do not marginalize people, greed does, whatever the character of society. Luddite reactions can never bring back a supposed golden age of labor-intensive, tranquil village life. Anti-industrial groups, however, do force us to focus upon the cost to human life and to the earth itself exacted by machine-intensive labor. Such reactionary movements do warn of the loss of direct and pleasing sensory experiences: the hands-on touch of craft work, breathing clean air unpolluted by industrial wastes, time spent on afternoon siestas and evening promenades in the village square. Primitivists forget the ugliness industry can erase: denuded forests, intertribal slaughter, plague arising from open sewers, an enslaved permanent underclass, death in childbirth, and backbreaking toil.

So let's think about how touch can be sensuous in respect to the artificial world, first by noting some philosophical observations, and then by making some practical applications.

Actually, it's not easy to separate these two spheres. They are aspects of a shared reality. The world of nature and the artificial world have been interfaced throughout human history, as soon as God wrapped our first parents in skins and drove them from Eden. Actually, all creatures rearrange their environment as well as accommodate to it. Human beings must do so in order to survive. It is natural for intelligent beings to shape their environment. Ever since the discovery of fire human beings have shaped the received natural world according to physical need and mental desire. Much inert stuff is modified by the touch of sentient creatures, including human beings. Is the modification done by an animal natural while that done by a person artificial? Are nests natural and houses artificial? Certain ecologically concerned people forget that humanity is part of nature, too. The human need to build shelters for themselves, to secure food, or to use tools differs only in degrees of sophistication from that of other creatures. Beavers use their intelligence to build dams, so do human beings. The activities of both may have good or bad consequences for other creatures. When a major fire burned much of the forest within the Yellowstone Park not long ago, people argued that it was a natural event from which much good would come. Let nature alone; with the overburden removed, the soil would be stimulated for new growth, so the argument went. The destruction of animals and their habitat was considered an acceptable cost. Only a few deep ecologists would apply that logic of beneficial fire to a blaze threatening to destroy Los Angeles and its inhabitants, although similar benefits would surely accrue to the land. It is good to collect nature in bits, as a preserve here, a wilderness there, like an art museum, for enjoyment not utility. But a larger question persists: How can we live righteously within nature as a whole?

We are not primitives, whose small numbers could not threaten primitive forests on a global scale, and whose lack of intelligent control made them fear the wilderness instead of harvest it. We are modern people with an incredibly complex technology for adapting the environment to our ends. To do this wisely is our task. And it is a major problem, because extended by powerful tools our hands can destroy our earthly habitat. No other species has that power. We can be destroyers or creators. Which will we be?

Human touch has altered the natural world to such an extent that little of the planet is "untouched" by human thought or hand. It is humbling, however, to reflect that most of the cosmos remains untouched by us! This conditioning touch involves more than technical rearrangement of earth's things. There is a malevolent aspect. Christian theology teaches that the creation has been marred by evil and awaits human redemption in order to find its own reordering. Wrote Paul, "The creation itself will be liberated from its bondage to decay and brought into the glorious freedom of the children of God." (Rom. 8:21 NIV) Because of evil and its consequences the divine image in creation has been frustrated. The earth suffers from human sin. Delegated authority has been misused. The steward has succumbed to arrogance and to greed. Humanity demonstrates plurality and sexuality, but not the mutuality required for human society and by the earth itself. Sin has put us out of touch with the cosmos. We are, as C.S. Lewis described it, "the silent planet" in a universe that otherwise sings for joy. Christianity proclaims that under the saving power of Christ "an ecology of agapic (self-giving) love and servanthood" will replace botched human dominion.[4]

The issue of ecological responsibility is an enormous one—with much written on the subject. The sins of our pollution are flagrant and much discussed. One *can* say this: To whom much is given much shall be required. We human beings cannot escape the responsibility for right care of the earth. God opts to use our hands and feet in the history of the cosmos. Surely the angels traveling neuron pathways from skin to brain carry some messages from God about how to handle the earth! Will we heed them?

Although not always sure why we have been so privileged, having so often failed, we are co-creators with God. Nature is not a prefixed order but rather a process of holy purpose. There are rhythms in space/time, but no necessary cycles of return. Templates for things, ideas, and persons are not fixed. They develop creatively under the dominion of intelligent purpose. One universal model, however, persists through time and in space as a call into the future: love. Divine and human. Love is the one enduring template for all thought and action occurring in the interface between the natural and the artificial worlds. And so the earth, at least, is being changed dramatically under the will of God, who is active through the agency of sentient creatures, including human beings made in the divine image. Even wrath and sin are turned by love into praise for the Holy One. Such is the significance of divine grace. Though the earth melt because of human miscalculation or evil purpose, love will prevail.

Every event, then, is a new page in time. History does not repeat itself. The universe is open and the future contingent. Within finite limits of existence and thought, humanity joins God in shaping the universe. Our hands and feet, with all their technological extensions, are God's instruments, whether offered freely in righteousness or suborned in divine judgment. The redemption of the earth from its oppression is speeded by the sanctified use of human hands and feet, and by the thoughtful interrogation of how, and to what purposes, our bodies intersect with the creation. The church proclaims that earth's redemption has been authentically witnessed by Christ, the Word of God incarnate, at the midpoint of time.

So, given the wonder of human cooperation with the Divine in the creation of the future, how, practically, may human machines do good to the earth and its creatures, and not harm? Some decisions are social ones, requiring political consent and power. Others are personal. And the larger decisions of the group reflect the smaller, day by day, decisions of individuals. Culture indeed molds individuals, but in the last analysis culture itself is molded by the will of persons. And within culture, although evil may seduce in the short run, its consequences are so ruinous that in the long run goodness triumphs. Good prevails when persons shape things constructively, when the messengers of God instruct their hands as fully in the artificial as in the natural world.

Here are some examples of sensuous touching in respect to the world conditioned by human hands. These applications of stewardly principles suggest how to overcome the evils of a materialistic culture, and turn it to good.

1) *Consecrate the tools our hands use.* Tools are extensions of our hands in kitchen and shop as well as in office or factory. Word processors and pneumatic drills alike reconstruct the given world. Respect toolmakers and those who use the tools, aware of how their creative insights and technical skills have provided us with things needful to our existence and useful for the good life. Tools may be instruments of wickedness or instruments of righteousness.

This poem, "The Carpenter," is based upon an early and pivotal experience that jarred me loose from a preoccupation with the nonmaterial as opposed to the spiritual.

> *Odd prayer, I thought,*
> *somewhat bemused—*
> *"God bless my tools."*
> *The man's confused:*
> *such prayers aren't taught*
> *in Sunday Schools.*
> *In worship ought*
> *such words be used?*
> *Then I recalled how,*
> *on another carpenter,*
> *nails and hammer were*
> *misused, and are so now.*
> *...Lord, forgive us fools*
> *God bless my tools.*[5]

2) *Construct houses for good touch.* Houses are to be lived in, not just to be looked at. A house is a home not just shelter, not just a convenient place to secure food, sleep, and clean clothes. Houses provide safety and

comfort, as well as the necessities of life. A house is a nest for nurturing the young, a playground, a school, a clinic, a sanctuary, a hideaway for love, a hallowed place for prayer. A house is a hostel for entertaining friends and sometimes strangers. A house should be a place where hands and feet are comfortable and have useful and enjoyable things to do, where furniture fits the body, where activity of mind and spirit is aided, not hindered. A home should be a place where guests feel at ease.

Functional furnishings and efficient home machineries save time and energy. Ethically speaking, a house should avoid ostentation, so as to conserve the earth and to sustain its resources for our use. Luxuries often come at a cost to the poor. One's house should not be so expensive as to be a financial burden or so cheaply made as to require inordinate energy to keep it functional. Materials chosen should be durable and authentic. Aesthetic aspects of housing are important, too. Good simple lines offer enduring satisfaction, beyond faddish styles. Paintings and sculpted pieces offer a close affinity with persons who work artistically with their hands. To use their artistry constitutes an acknowledgment of their giftedness. The same can be said for handcrafted artifacts, from doilies to baskets to clocks to wall hangings. It's important to have some sculpted things the hands can feel from time to time. It is a good discipline occasionally to ask questions about our houses. How have artists instructed our senses in eternal values? How do texture, grain, color, and hue cohere in functional and decorative artifacts? It is good to touch lovingly what human hands have shaped artfully from natural objects such as wood and stone. By their tools carpenters and artists and craft workers have constructed what by touch can become icons for sensuous spirituality. In many ways thoughtful persons can make their houses habitats of the Spirit.

3) *Use machines to liberate.* Our hands and feet are extended by many mechanisms that we take for granted. Very early in my life I was taught to write, using the Palmer method of penmanship, with its monitored drills to ensure an easy flow of lines. Later I was taught to type. For decades now my thoughts have flowed best from my keyboarding fingers, first on a sturdy black Royal typewriter, later on an electric one, and then on a word processor. What wonders the mind and the hand can do when linked with these machines! Ideas are transmitted into word and print, and electronic mail! Machines are complex tools, human artifacts tapping into natural power sources beyond our muscles and producing motions much more intricate than what our fingers can do unaided. In factories robots do routine toil once reserved for human workers. We are over-

whelmed by the world of machines, and science fiction teases us about future cyborgs and artificial intelligence taking over the world. Already micromachines are off the drawing boards and into technology, ready to reach into inner spaces of human and other creatures where no one has gone before.

Adults find it hard to remember when they didn't drive a car. But not their first efforts to program the VCR! Surgeons repair the heart of a fetus within the womb and we marvel only briefly, as if we expect this sort of thing. We have become a bit jaded, I fear, so immeshed into the machine age that we forget to applaud the human ingenuity that has put these machines into our hands. Maybe we're not jaded, but afraid. Some people are so enamored with machines they buy every latest gadget. This is materialistic idolatry. Others hang back from trusting their bodies to the latest machines. They're not impressed with electric pencil sharpeners. Most of us are a bit wary of a technological culture that can make computers and do angioplasty, yes, but can also bomb cities and alter the genetic code.

In our religion we have been too gnostic. We have failed to see the glory of physical bodies, and the reflected glory of machines that bodies construct and use as extensions of ourselves. It is a form of praise to God and to humanity made in God's image to enjoy and use machines appropriately.

4) *Let clothing enhance the body.* Let's think about clothing. People's clothing styles are manipulated not only by commercial and political interests but also by cultural forces. Sometimes those forces are in compliance with our interests, at other times not. We respond willingly to certain demands and balk at others. Consider the ordinary business suit. Does it signify a "conspiracy" to mask individual identity? Or is the suit a way to serve others more self-effacingly? A sign of dominion or of humility? Do commerce and governance require suits and ties to accomplish their purposes? At best such cultural demands symbolize the dignity of professional service. At worst they demean personal preference. Profitability is the corporate goal, national interest the political goal; so individuality, with its complement of private judgment, always faces subordination. At question is how much.

The clothing industry juggles many factors involving human choice. It initiates or responds to a culture that seeks a symbiotic relationship between the corporate need for impersonality and the personal need for recognition. Aesthetics vie with practical concerns. Thus endless variations of the business suit, the constant snob appeal in advertising, the cyclic modifications of style from single-breasted to double-breasted to three-piece suits, with fluctuations in shape and color of the necktie—that persistent cultural symbol of corporate servitude. If people must wear a harness then the clothing industry ought to give much attention to fit and feel.

The shape and appearance of the human being is driven both by culture and market. How clothing *feels* to the wearer is often sacrificed for public expectation of what looks appropriate. I remember once arriving at Chicago's O'Hare Airport on a very hot day. During the long wait on the tarmac the air-conditioning faltered. With other lightly clothed passengers, I watched those ahead of me deplane. From the business class compartment emerged two aspiring—and perspiring—executives. They retrieved raincoats and cases from the overhead compartment, slamming the doors noisily. A three-piece suit encased the fattening frame of each man—five years distant from football fitness. They were "dressed for success." They shoved their way out, saying "Let's keep in touch" to the other as they departed to separate offices to negotiate with other overdressed males for power and privilege, all climbing the corporate ladder. What were they in touch with?

Putting cultural glasses aside, these men looked plain silly. They were not in touch with the physical environment, sweltering as they were. Why should office men wear several layers of clothing on a hot day, turning air conditioners on high, while lightly dressed female employees shiver? Because the attire we wear is conditioned by societal demands. Craving recognition and status, or acknowledging that of others, the self accommodates to ridiculous social norms. We dress for others, sometimes happily, sometimes grudgingly, sometimes with useful conventions, sometimes otherwise. This accommodation takes various forms, such as the following.

1) The sexy persona. Those who want to be considered sexy, or are impelled by social expectations to be so considered, choose garments such as leather jackets over bare chests, risqué dresses, or other clothes that convey that image.

2) The military persona. The military uniform for police and army personnel signals both hierarchical order and depersonalization. The body of the individual is subordinated to an abstract body, i.e. the state.

3) The educational persona. School uniforms symbolize group order conducive to rational inquiry. Aimed at avoiding social snobbery, uniforms, ironically, can become themselves elitist. Academic hoods and gowns offer visual and tactile evidence of intellectual achievement.

4) Stage persona. Athletes and musicians accommodate to social expectations in guild uniforms that set them apart. Actors accommodate to dramatic roles on stage, and offstage wear unconventional garb that accents an avant-garde role in society. Media often define these roles and their imitations.

5) Judicial persona. Judges with gavels in their hands wear robes to signify dignity and objectivity; on the other hand, prisoners in handcuffs wear an ugly uniform to identify them readily as deviant to social norms.

6) Service persona. Service persons with appropriate corporate logos wear uniforms that signify competency and trustworthiness.

7) Religious persona. Religious dress includes robes, collars, and other symbols for clergy, and head coverings, prayer shawls, and special clothes for communicants. Here, too, clothing signifies a desire that touch and appearance inculcate reverence and respect.

During the Vietnam era some people rebelled stridently against culturally imposed norms, including those for wearing apparel. This movement viewed uniformity in dress as depersonalizing to the individual. Counter-culture rebels charged hypocrisy in a society that covered ugly systemic evils with conventions of clean, neat clothing. They felt that the aesthetically beautiful hid the ethically ugly.

The counter-cultural movement believed that socially approved clothing blunts conscience and dampens dissent. In reaction, customized garb, even drab and ugly apparel, signified a defiance of convention, a freedom to be creative with one's own body, and a way of challenging bad social policy. Whatever its other effects, the movement did deflate the balloon of social snobbery. It reduced the number of occasions for dressing up. It exposed the petty tyranny exercised through dress codes in offices and schools. It signified that clothing should feel good to the wearer's skin.

The movement's lasting legacy is a wider freedom for persons to be comfortable, and to follow their own tastes in clothing. But the movement, like so many revolutions, succumbed to subtle manipulation by a power structure of the sort it had originally protested. In short, it got blindsided. New style-setters emerged from the conjoined efforts of entertainment and media industries. New cultural gurus replaced business and professional authorities in dictating what people should buy and wear. Protest collapsed into a fad. MTV made it chic for rebellious teenagers to costume their defiance. But there was a price. Those who abandoned convention were led like lemmings to the sea by the clever manipulators. These new style-setters replaced parents and teachers. Peer pressure became an increasingly potent force when manipulated by commercial rather than educational leaders. In the 1990s, in reaction to a pluralism of styles that seemed to permit anything and everything, society once again began signaling social correctness through conventions of garb. Uniforms were touted for school children to counteract media tyranny, economic bondage, gang modeling, social anarchy, and violence. If kids dress right they will act right, said the elders, viewing with alarm the grungy ways of the skateboarding set. Maybe; maybe not. Perhaps some children will find the right balance between individual and corporate culture. But others will just conform pragmatically and sequentially to clothing styles set by others without becoming either more creative or more ethical. Among our institutions, higher education and the medical profession have most easily accepted clothing styles that both symbolize corporate accountability and respect individual expression.

These cultural shifts show how symbolic clothing really is and the difficulty it brings to persons and groups. With a finger to the wind, someone quickly responds to cultural change, whether that change is creatively or rebelliously induced. Someone is always ready to narrow or widen pant legs, shorten or lengthen skirts, and to peddle this or that athletic shoe. Someone will leap to the chance to hype bright or dull ties, leather or serge fabric, fashion gown or everyday wear, as soon as some entrepreneur targets a market, pays a celebrity to model the goods, gets advertisement agencies to crank out ads, and lines up merchants to hawk the goods. Dressing isn't just accommodating to personal tastes or social norms, unfortunately. It's also having our bodies clothed at the whim of others, through conditioned expectations and manipulated consumption. We aren't as free as we imagine we are, in respect to our second skin.

How then might we respond to the constant pressure for what we should wear? Here are a few suggestions.

1) Accent gender in ways that please the senses, within reasonable social and religious boundaries. At its best, clothing acknowledges the complementary nature of humanity: In God's image we are created, male and female.

2) Choose service uniforms that offer a reassuring statement to persons served. If the job requires uniforms for employees, whether serving at the lunch counter, repairing household appliances, or nursing the sick, let these clothes signify pride in work and accountability of others. Employers should not debase the dignity of employees. Workers are persons not signboards. They deserve clothing that complements their bodies and respects their dignity.

3) Defer to others in clothing styles, rather than to offend them, "to please others and not just our own selves." This applies to aesthetic taste, and not just to concern for what is morally prudent. It wouldn't hurt grandpa to throw away that old green plaid polyester suit in favor of something more pleasing to the eye of the beholder. It wouldn't hurt grandson to wear clothes that complement the natural body rather than make it look bizarre. Travel agents warn visitors to foreign countries not to offend local standards. Such advice is applicable in one's own land.

4) Choose clothing that enables the body to function well, clothes that enhance self-esteem without succumbing to vanity. Sweaters may make more sense than suit coats for example, and low heeled shoes than spike heels. Women have been liberated from the corset for half a century now. They are becoming liberated from bone-jarring shoes.

5) Accent ceremonial occasions. Rhythmic highlights of life are dignified by dressing up for weddings and funerals and inaugural functions. Worship is a rhythmic weekly ceremony, too, and the church calendar includes special occasions such as Advent and Easter. It is said that in worship the poor dress up and the rich dress down. Does this mean poor people are more humble before their maker than the rich? Perhaps. Traditionally worship offered blue-collar workers an opportunity for dignified appearance denied during the work week. But things have changed. "White-collar" attire can signify low-paying work as well as social elitism. A clerk may be dressed much like an executive officer. Perhaps many people are overdressed at work.

Would it be better if for all tasks clothing were simpler, less ostentatious, more functional? Probably. People would be freer. Ceremonies would serve more effectively. Why should commerce rather than cultural ceremony dictate "dressing up"? In reaction to daily work demands, some families now "dress down" for church, seeking to show reverence in ways other than attire. Not every occasion for worship needs to be an Easter parade, nor is a uniform required in worship; but it is probably good to approach public worship scrubbed and dressed in one's better clothing. Those too casual in dress may fail to approach the Holy Presence with reverence. The worth of ordinary things is affirmed by those sanctifying occasions that celebrate the special triune presence of God, the self, and others.

These suggestions lead us to consider the role of the ego in respect to touch.

Egoistic Touching

Egoistic touching means tactile sensations willfully selected and self-consciously experienced. To repeat, to be egocentric is not necessarily to be egoistic. We cannot love our neighbor rightly unless we love ourselves. All sensations and reflections are routed through the self at its center. So it is appropriate to ask about the personal satisfactions that come from touch.

In aesthetics, as well as in ethics, it is helpful to distinguish the intrinsic from the instrumental good. To illustrate, work is generally considered instrumental and play intrinsic. That is, some activities are done for the sake of other ends, such as providing food and shelter, achieving mastery, power, or prominence. This is work. Activities done for their own sake are considered play. If we exclude professional athletes, play needs no justification; it carries its own value within it. It needs to yield no practical consequences. This is an oversimplification, however, for necessary work provides its own bodily rhythms that yield intrinsic values, and play may be engaged in for instrumental reasons such as good health and social interaction. Personally satisfying touch, then, involves both those activities that are instrumental and those that are intrinsic. Many of these activities involve the use of hands.

It is a sociological commonplace to attribute human achievement to having an opposable thumb. Of course, *homo sapiens* isn't the only creature so endowed. Human beings do have a greater capacity than other creatures to ponder what their hands grasp. Surgeons and artists know the importance of hands. One surgeon agreed with Isaac Newton that in the absence of any other proof, the thumb alone would convince people of the existence of God.[6] Those of us who depend upon the skills of both artists and surgeons for our physical and spiritual well-being appreciate the wondrous complexity of hands. Indeed, all we have to do is break a wrist to discover how dependent we are. We ought to reflect occasionally upon what our hands do all day and ask how they might serve more constructively in the body, the temple of the Almighty. What activities are instrumental, means toward purposeful ends? What activities are intrinsic, doing playful things for their own sake? Work and play are not really opposites. They can be comingled. Playfulness at work does not mean clowning around to avoid serious effort but rather the conscious enjoyment of physical motions instrumental to purposive activities.

Jesus said we should be childlike. Does that imply adults ought to cherish the freedom to play? Most play involves bodily motion, whether it be carving things with hand tools or swinging golf clubs. There are mental games, of course, but even Scrabble involves sitting on the floor, moving the pieces, and getting up to get snacks from the refrigerator.

Goal-oriented persons must often learn relaxing techniques before they can participate in play as play and not as another job. Take golf for instance. Some high achievers require fierce competition. They must toil in order to play. They ought simply to enjoy the game, body, soul, and spirit, breathing in the fresh air, stretching the legs, feeling muscles ripple through the rhythmic swing of clubs, feeling through their feet the softness of the turf, and accepting with a kind of holy wonder the pleasure of shots well-executed. If a rival must be overcome one has really not remembered the simple joys of play. I am not discounting rivalry in team sports, but only recalling how children are often less fixated upon a Little League score than are the cheering adults. The children remember better the aesthetics of their own performance on the team. A single to right field, like a rose, is a thing of beauty, and a joy forever.

Touching Ourselves

There are various kinds of self-touch. One is grooming our bodies: combing and styling the hair, brushing teeth, rubbing lotion on the skin, trimming fingernails, bathing. Another kind of self-touch is exercise, calisthenics aimed at physical fitness. Narcissistic touching involves sexual stimulus, muscle flexing, and preening. Self-touching may become obsessive and misdirected. Much of it is media induced and self-indulgent. Through this kind of self-touch the sin of vanity profanes God's temple. Our materialistic culture caters to the worship of one's body. Whenever the ego usurps God's throne, the temple becomes a den of thieves, a grove of idols. Reacting against the vanity and hedonism that reached an apex during the decadent years of the Roman Empire, medieval mysticism sought to denigrate the body. Some of these mystics abused the body with hair shirts and denied its appetites. They punished it with hard beds, coarse foods, and even with flagellation. If they were no longer to be flogged for their Christian faith they would flagellate themselves in order to keep the body from betraying the spirit.

Later, Protestant spirituality modified self-discipline by turning it into prudery. But flagellation and prudery, like vanity, fail to honor the body as a temple of the Spirit. When the self rightly heeds the messengers of God that speed along the neurons of the body, then touch offers a way to honor the creation and to worship the Creator.

In various ways we modify our first covering, the skin, piercing or encasing parts of it with rings, or draping it with ornaments. We do this to enhance individuality, to tell people who we are. To "put our best foot forward" to use a tactile metaphor. Cosmetics enhance color and disguise blemishes. Ointments and unguents soothe the skin and provide refreshing smells.

Clothing is an important way in which we touch ourselves. As noted above the individual and corporate aspects of selfhood stand in a tension, sometimes skewed one way sometimes another, toward social conformity or individual idiosyncrasy. In the Genesis account when Adam and Eve sinned they discovered shame. To cover their nakedness God clothed them in the skins of animals. This second skin is more than genital cover. It protects from the elements. It facilitates work and play, and elicits recognition by other persons. And it does protect from shame. There may be such a thing as false shame, like false guilt, but generally, and particularly in the case of clothing, shame serves a useful function: It protects our personal boundaries. Like a medieval moat shame guards the castle of the self from uninvited guests and unwelcomed intrusion. Through clothing we can become co-creators with God in defining how we are to be known and received. A certain freedom is experienced in learning how to clothe this temple in which God chooses to dwell. One can choose to dress sensuously, not just to impress or entice, not just to imitate or to shock, but to provide personal delight. One can choose clothing that feels good to the skin and empowers movement, shoes that are comfortable for walking, sweaters that rest easily upon the shoulders, outfits that accent the aesthetic orders of creation, and fabrics that offer a wide comfort level. Simplification of design always results in energy conservation. So it is with clothing. The temple of God does not require closets full of impractical, uncomfortable, or faddish clothing. It is a minor triumph of the spirit to find simple, beautiful, creative ways to dress ourselves, ways that dignify the self, respect others, cherish the earth, and honor the Creator.

Touching Things

One can touch material objects as irrational pawns in the kingdom of the ego, objects to be adjusted to our desires. Or one can touch them as partners in the glory of God's creation. To touch things with the latter sensitivity is to experience a triangularity of touch, wherein sense perception embraces the self, God, and material substance. We do not treat things as persons—nor persons as things—but we ought to treat things as part of God's creation, to be understood and respected. To worship things is idolatry. This is the case whether those things be possessions desired or clung to, or their monetary symbols—money. In the last analysis we hold title to nothing. God holds the title to all, even the things we make with our minds and hands. God holds title so that we might not worship or misuse the creation, but share their created glory.

We can, nevertheless, by the gracious invitation of the Almighty, take pleasure in the touch of ordinary things. There is a difference between making a fetish of an object and relishing it. Whether it be teddy bears for children or tools for adults, we all find our psyches reinforced by certain things that enter our lives. These things include natural objects such as stones and rocks, garden soil, and trees. They also include constructed things such as clothing, furniture, cars, jewelry, and the tools we use in work. Managers often fail to appreciate the artistry demonstrated by machine operators, including those who run the office machinery so vital to company success. The dexterity of surgeons is much admired, and ought to be. So also should be admired the dental technician who cleans our teeth, or the waitress who carries our orders to the table, or the carpenter who installs a new door in our house. Honor also the skills of a truck driver who backs his rig up to a crowded loading dock, or a crane operator whose fingers delicately manipulate the controls in order to lift heavy objects to the roof of a building. Admire, also, a mill worker who saws lumber into the maximum number of functional pieces, the bulldozer operator who clears a steep hillside to widen a highway, a violin maker laboring out of the spotlight. And the farmer who discs a field.

Whatever we touch, the thousand nerve endings of the skin send their messages to the brain for reassuring feedback. These things all shout: This is your habitat, you are at home, this is who you are, this is what you do. Often we do not so much need new things as we need a quickened sensuous relationship to the things we already have within and about our habitat. Failure to acknowledge the spiritual value of ordinary work may make us search restlessly for fulfillment. A culture of abundance, so appealing to the eye, however, jades the sense of touch. That may be why persons whose wealth has afforded them many and fashionable possessions at mid-life patronize antique stores. In the touch of old things they hope to recover a surer habitat for the soul. Greater peace might come were they to let God sanctify the ordinary things they possess.

To touch sensuously the things one works with daily is a contemplative exercise, a form of tactile prayer. It can sustain us through cultural changes and through changes in physical environment. Good touch reaffirms purpose. As one author wrote:

> Contemplation can sanctify work, provide its reason, give it purpose, harvest its fruits. I have seen it in a farmer. He was a good farmer, he enjoyed farming, but he was not a soil-grubbing, money-mongering farmer. For him the purpose of work was not to make money. It was not even to provide food, shelter, and clothing. Those were but the means. What he got from his work was the knowledge of God. After supper, evenings, he liked to saunter around his fields....a kind of Sabbath journey in which he placed his effort on the altar, and gleaned its spiritual benefit. How different, such leisure, from the entertainment we moderns have provided as an escape from the drudgery of work.[7]

Touching Other Persons

One affirms the boundaries of the self through touching others. Interpersonal touch may be benign or malign, or neutral. "He is touchy," we say, referring to someone who is easily offended. Some persons are even described as "sore heads." Well, these allusions may relate to how warmly one received the literal touch of another person, especially those outside the family circle. Some people don't like to be touched. Why is it some like to be greeted with lots of physical contact such as hugging, kissing, and backslapping, while others prefer no casual touch at all, except sound waves of oral speech hitting the ear? Probably because of how the skin sensors have been habitually instructed by the brain to send and receive messages. Perhaps this is how they were nurtured at home. For some people the proffering of casual touch threatens a breach of the moat: One's autonomy is put at risk. To others effusive physical affection affirms one's value as a person. All touch is not fully altruistic; much of it is ego centered, but it need not be selfish.

Interpersonal touch is reciprocal. Our nerve endings greet each other in touch. Bodies overlap their circles of private space. Physical affection is the moral use of touch. Violence is the immoral use of touch. Good friends long separated, who unexpectedly show up at the same place often will greet each other with vigorous touching, even pounding each other on the back, slapping hands together, or hugging each other tightly. Violent? No, loving. But an indulgent pat on the head can be a violent encroachment by a dominant person into the territory of a dominated person. All violence is not physical although physical touch is a major form of violence. This distinction helps us separate police action from warfare. God has not delegated to any the task of torturing or killing, but only the task of restraint, of guarding the space of everyone for the common good. The so-called violence of the magistrate, ideally, coerces without violating the person. It preserves space for all with minimal restraint upon the individual.

Denied sufficiently supportive, primary, tactile experiences, society becomes fixated upon touch as power over others instead of action with them. Sexual touch becomes elevated, fantasized as the ultimate expression of personal power. Persons so fixated become obsessive, yearning for the ultimate in sexual experience. And of course they are then easily exploited. Sex is dangled before them at every turn, taunting them for failure, luring them to exotic hedonic heights. Anxiety accompanies this social pressure, disappointment looms, and people are frightened and hurt in this social charade.

Because television is dominated by market forces, programs and advertisements are calculated to gain and hold attention. What sort of scenes and sounds grab attention? Violence, sex, and humor. So television is drenched in these attention-getting ploys. The effect of such merchandising, however, is not measured by sales records but by the modification of social values. For children, especially, who imitate in action what their eyes see and their ears hear, the effect has been devastating. Aggressive behavior is evoked in children before they have acquired rational discipline to handle relationships with others. Fantasy and entertainment dominate over inquiry into reality. Latent sex drives are prematurely awakened by a rapacious society. No wonder at younger and younger ages children can't sit still in school, hit, steal, and kill. No wonder they irresponsibly engage in sex before they reach their teens, and become promiscuous thereafter. Such children have a difficult time distinguishing reality from fantasy. The sensory deluge they experience blurs social norms that ordinarily guide the young.

As a result of these social forces, in our culture sexual touch has become separated from love. This is a tragedy. For many persons sex is associated with aggression, if not violence, and with ribald and superficial entertainment. Sexuality has lost its context in gentleness. Sex organs become aggression machinery rather than temple tools for loving intercourse. Where are the social rituals of slow developing intimacy? Driven underground by the model of immediate gratification. Sex is touted as a form of physical conquest—an alternate to football, a sequel sport to volleyball on the beach, inevitably linked with alcohol. Such are the results of the commercial decision to hype violence, sex, and humor.

Love is the true setting for the jewel of sexuality. That ideal has been blurred for modern children, to their hurt and to the shame of the perpetrators of this secular mythology. Human beings have enough problems with sin without another snake in the garden seducing them into idolatry with video images of power.

The most violent form of sexual touch is, of course, sexual rape. Rape of any kind, however, violates the body and the community. It threatens social interdependence. A woman caught alone at night and physically assaulted, a hardworking father unable to defend his daughter against lewd sights and demeaning advertising, a young couple unable to prevent their pre-adolescent boy from shooting a transient, these are signs of social failure. What a travesty upon education that well-trained entrepreneurs would violate the fruit of those parents' bodies, sneaking into the center of a child's self through gates of the eye and ear with obscene movies, arcade shows, and electronic games. And how appalling that they would wash their hands of the consequences of their labor, or just vote for more prisons to house the violence that is in part their responsibility. Every purveyor of pornography and obscene video images is an accessory to sexual violence.

To reconstruct acceptable norms for touch that gratifies the self without offense against the other person is a major task for our culture. Can a Christian theology of personhood become a catalyst for that reconstruction? I hope so. At least we can take charge of our own bodies so that what and who and how we touch pleases the Holy Spirit.

Certain disciplines help us be better touchers of ourselves, of things and of people. Two of these disciplines, the more philosophical, are learning how to bear pain and how to experience joy. The third involves skills in practical tactile behaviors. Other disciplines for affectionate touch are described in the other sections.

Bearing Pain

Pain tests the limits of humanity. These finite limits are manifested in various ways, as physical hurt, weakness, ignorance, victimization, diminishment of power and function, as failure, loss, and despair. Pain is a barometer of the Spirit. Sometimes it indicates the silence of God. But pain can also signal the presence of God. Christ crucified signifies that God shares our pain, even to the point of agonized and undeserved suffering. The Messiah is one who bears our grief and pain as well as our sins, and offers redemption.

Chronic pain is often a difficult journey along a narrow road bounded by the polarities of divine presence and absence. During times of pain one prays that the Creator of the body and mind will send the messengers of comfort along the neural pathways and offer the shalom of divine grace.

Experiencing Joy

It is a hedonic myth that self-fulfillment is found in seeking happiness. Happiness is not an end, it is not a goal; it is rather an emotion concomitant to the good living that follows loving God, self, and others. Happiness is background music and scenery along the way, but the route taken, whether over rough or smooth terrain, is a journey of the Spirit. It is a trek from and toward God. Pain is part of the discipline whereby we attain the holiness for which God has created us. Joy is the upper side of that discipline. Only superficially can our sensory apparatus be said to flow along a pleasure-pain continuum. Hedonic tone doesn't explain adequately the breadth and height and depth of that sensory range. Bodily pleasures are subordinate to spiritual interrogation that transposes them into joy, or casts them aside. Bodily pains are subordinate to spiritual interpretation that transposes them into sorrow, or casts them aside. Joy and sorrow thus mark the intuitive use of the senses to discern the will of God within creation, and in one's own life. These terms witness moral maturity.

Practical Tactile Behaviors

Although much that our bodies do is not learned self-consciously, we can teach our bodies to function more smoothly. We can achieve tactile competency. Some years ago, school administrators in the state of Oregon established competency based goals for public education. Some competency objectives were academic, like reading at a certain level, others were more pragmatic, like balancing a checkbook. The debate among educators over the value of performance based objectives continues. My point here is to suggest a few minimal tactile behaviors expected of educated children:

1) to walk gracefully, not pounding, not scraping anklebone on heel, not hunched over, but flexing the foot and striding rhythmically
2) to close doors without slamming them
3) to shake hands with appropriate pressure
4) to embrace other persons, young or old, tenderly, not clumsily, and to receive graciously the touch of others
5) to use machinery with a feeling for its proper function and limits

6) to walk among crowds without shoving and pushing
7) to handle a pet with sensitivity to size, needs, and characteristics
8) to care for shrubs and flowers with sensitive fingers
9) to exercise or massage body muscles for the relief of tension
10) to demonstrate skill in working artistically with natural substances

Empathetic Touching

I said earlier that affectionate touch is reciprocal. In contrast, violent touch is unilateral, the imposing of one's will upon another. For physical affection to be reciprocal means that each person touches to the other's good. In empathetic touching we unite emotionally with others, we share equitably in tactile experiences. These kinds of touching focus on the good of the other person. They are given with the hope but not the requirement that touch be equally reciprocated, or that it be fulfilling.

What power touch has! We stand so vulnerable to the hand of everyone. Perhaps the wonder is not that there is so much violence but so little, given the carnality that darkens every soul. Ordinary people respect and even guard the bodies of others, even to the risk of their own safety. Most of us are not predators but neighbors to each other. A good neighbor is alert when appropriate touch is required, not simply to rescue persons from a flood, or to offer a hand to an elderly person, or to bring a meal to a sick family, but also to use touch anticipatorily, to stave off trouble and to affirm others before trouble strikes.

This general civility may lull us into complacency. On occasion, a well-esteemed couple suddenly separates, ending the marriage, to the astonishment of family and associates. Or violence erupts within a family uncharacteristically. Then friends, extended family, and the faith community ask each other, what might we have done? Did we miss the warning signs? What could we have said? Or done? Perhaps friends, family, and church members should have asked: How might we have provided sustaining touch, friendly touch, to strengthen stressed people during tough times? Often an arm about the shoulders signifies more than verbal advice.

Family Touch

Early experiences determine the chemical configurations of the brain. A template is established, and if sensory deprivation occurs because infants and children are not touched in a loving and affirming way, that template is poorly developed to accommodate interpersonal needs. Without good touch the brain can be impaired, sometimes irreversibly. In ordinary language, children who are hit become hitters. Children who are inadequately and insufficiently touched wither psychologically and physically. This is more than just learned behavior. There are chemical and biological roots for dysfunctional behavior arising from touch deprivation. Scientific tests give support to the hypothesis that low levels of the biochemical neurotransmitter seratonin correlate with violent temperament.[8] It is also the case that loving touch can overcome some early deprivations, can change the chemistry of the brain, can make the psyche whole. Some foster and adoptive parents have found this to be so, although for some children impairment remains. In ordinary families wrestling among siblings and play with parents support affection and teach the limits of responsible touch. This kind of responsible touch is also taught through athletic activities and games, although the cultural pressure for violence often pushes play beyond acceptable limits.

Culture influences us so strongly that parents often experience powerlessness in respect to their children—watching helplessly as the Pied Pipers of our day lead offspring away from the nurturing shelter of the home. In older cultures, the classical Chinese society for example, a family might inhabit the same location for thirty or forty generations, with the living generations sharing the homestead with departed ancestors.[9] In such a society familial touch is ritualized in many ways, often becoming so stylized that freedom and creativity are lost. The future is held hostage to the past. In striking contrast, our highly mobile society means that children experience several moves, several houses, and sometimes several parental pairings, before they mature. What and who they touch changes frequently. In consequence, nurturing tactile experiences may arise from non-family adults and peers more than from parents and a stable extended family.

Some children hardly ever say hello to their grandparents now, let alone touch them physically in any enduring manner. Some never sit on grandparents' laps to cuddle and have stories read to them. Many children grow to adulthood never having attended a funeral or read the headstones of deceased relatives. Even in China modern children no longer bow respectfully to thirty generations of departed ancestors buried in the courtyard of the family home. Currently in Japan busy adult parents rent professional grandparents as surrogates to increase the amount of touch within the family circle. Surely thoughtful consideration of the mechanics of good family touching is in order.

We conclude this discussion about family touch with these queries:

1) Parents and grandparents, do you touch your children and grand-children in loving ways, according to their needs and not just to establish control?

2) Children, do you touch family members and friends gently, not cruelly?

3) Husbands and wives, does your casual, playful, and erotic touch compliment rather than put down the other person?

4) All of you, do you touch animals and plants according to their status as creatures of the most high God? And do you touch the earth tenderly, as your habitat?

Erotic Touch

A character in one of Graham Greene's novels blurts out a question anguished persons have asked, inwardly at least, "Why did [God] give us genitals then if he wanted us to think clearly?"[10] How to bring sexual passion under the control of mind and spirit is a struggle for many people. It ranks with money and power as a major test of spiritual discipline. These disciplines are treated helpfully in a definitive work by Richard Foster, who considers the divorce of sexuality from spirituality to be one of Christianity's major tragedies.[11] Foster makes the case for right use of sexuality rather than for monastic proscription. He uses as a metaphor for sex that of a great river, rich and deep when it stays within God-given banks, damaging when it does not. Foster argues for distinguishing between erotic attraction and erotic faithfulness.

If erotic touch is accepted as God-given rather than ego-driven, then one can receive its message as heaven-sent. Sex is good in godly context. One only has to scan sophisticated national magazines advertising erotic paraphernalia or low-brow pornography to know how passion threatens reason. This judgment about the strength of passion occurs when "respectable people" like Little League coaches or Sunday school teachers are indicted for seducing children, or famous ministers are caught in adulterous situations. The "burnt out" priest's lament rings a bell in the psyche of thoughtful adults who reflect upon their own struggles to bring sexual passion under the discipline of reason.

Given the force of sexual passion, nurtured by powerful body chemistry, abetted by constant cultural pressure, how can healthy persons fulfill the biblical commandment, summarized by Jesus, to love the Lord God with the whole heart, soul, and strength, and one's neighbor as oneself? One way is to make eros a respected partner with other forms of love: family, friendship, especially with unconditional (agapaic) love. This way asks us to direct all neural impulses for affection, genetic and environmental, toward the will and purposes of God.

Who and what we touch is governed by how we touch. There is a popular view that modern people have at last been liberated from restrictive sexual mores of the past. It is generally assumed, for example, that sex for pleasure was taboo during the Middle Ages and that somehow the church was a dour spoilsport in this regard. Some Medieval theologians *did* argue that the Fall had impaired human reason, thus removing the rational governor to animal passion. In consequence, following Jerome, some theologians thought all sexual activity was contaminated with sin even when necessary for procreation. Others demurred, considering the necessary function blameless. There were other voices, however, in support of the view that Edenic sex was probably even more pleasurable because good will and reason regulated passion. These were influenced by a book by Constantine the African, *De Coitu*, written in the eleventh century. Constantine followed the authoritative physician Galen, who believed that sexual intercourse was not only pleasurable but "beneficial and an aid to health."[12]

That the modern world does not suffer from prudery is very evident! Indeed, it may suffer from exhibitionism, and a lack of privacy. Roman Catholic as well as Protestant couples practice artificial birth control, and the joys of marital bliss are extolled forthrightly in various church-sponsored conferences and writings. Radio and television programs focus upon how to enjoy sex. Significantly, despite what popular literature suggests, even in our permissive culture most couples are faithful to each other. Sexuality studies even suggest that monogamous Christians experience heightened sexual enjoyment. (Now here is an evangelistic ploy: Come to First Church and jazz up your sex life!) Anyway, our culture is certainly hedonistic, with sexual activity topping the list of fun things to do. Accordingly, how to affirm the body erotic without worshiping it as an idol is a prime goal for spiritually sensitive persons. Here too is a test: how to be sensuous without becoming sensual.

At best, sexual touching is a form of intimacy. Erotic experiences should be private, privileged information not trade goods. The current yen to make erotic pleasures public does not enhance but rather destroys intimacy. "Intimacy," according to one author, "is a mutual sharing— both giving and receiving—by two people of their innermost thoughts and feelings, with affection and respect, for the benefit of each."[13] I like that definition. The sensory experiences of skin on skin and the coital touching of sexual organs signify erotic love in a special, intimate way.

These forms of touch also foster friendship. Friendship is a characteristic of married intimacy. As another writer puts it "...the deepest forms of erotic love involve more than one's physical characteristics, a longing for what amounts to a recognition of one's worth."[14]

Friendly Touch

Intimate touch, then, is to be found in more ways than through sexual intercourse. Intimacy occurs significantly among friends through manifold sensations of touch. Indeed, the current preoccupation with sexual touch may be a result of a society that has stifled intimacy through friendship. For one person to be truly present to another some form of interactive touch is required. The other senses are important, but they simply do not suffice. To see a friend is good. A letter or a phone call supports friendship. But touch offers powerful sensory closure to friendship. The circles of our beings intersect. We share personal space. Touch gives intimacy to friendship.

If in contemporary American culture the focus has been upon sexual intimacy, in other times and cultures it has been upon friendship. Recently a physician friend of mine found an old photo of the two of us at a summer church camp. We had our arms about each other. It is just a snapshot of two kids who enjoyed each other and have remained friends for more than half a century. The remarkable thing about it is that the physical affection seemed normal then, and should now. This display of affection had no sexual overtones. It portrayed a powerful, sensuous, and godly intimacy.

I would like to see intimacy recovered within larger circles of friendship. Sensory deprivation arises when people are not sufficiently touched in their adult lives, as well as when they were babies and children. Consider some ways that the current preoccupation with sexual touch as *the* locus for intimacy, aided and abetted by commercialized media, has impoverished our lives. First, by minimizing friendship as an experience basic to social civility it maximized adversarial processes. Second, by narrowing perceptions of sexuality to genital intercourse it has fostered predatory tactile behavior; touch becomes a demonstration of power instead of affection. Third, a stereotypical focus upon genital sex brings role confusion to persons who otherwise might be content with non-genital friendships. Men, it seems, can't be close friends with other men without being labeled gay. Women can't be close to other women without being labeled lesbian. Men and women cannot be close friends without being suspected of having a romantic affair. Given the force of these stereotypes, role models for intimacy in friendship are not easily provided to the young within our culture. These stereotypes must be overcome.

We ought to lighten up in respect to friendly touch. Teachers should be able to show physical affection to their students without the risk of being sued. Likewise, for students with teachers. Conflict-resolution classes might be more effective if there were more nonadversarial role models. Perhaps every school and church curriculum for the next decade ought to include a class on effective and affirming touch, so that our culture can correct an aberrant course.

In the sixties the emphasis in the counterculture was upon touch as an emotional offering of one's body to another on request in whatever form desired. That openness to touch on demand degenerated into sexual permissiveness. But at its best the countercultural movement groped for a nonexploitive, nonadversarial community where friends touched each other and personal space was sacrificed to in-group space. Now a reaction has set in. Touch my turf and I will sue, seems to characterize the current mood. To preserve the autonomy of the self while affirming the integrity of the group is a major goal for a better social order. The right use of friendly touch is one means toward that goal. Now is the time to learn again the social importance of disciplined, friendly touch.

So, family, friends, neighbors, let's touch each other in affirming ways—a handshake, a hand on the shoulder, an arm about the waist. Colleagues, let's not touch each other in an autocratic pecking order nor in demeaning tactile power plays but in the unity of common tasks. In such a context affection is demonstrated as caring touch. Let touch be sensuous not sensual. Greeting cards are nice but are no substitute for personal touching. Let us care for others in deed as well as word. Much of the loneliness of urban dwellers, retirees, and elderly persons in nursing homes comes from the absence of significant and affectionate touch. Mutual caring is a mark of friendship and good touch is a mark of caring. As Myeroff writes:

> In a meaningful friendship, caring is mutual, each cares for the other; caring becomes contagious. My caring for the other helps activate his caring for me; and similarly his caring for me helps activate my caring for him, it "strengthens" me to care for him. The man who is not needed by someone or something does not belong and lives like a leaf blown about in the wind. I have a need to be needed, and the need of others for me goes hand in hand with my need for them.[15]

Animals can be our friends, too. Tactile experiences with friendly animals is reciprocal, and important to both creatures. Dog owners know how much affection these creatures can soak up. So do cat owners, although cat style differs from that of their canine friends—they are more subtle, perhaps. Some people have found this desire for creature touch to be true with certain sea animals also, such as the dolphin and certain whales. For thousands of years seagoing persons have struck up friendship with the dolphins, who like to ride the crest of a wave, who cooperate with fishermen and sometimes nudge drowning people to shore, or form a breakwater to protect ships from capsizing in storms. Recreational parks (like Seaworld) where children can touch dolphins and whales, and the animals can touch human beings, capitalize upon these relationships. For most of us, however, animal friendship will be limited to those creatures who share our homes. The value of such friendship is sometimes accented by an annual religious event, "the blessing of the animals," which affirms the mutuality of this relationship. It is an appropriate ceremony; it should be used more widely.

Healing Touch

Some persons believe affectionate touch may often do more good than medicine. Most of us would at least agree that healing is helped by the touch of compassionate caregivers. Of course, the healing arts have always involved sensitive touching, whether it be physical therapy or surgery.

Galen and the Greek physicians who followed in his train used touch and sight primarily in their practice, with touch involving pulse taking, temperature, and palpating the body, particularly the abdomen.[16] We patients take for granted the sensitive hand of the examining physician, particularly in the annual physical examination. A certain code of ethics prevails in this examination, combining a respect for privacy with a need for objective analysis. This tension can be particularly acute in gynecological examinations and in childbirth. Centuries ago this tension led to a division between physicians who use their intellect and surgeons who use their fingers to cure.[17] Midwifery is an example of one cultural response to the tension between respecting privacy and receiving professional assistance. In our own culture professional healers follow certain codes of conduct, for example having a nurse present and covering the body with a sheet.

Professional healing depends upon a fruitful interaction of all the senses. The physician must listen carefully to what the patient says, and look carefully, often needing to interpret ordinary speech into scientific analysis. The introduction of instruments has obviously increased the power of these senses, including touch. Surgery depends upon that technological refinement of touch. Professional healers also depend upon reassuring touch, ordinary touch, to heal the person. Wise nurses and doctors understand that touch is important, sometimes vital for healing. We want our caregivers to be competent technicians, knowing how to use their hands and their instruments skillfully. We also want them to be caring persons who do not just disappear quickly into the next consulting room. Physical touch is one way to demonstrate that caring. A hand on the elbow or an encouraging handshake may relieve anxiety.

The hand can be a metaphor for healing, "the healing touch." But it also can be a figure for death. The hand has been portrayed in art as the loving Creator reaching out to humanity. But the hand is also a symbol of the scourge of God. Transcendent touch has been portrayed as the grim reaper harvesting the earth through this or that plague. In Bible times leprosy induced a horror of touch, a phobia Jesus dealt with fearlessly, as recorded in the Gospels. Other diseases have reached epidemic proportions, resulting in wide-scale death. The bubonic plague of the fourteenth century was one. Regionally, smallpox is another scourge that has devastated communities of people.

These plagues have had their impact upon cultural memory. Fear of contagion has always made some persons particularly squeamish about touch, even friendly touch. This fear can become a phobia if the epidemic is of a sexual sort. Once the disease was syphilis, now it is AIDS. According to Sander Gilman sexualized touch has been variously depicted artistically both to accent the good of sexuality but also to show its evil side. Touch as an artistic metaphor changed in consequence of the first of these plagues. Perhaps it's changing now. Because of the scourge of syphilis in the fifteenth and sixteenth centuries, some artwork was designed, like contemporary posters about AIDS (one poster shows the hand of death holding out a syringe to an open hand), to warn of the health consequences of profligacy. Gilman writes:

> The great syphilis epidemic of the late fifteenth and early sixteenth centuries made the sexualized touch also the sign of death. What had been in Christian iconography an association between the sense of touch, the materiality of Christ and the act of crucifixion (and eventual resurrection), was secularized as the association between images of touch, images of disease and images of polluting sexuality....Over and over again, the hand, which is

the icon of touch, comes to stand for the potentially deadly touch, just as the erotic touch has hidden within it the potential for pain.[18]

In the ancient church the hand of God (*magnus Dei*) was a significant symbol of life, not death; salvation, not damnation. Often God's hand was depicted within the circle of a tri-radiant nimbus, to show the completeness of divine caring. This hand conveyed divine blessing. In using this symbolism Christians drew upon the Old Testament, in which God's dealings with people uses the imagery of the hand, e.g. "The gracious hand of our God is on everyone who looks to him, but his great anger is against all who forsake him." (Ezra 8:22 NIV) Israel celebrated deliverance from oppression by "the hand and the outstretched arm" of the Almighty (Deut. 7:19). Scores of references suggest that by the hand of God we are brought to freedom and life.

Michelangelo understood this powerful tactile symbolism. He used the hand on the ceiling of the Sistine Chapel to depict God reaching out to humanity. Good metaphors have their roots in ordinary experience. Our hands, like God's, can reach out to help and to heal.

Healing touch comes to a hurt person as the "hand and outstretched arm" of the Almighty. The competence of professional caregivers is enhanced by the hope they transmit through other kinds of simple touch. Physicians are gifted of God as healers, and the best of them acknowledge that gift humbly and with a sense of service to others. They are the outstretched arm of the Almighty.

Healing comes in other ways. A cuddly kitten offers soothing therapy for a child. A warmhearted dog is a godsend for a shut-in. I have read about the therapy some cancer victims gain from going into the woods. They discover themselves to be nurtured by the touch of plants and trees and by the solitude offered. Many persons have discovered what scientists are now affirming: In some mysterious ways the mind does exercise control over the immune system. Blood pressure can be reduced when one's mind touches one's body through biofeedback. Illnesses of the body can be headed off by meditation and prayer. Not always, but sometimes. Wholeness is a condition of mental and physical balance, a condition of health. For all of us the touch of friends supports us during the trauma induced by accident, disease, death, or other losses. Support groups are helpful kinds of sensory therapy.

Spiritual healing is a special God-anointed kind of touch. There are many ways in which this healing occurs, some of it quiet, some theatrical.

Some misguided, some offered in intercessory prayer and Spirit-guided wisdom. Many years ago my wife was ill, and we were very discouraged. Young, poor, uncertain, we stood ready for the wisdom of healing touch. This occurred, unsolicited, one day as an older minister came over and asked quietly if he could pray for my wife's healing. Well, his discerning spirit seemed to us a heaven-sent answer to our anxious prayer. And she was healed. How to explain this? I don't know. Other prayers of ours for healing of loved ones have not been answered. There is a mystery here that ought to be respected. That's why religious healing ought to be a quiet affair rather than a theatrical performance that presumes upon God and treats the Almighty as a star actor who must enter stage on cue.

Often religious healing is accompanied by the laying on of hands or the anointing of the head with oil. These actions constitute a tactile form of prayer. We say with our hands what our mouths cannot fully convey. Touch is a human means for the conveyance of God's grace, whether for healing or for other purposes. In religious ceremonies we discern how the Spirit of God flows among and within us for our good and God's glory. In personal devotions some persons use prayer beads, or special objects such as holy water, altars, prayer shawls, or even the Bible, as things to handle in private worship. Less liturgical persons find the same access to the Holy Place through painting, sculpting, caring for their tools, knitting, and the like. It is surprising how much touch can be an investiture of God's grace, whether through specially dedicated things or ordinary objects of our hands. We can let them be God's messengers.

Touch as Investiture

Investiture literally means to clothe persons with symbols of authority or recognition. Kings are crowned, athletes have wreaths draped over their necks. Medals are pinned on heroes. With pomp and ceremony deans and presidents drape colorful hoods over the shoulders of degree candidates at graduation time. Forms of investiture occur in many organizations. Fraternal orders invest new leaders with special garb, service club leaders solemnly hand over a gavel to new presidents. Ritual handshakes link even political opponents in civic ritual that transcends partisanship. Judges are robed. So are choirs. A chaplain marches to the podium of the Senate and prays before the United States Senate even though a ritual prayer at high school commencement is considered untenable in a multicultural society.

The laying on of hands was an important ceremony in the early Christian community. Persons specially called of God to be ministers of the Gospel received affirming sanction by their peers through a service of worship involving the physical laying on of hands. This gathering round for dedication and blessing has occurred in various ritual formations throughout the history of faith communities. To lead others is more than a political arrangement; it is the consensus of thoughtful people. And so divine sanction and blessing has been sought for appointed leaders. This ceremony has its roots in ancient Israel's practice of the Lord's prophets anointing the people's rulers. It also has roots in the Roman world. The Roman emperor was dubbed *pontifex maximus,* the ultimate bridge between humanity and deity. What was idolatrous to the Jews was reverent honor for the Romans—an ideal of empire divinely anointed. When the empire lost credibility and control, the church-state sought to preserve the force of such investiture without idolizing the ruler or deifying the state. This was no easy task. Roman pomp didn't fit well with prophetic simplicity.

During the Middle Ages the principle of investiture evolved into a divine rights theory of political governance and an episcopal theory of religious appointments. Presumably the Almighty should have something to say about who leads other people, politically or religiously. Presumably church leaders were the seers who, like Samuel, knew who should be king. A long-running controversy erupted over who should do the investing, the state or the church. The impasse between pope and king was broken by the emergence of more egalitarian ideas; consequently social contract theories generally superseded the divine right principle, and parliaments demoted kings to figureheads.

Let's look a bit more closely at the New Testament accounts of the use of hands. Maybe it will help us reflect more thoughtfully about that kind of touch we call investiture. The early believers followed Jesus' example of compassionate, healing touch, and the lonely and the ill responded to this touch of love. A nervous but obedient believer, Ananias, placed his hands upon Saul, who had been blinded on the Damascus road, and sight was restored, literally, to this one who turned from harassing the church to being a major proponent. Investiture also confirmed his inner vision and conversion (Acts 9). The laying on of hands by the apostolic leaders Peter and John confirmed the baptizing presence of the Holy Spirit upon new believers. Hands were the messengers of God to confirm to the mind the transforming work of God (Acts 8:14-18). Gifts of money and possessions were sanctified for outreach purposes by being laid at the apostles feet. And to seek prestige out of giving was severely rebuked. The term simony, that is, the sin of trying to buy spiritual power, is named for Simon who first sought to do so and was severely rebuked by Peter.

You can't buy the gift of God with money, he said. (See Acts 8:9-25.) Sacred touch is no commodity, but a gift of God, and our hands are but the messengers delivering the gift.

By group touch the early Christian community of faith confirmed the call of God for special ministry, as in the case of Saul (Paul) and Barnabas, who were commissioned by the Antioch church to begin a missionary journey (Acts 13:1-3). Such hands-on action gradually became a more formalized church ceremony, with the words themselves conveying both the ritual act and its signification. So when an older Paul admonished a younger church administrator, Timothy, "Do not be hasty in the laying on of hands" (1 Tim. 5:22 NIV), he was simply urging caution in the confirmation of persons called to special ministry. To recognize what God has ordained ought to be a serious matter. It calls for a bit of solemnity.

Godly Disciplines of Touch

I have already suggested certain responses in the sections dealing with passive, conditional, egoistic, and empathetic touching. Suffice it to note a few general and practical disciplines for the right and sensuous use of touch.

1) Religious instruction for children should include teaching them how to touch. My friend Gary Fawver, widely experienced as a camp director (former president of Christian Camping International, USA) has conducted what he calls the "Five Sense Tour," which includes exercises to help children intensify their tactile sensations in a way that affirms the creation and the Creator. He has them reflect on what water is like, and the sun, and the bark of a tree. He has them feel another's face and hair, and feel the flow of energy from finger receptors by clapping and touching natural objects. There is wisdom in what Fawver recommends.

2) An inventory of one's tactile habits may be a useful prelude to spiritual renewal. Because many persons have depended so much upon the languages of the eye and the ear it may be helpful for them to discern the voices of touch, to learn about the messages they have been sending and receiving.

3) One's spiritual journey can be significantly enhanced by disciplines of touch, involving the right interrogation of passive and conditioned touch, the deliberate selection of egoistic touch that dignifies the body as God's temple, and by dedicating ones body—hands, feet, instruments—to the good of others. People brought children to Jesus for him to touch. May the disciples of Jesus carry about them the same charisma

that makes people want their touch and expect it to be kind, loving, and healing.

4) Interact more thoughtfully with the creation. As you understand your physical body in spiritual terms, so understand the creation, to enter more fully into the wonder and joy of it. Isaiah wrote: "You will go out in joy and be led forth in peace; the mountains and hills will burst into song before you, and all the trees of the field will clap their hands." (Isa. 55:12 NIV) The language suggests an "I-Thou" relationship, to use Martin Buber's well-known terms. Together the human and nonhuman creation worship their Maker. The metaphors are meaningful not because trees literally have hands and clap them, but because we have hands that clap, we have the capacity to receive their presence and movement in that way. We have eyes to see and ears to hear and hands and feet to feel.[19]

5) Let touch be a vital part of your friendship with others. Discover the ecstasy that arises from touch that wants to affirm and not control. Help contemporary culture recover the affirming use of touch in friendship.

Touch

Times there are to wrap up in silence,
sun above, earth below, or even to draw
darkness down around, and be alone.
And there are times
when friend and friend touch friend
without much noting
the mechanics of it all,
as life drums out a rhythm
fast and slow.
There are such times...
But there are other times:
times when to live one day even
untouched by someone who cares
can scarcely be endured,
times when watching
the cat rub against the dog
renews that ache to feel
an arm about the shoulders
or the hand grasped,
establishing again
the borders of the soul;
desperate times,
pretending touch

has been initiated,
or at last reciprocated,
but knowing it's not so;
times when each handshake
is unilateral and foreigners
hoard affection's currency,
when home tangibles
seem not to reach and
passion only briefly quiets
that yearning for a community
of love. These are times
to be lived through.[20]

Notes

1. I found this story in an article by Elizabeth Sears, "Sensory perception and its metaphors," *Medicine and the Five Senses,* edited by W. F. Bynum and Roy Porter (Cambridge: The University Press, 1993), pp. 29ff. Sears also notes the use of architectural metaphors, e.g. the senses as portals, as used by Richard of Fournival, 13th century mss. The castle with its sensory gates is a metaphor used, based upon Aristotle's *De Anima* and *De sensu*, which depict bodies (even of animals) as instruments of the soul. This view was variously elaborated in the Middle Ages, citing ancient worthies such as Aristotle, Cicero, Galen, to show that the senses are messengers which bring information to the soul that acts as judge. p. 27.

It is interesting that the editors of this volume also begin the book with Augustine's musing about the senses, noting "If Augustine could not describe the love of God without recourse to the senses, it is little wonder that the history of a more mundane subject like medicine is rich with reflections on, and concern with, the body's gateways." p. 1.

2. Phyllis K. Davis, *The Power of Touch* (Carson, CA: Hay House, 1991), p. 9. Her list of idiomatic expressions enabled me to expand my own. This handbook offers practical suggestions for therapeutic and loving touch for persons of all ages. The author is particularly concerned that infants and children are appropriately nurtured by loving touch. In regard to sexual touch, she feels that satisfaction comes through completing the rituals of touch culminating in coitus, and is hindered when touch is considered only the trigger for sexual coupling. She asserts that often sex is substituted for touching, "when people consumate their relationship sexually the loving touching soon stops." p. 105.

3. See Robert Kaplan, "The Coming Anarchy," *The Atlantic Monthly* (February 1994). Kaplan's thesis is that we have to accept environmental causality, not just social causality. Too many people leads to the exploitation of the earth. Refugees are a social sign of the turmoil abetted by overpopulation.

4. See Gerald Wilson, "Restoring the Image: Perpectives on a Biblical View of Creation," in *Quaker Religious Thought* #74 (December 1990), p, 20.

5. See *Drawn by the Light* (Newberg, OR: Barclay Press, 1993), p. 86.

6. Paul Brand, "The Scars of Easter," *Christianity Today* (April 5, 1985).

7. Henry Zylstra, *Testament of Vision* (Grand Rapids: Eerdmans, 1958, 1965 edition), p. 138.

8. David Susuki in the television series *The Brain*, Discovery Channel, 1994.

9. Nora Waln described such a society in pre-revolutionary China of the 1920s in *The House of Exile* (New York: Little, Brown and Company, 1933; New York: Soho, supplemented edition, 1992).

10. Graham Greene, *A Burnt-Out Case* (New York: Penguin, 1960), p. 76.

11. Richard Foster, *Money, Sex, and Power* (New York: Harper & Row, 1985), p. 91. Foster notes the wall and door imagery in the Song of Solomon, which praises the attractiveness of sexual purity in the betrothed. This picture of the integrity of the castle accords with the New Testament vision of the body as temple of the Spirit.
"We have a young sister, and her breasts are not yet grown. What shall we do for our sister for the day she is spoken for? If she is a wall, we will build towers of silver on her. If she is a door, we will enclose her with panels of cedar. I am a wall, and my breasts are like towers. Thus I have become in his eyes like one bringing contentment." (Song 8:8-10 NIV)

12. Cited in "Sexuality and Spirituality: The Intersection of Medieval Theology and Medicine," in *Fides et Historia* (XXIII:1, Winter/Spring 1991), p. 27.

13. James R. Averill and Elma P. Nunley, *Voyages of the Heart: Living an Emotionally Creative Life* (New York: The Free Press, 1992), p. 235.

14. Francis Fukuyama, *The End of History and the Last Man* (New York: Macmillan, 1992), p. 176.

15. Milton Mayeroff, *On Caring* (New York: Perennial Library, 1971) pp. 69, 37.

16. See "Galen at the Bedside" by Vivian Nutten, in *Medicine and the Five Senses.* edited by W. F. Bynum and Roy Porter (Cambridge: The University Press, 1993), p. 11.

17. In *Medicine and the Five Senses,* Chapter 10, "The Rise of Physical Examination," Roy Porter shows cultural variants in the use of touch by healers.

18. Op. cit., "Touch, Sexuality and Disease," especially pp. 202 and 224.

19. An article by Brian J. Walsh, Marianne B. Karsh, and Nik Ansell, "Trees, Forestry, and the Responsiveness of Creation," *Cross Currents* (Summer 1994) provided this insight.

20. By the author, in *Sunrise and Shadow* (Newberg OR: The Barclay Press, 1985), p. 11.

CHAPTER SEVEN

CONCLUSION

God has given us all our senses for our pleasure; yet reserved to Himself their use as medium and avenue for His larger purposes to play upon our minds.
—Thomas Mann

In this book we have considered how to be spiritual in sensory ways. It is our view that neither narcissistic adoration of the body nor platonic denigration honors the body as the temple of the Holy Spirit. Thoughtful interrogation of the sensory messengers of God, however, shows respect for the creation. Prayerful interrogation of the senses opens the door to significant disciplines of spirituality. Constructive use of the senses constitutes acceptable worship of the Creator. This can be affirmed without putting down the importance of certain disciplines of sensory denial such as fasting, celibacy, and voluntary poverty. Those spiritual disciplines that mute the senses and those that liberate them share a common goal: the transformation of the self into the image of God. Brenda Meehan puts it succinctly: "The goal of the monastic life is the transformation of self, from ego, anxiety, and alienation to compassion, freedom, and union."[1]

Isn't such transformation a goal for spirituality whatever one's vocation, and whether that goal is sought through disciplines of sensory denial or through disciplines of sensory affirmation?

Sensuous spirituality counters a sensate culture. Current culture is generally sensate. Seduced by some media images and celebrities, it is becoming increasingly debased. Aesthetic norms are supplanting ethical ones. The new barbarism is sensual rather than sensuous. It is aimed at immediate ego gratification rather than enduring self-fulfillment. Such barbarism is already becoming normative for our era, according to a commentator, Steven Stark,[2] who opines that American pop culture is fixed at a young teenage boy's level: filthy jokes, fascination with violence, irresponsible obsession with sex, gossip masquerading as news. In the same way that powerless boys are destructive, so, he thinks, the popular culture reflects a glee at pulling down authority. This uncivil oppositional anger, this exhibitionist mentality, has arisen, he believes, because "a nation of couch potatoes feels like a nation of fifteen year olds." Journalists *and their corporate sponsors* demonstrate and abet this immaturity by their own fascination with hypocrisy and violence.

Fundamentalist militancy is one reaction to the new barbarism. This militancy takes various religious, ethnic, tribal, and nationalistic forms. At best such militancy challenges the relativism that marks secular pluralistic culture; it seeks a return to authoritative moral standards. At worst such militancy encourages people to be cruel, intolerant, ethically selective, fearful, even paranoid. And like the Crusaders of the Middle Ages or Cromwell's New Model Army, such militants use the wrong weapons to support their transcendent ethical principles. Jesus rebuked Peter for trying to do with the sword what can only be accomplished by the Spirit. True believers find that lesson hard to learn.

There are alternatives to these militant reactions. Disciplines of spirituality offer better responses to social disorder than do strident crusades. Disciplines of denial such as Judeo-Christian asceticism and the Buddhist eight-fold path offer nonviolent prophetic protest against this current militancy. Through retreat from worldly engagement monastic groups often bind up the broken and offer a haven for persons crushed by the evils of the present world. Assuredly, a loving retreat and a safe house is better than paranoia or violent confrontation.

Most persons cannot reasonably enter such restrictive vocations, however, or can only do so briefly, as interludes in ordinary life. They have responsibilities to family, to their employers and employees, and to neighbors known and unknown whom they serve by faithful exercise of their vocation. Theirs must be a worldly spirituality. It offers a more viable alternative than does monastic retreat. Such affirmative spirituality links the self, God, and others in a sensory network through which the will of God is perceived, conceptualized, and obeyed in life's ordinary modes. Each of the senses can be an instrument of such active spirituality.

Sensuous spirituality honors the creation. This more affirmative approach honors the world apprehended by the senses, the world God creates, sustains, and loves. It does not disdain material realities, nor limit the spiritual world to mental constructs and immaterial entities. It does not construe the world of things and creatures as evil but as a good creation, which God patiently is redeeming from fallenness and sin. It includes ecological concern within the scope of redemption.[3] Such spirituality poses a realistic alternative to encroaching barbarism. Like David of old, believers in God have five smooth stones to slay the Goliath-like monster who tramples, seduces, and terrorizes our culture. What are the five smooth stones? A vision of God, a word from God, a taste for righteousness, the smell of a new creation, and the touch of heaven. This pro-active position affirms the body as God's temple, and the senses as divine messengers. Such disciplined spirituality gives realistic testimony to the presence within time and space of the Kingdom Jesus announced.

The Christian community of faith is often referred to as "the body of Christ." Christ is the head; believing persons are the members of this body. They share the mind of Christ. Like all good metaphors this term is based upon perceptual reality. It is not an allegory. The Church is composed of actual embodied persons, not immaterial ideas or disembodied spirits. The Church as the body of Christ consists of persons who see the creation and others through the eyes of faith, who hear with the compassion of Jesus, whose noses and palates are sensitive to the needs and longings of others. The Church consists of persons who keep in touch with others in ways that reflect how God keeps in touch with them.

Sensuous spirituality provides a practical context for belief. It keeps belief in God from becoming too theoretical, too notional. It prevents theology from lapsing into just an academic study, a branch of anthropology or sociology. Thus it guards against verbal idolatry. To know God as object—even a verbal object—would be idolatry. We cannot attain the knowledge of God empirically. Indirectly, however, we do know God, analogically and symbolically. We find God's tracks. We see, as it were, the "back side of God." Through the senses, more directly, *we respond to God's knowledge of us.* Mind and spirit are not just ethereal things. They are neural motions within the physical body. Ideas take shape through sensory perceptions. Indeed, we know God co-naturally by sharing God's image and by feeling mutuality with creation. We love God because God first loved us. We know God because God first reaches out to us, first strikes the ear with sound, the eye with sight, the palate with delectable food, the nose with aromas. We know as we are known.

Intimacy with the Divine arises from cognition experienced as revelation. First, receiving the sensory messengers of God, then contemplating those sensory perceptions within the mind, and finally intuiting their significance in respect to being and doing. In each process the Holy Spirit, immediately or mediately through Scripture and the community of faith, is a personal and corporate teacher. Such is the modality of spiritual development. Such is the habitat of the soul. This is how the Blessed Community coheres.

The "soul" is not a thing distinct from body, not a "ghost in the machine," to use Gilbert Ryle's deprecating phrase, but rather an integrating center of body, mind, and spirit. The term connotes a reality that transcends material forms of reality, envelopes them but does not demean them. The soul is thus the integral self that exists beneath genetic and environmental shaping, experiencing reality and creating new configurations of it through sense, reason, and intuition. To be truly spiritual is to be fully sensuous, fully rational, and fully intuitive.

The fear of the Lord is the beginning of wisdom, said the psalmist (111:10). This fear begins with good sensing. Sending the senses as far out as they can go, as Augustine said, does not reach the Almighty, but such empirical inquiry does signal back to us the affinity of all sensed objects with their Creator. By inner questioning of the sensory messengers we commune with God and God communes with us. Things are not God but they point to God. Our neural networks are linked with divine revelation. God transcendent is also God immanent. The voice within accords with the voice without. Paul referred to Christ within us as the mystery revealed (Col. 1:27). Thus the Incarnate word inwardly received joins the verifiable event and the historical report, as a trustworthy intuitive judgment. God is with us. We know this in our heads. We experience this in our hearts. We feel this in our bones.[4]

Sensuous spirituality encourages hope. Despite the superficiality of our culture, many ordinary people await a hand out of the swamp of cynicism by heroes of faith who will then point them toward the highway of holiness appropriate for life's journey by children of the Most High God. Ordinary people do not want the desires of the body to betray them into compromise, deceit, and despair. They do not want people to trifle with their affections, to program their minds, to determine their choices. They do not want their spiritual yearnings to be ignored or dismissed by science. They do not want their quest for spirituality to be answered by entertainment. People want to experience life for themselves, at its fullness, not at second hand. They want their bodies to be free, not programmed. They want to be the elect of God, not the pawns of principalities and powers. Why should they be forced to buy a ticket for everything their eyes see, their ears hear, their noses smell, their palate tastes, and their hands touch? They are tired of having their yearnings programmed and auctioned to the highest bidder.[5]

Be reassured. A godly life is possible in an ungodly world. One's body can be the temple of the Spirit. The Spirit is at work in the world. Hope is more than a verbal construct, more than an emotion, more than an inference. Hope infuses the physical body, its muscles, bones, organs. It flows with the blood and lodges in the brain. At its best, hope is a sensuous longing for holiness, for God. Each sense is a thoroughfare for anticipated encounter with the person of God and the persons of others at the core of their being. In the experience of hope every neuron of the body tingles with divine fire. In the experience of hope the senses celebrate Sabbath rest. They lay themselves on the altar of reality as living sacrifices to the Creator and hymn praises for the beauty of life.

Hope affirms a bodily resurrection. And why not? However reconstructed, the body arising from the other side of death will be fully cognitive, fully alive. Such is the daring conviction inferred from Jesus' own resurrection. More of personal reality, not less; more of life, not less. The Holy Spirit is our pledge of life eternal. The earthly body is seed buried in the ground awaiting the flowering of the heavenly body. In this hope we greet each day as an opening into eternity. The world is going somewhere and we are part of that exciting cosmic journey. Jesus is the pioneer, the first one through the mountain pass, as it were. Knowing this, we are content, however difficult the struggle, however dim the light, however we might blunder. Because Christ lives, we, too, shall live. This is strong hope; the gates of hell will not prevail against people of faith!

It is not death that many older or terminally ill persons fear, but the dying. They need this word of resurrection hope. But they also need comfort in process. They experience pain, sometimes mental diminishment, and a loss of physical strength. To use a good old word, they need comfort—one to be strong with them. The call for comfort is expressed in this poem.

When I am very old and cannot walk,
come sit with me awhile, and talk
of paths where we have strolled
together, or apart.

When I am very old and cannot see,
could you read the Bible, maybe,
or a cherished book
to give light to my heart?

When I am very old and cannot hear,
do not shout, just stand quite near
and touch me while you speak,
so I can feel your words.

When I am very old and out of touch
with what used to matter much,
be patient, hold me then,
as once I held you.

When I am very old and do not know
even that you come and go
about my lonely room
your love will keep me true.

When I am very old, your love will guide
my body and my mind and soul
across the bridge of years
to Life, and calm my fears. [6]

Frederick Buechner writes this for our encouragement: "Be alive this first and holy day because order has been created out of chaos, light out of dark, so you can see, touch, taste, and smell and tell this day that you have never seen before because it has never been before."[7] What can one say to this word but "Amen!"

An old hymn says, "Our hope is built on nothing less than Jesus blood, and righteousness." Our hope! There is more beauty even in crude expressions of hope than in eloquent despair; and there is more human integrity to both hope and despair than there is in cynicism.

Have confidence in the senses! Care for them as visiting angels. They are God's messengers of hope. Spiritual reality drums its song bodily with each heartbeat. The eye, the ear, the nose, the palate, the hand—each throbs with the pulse of the Holy Spirit. Spirituality isn't just something saints do well while meditating. Within the body's temple the senses serve as acolytes of the Almighty. Or they can if we let them. Rabbinical wisdom says that whoever enjoys anything in this world and fails to offer a benediction robs God. Rejoice in the midst of darkness! Offer a benediction of praise! God's kingdom is within and among us in the ordinary activities of our daily lives.

Praise God for the instruments of peace:

for eyes
that linger
to see
how truth applies
for ears that gather
all the hurts
the joys the fears
for noses welcoming
whether scenting
sweat or roses
for lips
that promise
picnics parks
and other trips
for hands
outstretched
that offer love
a place to stand.[8]

Notes

1. From Brenda Meehan, *Holy Women of Russia* (San Francisco: HarperSanFrancisco, 1994), p. 148.

2. In an article, "Where the Boys Are," *Atlantic Monthly* (September 1994).

3. The magazine *Green Cross* is one example of Christian ecological concern; note for example Vol. 1, Number 2, Winter 1995.

4. For an evocative allegory about inward and outward sensory experiences see Emanuel Swedenborg [1688-1771] *The Universal Human and Soul-Body Interaction* in the *Classics of Western Spirituality* (New York: Paulist Press, 1984), p. 123. Emanual Swedenborg believed that the five outward senses had corresponding inner senses: "The sense of touch corresponds in general to affection for what is good; the sense of taste to affection for knowing, the sense of smell to affection for perceiving, the sense of hearing to affection for learning, and to obedience, and the sense of sight to affection for discerning and being wise."

5. Earl Shorris, "A Nation of Salesmen: cautionary tales from the life of *Homo vendens,*" Harper's (October 1994). "Selling," he writes, "in all its forms, has achieved dominion over the world in our time, not only determining the economic spirit of the nation but deeply affecting its social, political, cultural, and moral life....Under the dominion of *Homo vendens*, we are no longer free to know the world. The salesman now informs us. In the mix of mind and matter that is perception, the information comes not from our senses encountering reality but from the salesman. Thus we have lost the world." p. 40.

6. "When I Am Old," by the author, 1994, previously unpublished.

7. *The Alphabet of Grace* (New York: Harper, 1989), p. 38.

8. Arthur O. Roberts, *Sunrise and Shadow* (Newberg, OR: Barclay Press, 1985), p. 18.

[The following material supplements general descriptions about the psycho-physiological aspects of sensing found in Chapter One, and in the particular descriptions of neural pathways and processes of each of the senses. Notes in Chapter One and in the Bibliography list sources used in preparing this summary.]

NEURON STRUCTURE AND FUNCTION

The neuron, or nerve cell, is the basic unit by which we are able to perceive the world around us, and by which we are able to act to induce a change in our environment or maintain homeostasis, based on our sensory information. Like other cells in the body, neurons may be highly specialized to their particular area and function. They permeate every muscle, tendon, sensory organ and form the basis on which the nervous system exists.

Roughly, neurons can be divided into two classifications: those involved in *afferent* activity and those involved in *efferent* activity. Those that have mastered the "affect and effect" rule of grammar will infer that the afferent neuron is involved in reception and transmission of sensory information to the brain, whereas the efferent neuron transmits command information from the brain to another part of the body to initiate some kind of change.

This word distinction may be grasped analogically by considering the neuron's function. In short, the *afferent* neuron relays stimulus information from our eyes, ears, skin, etc. to the brain through a complex neural network. After the brain "makes sense" of the information, *efferent* neurons act as a pathway to a muscle or gland, for example, to create a change in the body's internal or external environment. Multiply this change by the myriad of movements and processes the body goes through to maintain equilibrium and function in response to cues from the environment, and one can imagine the constant bustle of information communication and transportation on the highways and byways of the body, the nervous system.

In order to achieve optimal functioning and complete the complex tasks required of them, neurons are assisted by another component of the neural network, helper cells called glial cells. Glial cells make up the bulk of neural tissue, outnumbering neurons in a 10:1 ratio. Glial cells vary widely in structure and function, just as neurons do. However, some basic functions of glial cells exist across the board.

Some glial cells produce a lipoprotein called myelin that creates a sheath around the axons of some neurons. Myelin acts as an insulator and aids in conduction of electrical current down the axon, which is part of the process by which neurons communicate with one another. The glial cells wrap themselves around the axon in concentric myelin layers, with many glial cells needed to cover its length.

Other glial cells are "phagocytic," meaning that they protect neurons from harmful viruses, bacteria, and toxic debris. They do this by acting as aggressors that envelope and digest the threatening elements in much the same way that the white blood cells work in the immune system. Still others act as a support network, aiding mechanical stability, regulation of the neuron's metabolism, and response to injury.

Cellular Structure

The structure of the neuron has many of the same types of internal bodies, or organelles, common to all cells. However the neuron's structure is specialized to its function in some interesting ways. For example, the cell membrane of the neuron is made up of two layers instead of one. This helps create the capacity for the membrane to carry an electric charge. This distinction is essential to creating the environment by which neurons transmit information to and from one another.

The nucleus is the information center of the cell. Within its DNA are instructions for every function that the cell will carry out in its lifetime, including energy production and regulating metabolism. These instructions are carried out by various protein structures that work in concert: messenger RNA, ribosomes, and transfer RNA. They interact in a system of folds and channels around the nucleus. Using a DNA template, the messenger RNA directs ribosomes to assemble appropriate combinations of proteins that are needed to produce energy, or perform a certain function within the cell. Transfer RNA acts as a supervisor, giving order and setting proteins in motion.

With the exception of receptor cells in the olfactory bulb, mature neurons cannot reproduce themselves. Therefore, the instructions within the neuron's DNA are concerned primarily with immense energy requirements of the neuron to keep its "communication lines" open.

Since communication with other neurons is its primary function, the neuron has developed highly specialized projections of its cell body for that purpose. The "appendage" that receives incoming information is called the dendrite and for greater surface area and sensitivity, it is split repeatedly into an increasingly fine network of branches covered with spines. At the opposite end of the cell, the axon transmits or conducts information. It can be very short or very long (up to one meter), depending on where the information needs to go. Axons may branch off, to a lesser degree than dendrites, depending on the number of other cells it needs to reach and it ends in transmissions structures called terminal buttons. Additionally, a single neuron can have more than one dendrite and/or axon in many combinations depending on their function. Neurons often have many dendrites entering a nerve cell body but only one axon will leave—although it may branch to several targets.

The terminal buttons of the axon contain chemicals called neurotransmitters. As an electrical impulse runs down the axon (transmitted from another neuron), its terminal buttons either are inhibited or excited. If the electrical impulse inhibits them, then no neurotransmitters are released and the impulse terminates with that neuron. If the impulse is excitatory, the terminal buttons release neurotransmitters into the small space that exists between the terminal buttons of one neuron's axon and another neuron's dendrites. This space is called a synapse. The dendrites of the neighboring neurons absorb the neurotransmitters from the synapse and a chemical reaction occurs that creates an action potential (an interchange of positively and negatively charged ions in the dual layered cell membrane), and sends an electric impulse down the length of the neuron and starts the whole process over again in a new neuron.

Neurons are the single units that make up bundles called fibrils and, in turn, nerve fibers. Nerve fibers are bundles of fibrils that generally serve a common purpose. Neurons, fibrils, and nerve fibers can be part of the afferent, sensation detection network, part of the efferent, motor network, or can act in an intermediate capacity between the two.

BIBLIOGRAPHY*

Ackerman, Diane. *A Natural History of the Senses*. New York: Random House, 1990.

Augustine. *Confessions*. Translation by Albert Outler, Vol. VII of *The Library of Christian Classics*. Philadelphia: Westminster, 1955.

Averill, James R. and Nunley, Elma P. *Voyages of the Heart: Living an Emotionally Creative Life*. New York: The Free Press, 1992.

Bartoshuk, Linda M. "Sensory Factors in Eating Behavior." *Bulletin of the Psychonomic Society*, 1991, 29 (3) 250-255.

Bransford, John D. *Human Cognition: Learning, Understanding and Remembering*. Belmont, CA.: Wadsworth, Inc., 1979.

Buechner, Frederick. *The Alphabet of Grace*. New York: Harper, 1989.

Carter, Stephen L. *The Culture of Disbelief*. New York: Harper, 1993.

Corwin, Jeffrey; T. and Warchol, Mark E. "Auditory Hair Cells." *Annual Review of Neuroscience* 1991. 14: 301-33.

Csikszentmihalyi, Mihaly. *The Evolving Self*. New York: HarperCollins, 1993.

Davis, Charles. *Body as Spirit*: *The Nature of Religious Feeling*. New York: Seabury Press, 1976.

Davis, Phyllis K. *The Power of Touch*. Carson, CA: Hay House, 1991.

Foster, Richard. *Celebration of Discipline*. New York: Harper & Row, 1978.

————. *Money, Sex, and Power*. New York: Harper & Row, 1985.

Fukuma, Francis. *The End of History and the Last Man*. New York: Macmillan, 1992.

Gilkey, Langdon *Nature, Reality and the Sacred*. Minneapolis: Augsburg/Fortress, 1993.

Hawken, Paul. *The Ecology of Commerce*. New York, HarperBusiness, 1993.

Heller, Morton A., and William Schiff. *The Psychology of Touch*. Hillsdale, NJ, Lawrence Erlbaum Associates, 1991.

Jacapone da Todi, *Classics of Western Spirituality*. New York: Paulist Press,   1982. Lauds 5 and 6, pp. 76ff.

Josephs, Robert, et. al. "Judgment by Quantity," *Journal of Experimental Psychology: General* (March 1994).

Mayeroff, Milton. *On Caring*. New York: Perennial Library, 1971.

Medicine and the Five Senses, ed. W.F. Bynum and Roy Porter. Cambridge: The University Press, 1993.

Meehan, Brenda. *Holy Women of Russia*. San Francisco: HarperSanFrancisco, 1994.

Osberger, Mary Joe. "Audition." *Volta Review*, Vol. 92 (4) (May 1990), pp. 34-53.

Owens, Virginia Stem. *A Taste of Creation*. Valley Forge: Judson Press, 1980.

————. *And the Trees Clap Their Hands, Faith, Perception, and the New Physics*. Grand Rapids: Eerdmans, 1983.

Postman, Neil. *Amusing Ourselves to Death*. New York: Penguin, 1984.

The Psychology of Touch, ed. Morton A. Heller and William Schiff. Hillsdale, NJ: Lawrence Erlbaum Associates, 1991.

Roberts, Arthur O. *Sunrise and Shadow*. Newberg, OR: Barclay Press, 1985.

————. *Drawn by the Light*. Newberg, OR: Barclay Press, 1993.

Romero-Sierra, C. *Neuroanatomy: A Conceptual Approach*. 1986: New York: Churchill Livingstone, 1986.

Safire, William. *The First Dissident*. New York: Random House, 1992.

Schiffman, H.R. *Sensation and Perception: An Integrated Approach*. New York: John Wiley and Sons, 1990.

Shepherd, Gordon M. *Neurobiology*. New York: Oxford University Press, 1988.

Susuki, David. *The Brain*, a television series on Discovery Channel, 1994.

Emanuel Swedenborg. *The Universal Human and Soul-Body Interaction*. Classics of Western Spirituality. New York: Paulist Press, 1984.

Toffler, Alvin and Heidi. *War and Anti-War*. New York: Little, Brown, 1993.

Waln, Nora. *House of Exile*. New York: Soho, enhanced edition, 1992.

Waite, Terry. *Taken on Trust*. New York: Harcourt Brace, 1993.

Zylstra, Henry. *Testament of Vision*. Grand Rapids: Eerdmans, 1965.

*Various magazine articles are also acknowledged in the chapter footnotes.